Virginia Higginbotham is associate professor of Spanish at the University of Texas at Austin. She is the author of a number of articles on the dramatic work of Lorca.

The Comic Spirit of
Federico García Lorca

Detail from Goya's **Entierro de la Sardina** *(reprinted by permission of the Real Academia de Bellas Artes de San Fernando, Madrid)*

The Comic Spirit of
Federico García Lorca

BY VIRGINIA HIGGINBOTHAM

University of Texas Press

Austin & London

The publication of this book was assisted by a grant from the
Andrew W. Mellon Foundation.

Appreciation is expressed for permission to quote poetry
and prose from the following: Federico García Lorca, OBRAS
COMPLETAS. Copyright © 1954 by Aguilar, S.A. de Ediciones,
Madrid. All Rights Reserved. Published in English translation
by Virginia Higginbotham by permission of New Directions
Publishing Corporation, Agents for the Estate of Federico
García Lorca.

Library of Congress Cataloging in Publication Data
Higginbotham, Virginia, 1935–
The comic spirit of Federico García Lorca.

Bibliography: p.
Includes index.
1. García Lorca, Federico, 1898–1936—Humor,
satire, etc. I. Title.
PQ6613.A763Z68   868'.6'209   75–16079
ISBN 0–292–71033–X

Printed in the United States of America

Contents

Preface

To remain alive, works of art must be reevaluated by each successive generation. If the art of the past is not reinterpreted in the light of social, moral, and aesthetic changes, it loses its vitality and becomes a relic until a new generation discovers in it reflections of its own image and values. In this way *Don Quijote*, for example, continues to live for twentieth-century readers who find in Miguel de Cervantes's novel not so much the foolish knight but the existential man whose search for identity produces the alienation and disorientation so characteristic of our own day.

Lorca's works have been read and enjoyed in many countries and languages by countless readers and theatergoers. The diverse views of his plays that are now emerging result not necessarily from previous misinterpretation but from changing values and viewpoints that reflect the experience of the years since his last play was written. It is not surprising that new views of Lorca's art directly contradict earlier opinions, for the special character of each generation is best defined in contrast to and contradiction of its predecessors.

Thus it is that a new interpretation such as this one is offered—not with a claim to insights denied earlier critics, but with the conviction that, if Lorca is to continue to grip the imagination of a contemporary public, critics must be alert to new perspectives from which his art may be appreciated. Not only is this the critic's right; it is also the critic's duty to keep great art alive by relating its values to the present generation.

Masterworks of art transcend not only the barriers of time but of national cultures as well. Humor, however, is not always so universal. Jokes are notoriously untranslatable and what seems funny in one language is often not so funny in another. Further, each nation has its own idea of the comic, so that English humor, for example, is often distinct from the French *esprit*. Yet, as Luigi Pirandello points out,[1] we must not make the mistake of thinking that, because the English call their national comic sense *humour*, only the English have true humor. Besides, as Vivian Mercier reminds us, the origins of humor are preverbal.[2] The spread throughout Europe of the comic masks of the Italian commedia dell'arte attests to the fact that the comic spirit conveyed in dramatic terms—gesture, mime, parody, and burlesque—is more easily exportable than that based on rhetoric and language. Humor dramatized in comic characters is perhaps more universal than that based on wordplay, puns, and other rhetorical devices. If the French thought Shakespeare mad when he included the gravedigger scene in *Hamlet*, their own Molière also succeeded in making comedy an ultimately serious business.

I became interested in Lorca's comic spirit as a graduate student of Professor Bernard Gicovate at Tulane University. His suggestion that the comic passages in Lorca's plays were important and related to the playwright's outpouring of fear and frustration seemed to me a treasury of ideas. Professor Gicovate may not recognize the conclusions drawn from his thought, yet I owe the initial idea for this work to him. I am also grateful to Professor Rodolfo Cardona, whose helpful suggestions improved my manuscript. Grateful acknowledgment of permission to reprint portions of this book that have appeared elsewhere is also due the editors of *Romanic Review, Modern Drama, Insula,* and *Hispanófila.*

Introduction

The Problem of Definition

This is a study of the works of Federico García Lorca from a new perspective. During the passing years since his death, Lorca, Spain's best known twentieth-century poet and playwright, has generally been considered a writer of tragedy. Three of his major plays are grim, fatalistic stories of suffering and death, and his poetry is filled with dread. Yet most of Lorca's dramatic production consists of comedies and farces. Throughout Lorca's poetry and prose, as well as in his most somber plays, there runs an undercurrent of humor—dark irony and satire—that is in no way contradictory to his tragic view of life. On the contrary, through humor Lorca defines, intensifies, and tries to come to terms with what he sees to be man's essentially hopeless condition.

The importance of humor has been largely ignored in the fundamental studies of Lorca's works, such as those by Arturo Berenguer Carisomo, Guillermo Díaz-Plaja, Alfredo de la Guardia, and Edwin Honig.[1] Jean-Louis Schonberg, more aware than most critics of Lorca's humor, stops short of analyzing its significance.[2] In isolated articles Susan Smith Blackburn and, more recently, David Bary, have discussed comic moments and techniques in Lorca's lyric poetry and dramas.[3] Guillermo de Torre and François Nourissier have identified the value of the puppet farces as a source of the themes and techniques of his serious plays, but the implications suggested by this idea have not been examined.[4] For the most part,

William I. Oliver's complaint that comic moments in Lorca's plays have been insufficiently understood[5] has not yet brought forth a comprehensive appraisal of Lorca's humor. The present study attempts to do this: to analyze the comic moments in Lorca's lyric poetry, imaginative prose, and drama and to interpret their importance in Lorca's view of life.

I have entitled this study "The Comic Spirit of Federico García Lorca" because I am interested not only in Lorca's use of comic techniques, but also in the attitudes they reflect. I prefer the phrase *comic spirit* to the term *humor* because, while *humor*—equivalent to the Spanish *humorismo*—can refer to a wide variety of comic experiences, it is less inclusive and does not necessarily imply a general outlook or attitude toward life. Lest the discussion become an investigation of terminology or a psychology of humor, definitions of the various forms of humor—wit, irony, satire —will be subordinated to my larger purpose: an investigation of Lorca's comic outlook. Following a general chronological plan, I shall try to show how Lorca's comic spirit develops from the melancholy, disturbing humor of his early poems and plays, deepens into the sardonic laughter of his surrealist prose and dramatic experiments, and, returning briefly to the slapstick antics of puppet farces, culminates in his master plays with the grim, often grotesque humor of despair.

Lorca's comic spirit is apparent in nearly everything he wrote. In his lyric poetry Lorca disguised his fear of brutality and death with satire, bitter irony, and caricature. Cruel and pompous humans are portrayed as frogs and lizards in the verse fables of *Libro de poemas*; childhood innocence and death are juxtaposed in the macabre verses of *Canciones*; the death of the young nobleman, don Pedro, is announced as an ironic joke in the *Romancero gitano*. Passages of sinister and satirical humor abound throughout Lorca's poetry. The two important exceptions are, appropriately, the elegy, *Llanto por la muerte de Ignacio Sánchez Mejías*, and the bleak and tortured *Poeta en Nueva York*. It is entirely fitting that these two lyric works, intense outpourings of personal grief and psychological depression, are devoid of comic value and that the poet should have been at these moments bereft of the strength that humor often provided him.

Lorca's comic spirit, evident throughout most of his lyric poetry, reaches its fullest expression in his drama. As a playwright, Lorca learned his art from comic theater. His delightful farce *La zapatera prodigiosa* is an adaptation of techniques used in the Spanish *entremeses* or short farces of the sixteenth and seventeenth centuries; *Don Perlimplín* is also in the ancient tradition of popular farce. In spite of the aura of popular tradition, however, there is in *Don Perlimplín* a new and disturbing juxtaposition of pathos and burlesque. In this short but complex piece, Lorca's dark comic attitude, which becomes characteristic of his dramatic art, dominates the tone of the play.

As he was completing his farces adopted from popular tradition, Lorca was at the same time learning the idiom of the avant-garde. The comic distortion and *humour noir* of surrealism corresponded to his own comic spirit, and he wrote a series of prose sketches, *Narraciones*, and the play *Así que pasen cinco años* in the surrealist manner. *Narraciones*, like the surrealists' jokes, was intended to shock the complacent reader and to ridicule conventional artistic values. In *Así que pasen* frustration and fear of death are dramatized with the macabre humor that parallels that found in the surrealist films of Salvador Dalí and Luis Buñuel.

In 1931, after his apprenticeship and his avant-garde experiments were concluded, Lorca returned briefly to the puppet farce when he wrote the final version of *El retablillo de don Cristóbal*. As a child Lorca had been intrigued with puppetry; as a mature artist he attempted to incorporate the crude comic devices of this primitive medium into serious drama. In his last two plays the coarse humor and physical abuse of the puppet stage are used to reveal the cruelty and distortion of Spanish social values and customs.

Thus, Lorca's mature dramas are derived from experiments with ancient and avant-garde farce. His tragic characters retain a certain puppetlike quality, and their suffering is enhanced by farcical detail. It is not merely incidental that the personification of death in *Bodas de sangre* is a grotesque figure who leers at her victims, for death is central to the meaning of the play. Lorca presents a comic counterpoint to his heroine's plight in *Yerma* and ridicules the imposing Bernarda Alba as a symbol of authority in decay.

Ordinarily a chapter dealing with historical perspective might be expected to introduce a discussion of the writer's works. An artist's historical significance, however, depends upon a full understanding of his art. It is my view that this has not yet been achieved in the case of Lorca, for the value of the comic in his poetry and plays has not been studied at length. Thus, I shall first present my view that Lorca's tragedies depend for their full impact upon farce. Then I shall attempt to explain how such plays could have emerged in twentieth-century Spain.

Critical opinion, stressing Lorca's debt to golden age dramatists, has often disregarded the fact that Lorca's dramatic vision is distinctly modern, a synthesis of the theater of his day. While Lope de Vega's *comedias* directly influenced Lorca's conception of theater and of *mise en scène*, the *tragedias grotescas* of Carlos Arniches, the attitudes toward women dramatized by Jacinto Benavente, and Valle-Inclán's vicious little parodies of society, the *esperpentos*, modernized Spanish drama and thus prepared the way for Lorca's plays.

Lorca's genius was to restore to the Spanish stage the sense of spectacle, lost since the golden age, while at the same time dramatizing the anguish and despair of present-day life. His comic spirit is another crucial link between traditional drama and the theater of today. While his folk wit and slapstick humor are inherited from the oldest European farces, his sardonic and ironic laughter announces the most innovative modern drama—the Theater of the Absurd. Lorca is not a humorist in the sense that he wishes to make people laugh. Satire, slapstick, whimsy, and *humour noir* are for Lorca means of revealing the human condition, which he presents as both amusing and hopeless. Thus, for Lorca, as for Eugène Ionesco, the comic has become "une autre face du tragique."[6]

SPANISH COMIC TRADITION IN NONDRAMATIC ART

That the comic and the tragic spring from kindred attitudes is what prompted Socrates' famous remark that a true artist in tragedy is an artist in comedy also.[7] For the comic spirit, like the tragic sense, arises from the perception of incongruity or the contrast between appearance and reality, between what is desired and what is achieved. But the comic spirit, unlike the tragic, is an attitude of defiance in the face of incongruity and defeat. As Robert W. Corrigan has said, "While tragedy is a celebration of man's capacity to aspire and to suffer, comedy celebrates his capacity to endure."[8] We have noted the Spanish laughter at misery and despair, both in the *entremeses* of the sixteenth and seventeenth centuries and in the more ominous farces of our own day. This comic tradition, to which Lorca was heir, is rich not only in drama, but in nondramatic art as well, primarily in fictional prose and in the drawings of Goya. While Lorca dramatized situations in his plays with gestures and jokes borrowed from ancient farce, his comic treatment of cruelty and suffering echoes the works of Spain's greatest creative artists. A brief review of some of the masterworks of Spanish nondramatic art should provide insight into Lorca's sense of the comic, for it is deeply rooted in the traditional Spanish response to life.

Spanish novelists have frequently reacted to misfortune with laughter and contempt and have retained an infinite capacity to endure hardship. The fierce assertion of survival instincts through mockery of adversity reaches its fullest expression in the picaresque novel, a genre cultivated nowhere more successfully than in Spain. Endurance of physical pain and hunger incites comic irreverence and satire of man's greed and hypocrisy in the anonymous *Lazarillo de Tormes*. Social inferiority as well as physical discomfort evoke a kind of frenzy of scatological and grotesque humor in Francisco Gómez de Quevedo's *La vida del buscón*. Clearly, picaresque humor is the defensive laughter of self-preservation; it proclaims man's indomitable will to rise above demoralizing circumstances. Although often admirable, laughter at pain is not the most humane expression of humor for it may lead, as it does in Quevedo's novel and often in twentieth-century surrealism, to a kind of perverse, sadistic pleasure in cruelty. The most profound expression of the Spanish comic spirit is not the bitter laughter of survival but a mixture of satire and grotesque distortion with tenderness and compassion. This is the complex comic attitude of Cervantes, Spain's greatest writer of prose fiction.

Unlike the picaresque novelists, Cervantes laughs at suffering not only in order to survive it, but also to portray it more forcefully and thereby increase man's sympathy for his fellows. Cervantes laughs at his hero's absurd and often painful encounters, but he never allows the reader to forget the essential pathos of don Quijote. The Knight of the Sorrowful Countenance is cruelly abused but is never driven to enjoy the abuse of others. On the contrary, don Quijote, like a comic Christ, is led to repeated disaster in defense of those whom he believes to be mistreated.

Portraying the tragedy latent in the ridiculous figure of Quijote, Cervantes combines two mutually exclusive moods and thus forges a new awareness of man's condition that is as complex and as moving as tragedy. Lorca, too, was intrigued by the humorous aspects of sacrifice. Lorca's comic martyr, don Perlimplín, like don Quijote, unexpectedly reawakens our awareness of the futility of life. That both Cervantes and Lorca found in humor a way to express the paradoxes—the similarity of opposites and the nobility of madness—that obsessed them proves the validity of Socrates' correlation between tragedy and comedy.

Cervantes's compassion humanized the hollow and cynical picaresque humor. He thereby greatly increased the range of the Spanish comic attitude, making it not only a defense against adversity, but also a means of revealing man's frailty and potential goodness. Yet it is the picaresque laughter at horrible circumstances and the memory of quixotic compassion that combine in the works of Francisco Goya to produce Spain's most harrowing portrayals of evil. Quevedo's laughter at physical abuse and Cervantes's attempt to arouse compassion through caricature assume monstrous, animalic proportions in Goya's art. In his series of etchings entitled *Los desastres de la guerra*, a conniving lawyer in Goya's "Contra el bien general" [Against the public welfare] sprouts bat wings, and a boasting priest in "Farándula de Charlatanes" [Troupe of charlatans] acquires a fowllike head and a squawking parrot's beak. Though Goya carries grotesquerie to the brink of madness, lament for human suffering remains his central concern. The horrors of war, the indignities of age, the death of truth, and man's inhumanity are the themes that most torment him. Yet, ironically, as Charles Baudelaire pointed out, Goya opened new horizons in the comic.[9] His vision of comic grotesquerie has haunted Spanish writers of the twentieth century, such as Valle-Inclán, who cites Goya as the source of his own bitter *esperpentos*. Lorca's Bernarda Alba is also a Goyaesque figure. Her comment that the poor seem to be made "de otras sustancias" [of other stuff] echoes Goya's image of two prosperous bourgeois in *Los desastres de la guerra*, who remark arrogantly that the poor wretches who lie about begging "si son de otro linage" [must be of another breed].[10]

While Goya's shrill grotesquerie reappears in the comic spirit of the twentieth century, the most direct descendant of Cervantes's benevolent humor is Benito Pérez Galdós, Spain's greatest nineteenth-century novelist. Like Cervantes, Galdós was preoccupied with paradox and contradiction and expressed his preoccupation by way of irony and satire. Incongruities abound in Galdós's four-volume series of novels about the miser Torquemada. The death scene of Torquemada, as well as that of his friend and kindred spirit doña Lupe, are tragicomic moments in which life's last thoughts are divided between the afterlife and closing market prices.

Galdós had a *farceur's* delight in and appreciation of aberrant behavior. With a dramatic flourish worthy of Lorca himself, Galdós created two of the most memorable fanatics of Spanish fiction, Torquemada, the archbourgeois, and doña Perfecta, the religious tyrant. Peculiarities of speech, vocabulary, gesture, and costume are recorded in a host of minor characters: Bailón, the zealous ex-priest and phony sage of *Torquemada en la hoguera*, whose furrowed brow and muscular frame recall the brooding figures of the Sistine Chapel, but whose nickname, *la sibila* [the sibyl], underscores the absurdity of his pose as a profound oracle; Donoso's hypochondriac wife, Justa, in *Torquemada en la cruz*, who enumerates her compendium of illnesses "con aquel dejo vago de voluptuosidad" [with that vague, voluptuous abandon].[11]

Galdós's satire of Spanish moral paralysis and social decay heralded in Spain a new generation of writers—those of the Generation of '98—who shared Galdós's critical view of the deplorable state of Spanish social and political life in the early decades of the twentieth century. For this generation, particularly in the novels of Pío Baroja, the charitable humor of Galdós became what Miguel de Unamuno called *malhumorismo*—the aggressive, insulting sarcasm that seethes in those who are outraged.[12] The comment in *El árbol de la ciencia* that the customs of a Castilian village "eran españolas puras, es decir, de un absurdo completo" [were pure Spanish, that is, completely absurd][13] is typical of Baroja's caustic humor.

Baroja found Spanish institutions not only useless but actually harmful. He is so anticlerical that even a dog owned by a character in *Zalacaín el aventurero* detours around the church. Another of Baroja's novels, *Paradox, Rey*, is a macabre fantasy satirizing the so-called civilizing influence of Christian culture. The novel tells the tale of a group of Western expatriates who join a tribe of natives in Africa and set up a utopian existence. European colonists soon arrive, sacking the village and slaughtering the natives. The bishop blesses these violent acts, thanking God that "la civilización de paz y de concordia de Cristo ha entrado definitivamente en el reino de Uganga" [the civilization of peace and Christian harmony has finally come to Uganga].[14]

Flashes of Baroja's sardonic wit can be seen in works of other writers of his generation. The poet Antonio Machado parodies the Spanish notion of respectability in verses about the falsely elegant don Guido in *Campos de Castilla* (see "Llanto de las virtudes y coplas por la muerte de don Guido"). Machado's disillusion and metaphysical doubt are expressed in the ironical musings of his two self-caricatures, Juan de Mairena, a local gym teacher, and his mentor, Abel Martín, in *Cancionero apócrifo de Abel Martín* and *Juan de Mairena: Sentencias, donaires, apuntes y recuerdos de un profesor apócrifo*. Even the anguished philosopher of the Generation of '98, Unamuno, is not devoid of humor. In the prologue to his novel *Niebla*, Unamuno characterizes his own thought as "la preocupación del bufo trágico" [the musings of a tragic clown] and proclaims his intent to write one day a "bufonada trágica o una tragedia bufa" [tragic comedy or a comic tragedy] in which humor and tragedy are indistinguishable.

The bitter humor of Baroja, Machado, and Unamuno not only reflects the hopelessness of their own generation but also provides the philosophical orientation for the succeeding generation that is Lorca's. The clash between Spanish traditions and the twentieth century disoriented the Generation of '98 and caused them to vent their sense of spiritual paralysis in works replete with cynical laughter and self-disparaging wit. Only the English, asserts Baroja, have produced works of humor comparable to those of the Spanish. For humor, he explains, is deeply rooted in melancholy, and the insular man, like the peninsular inhabitant, is isolated and antisocial.[15]

The skeptical and alienated Generation of '98, uncertain as to Spain's role in modern society, seemed to sense the specter of disorder and confusion looming in the not-too-distant future. For avant-garde artists and intellectuals, however, disorder had a mysterious appeal; some diligently cultivated it. One of the most assiduous practitioners of disorder was Ramón Gómez de la Serna, who in the 1920's and 1930's brought about almost singlehandedly a revolution in Spanish letters. As an indigenous and authentic avant-garde writer, Gómez de la Serna introduced new developments in art to younger Spanish poets and artists, including Lorca.

Humor is central to *ramonismo*, or Ramón's way of seeing things. The sardonic *malhumorismo* of the Generation of '98 represents for him a point of departure into the realm of nonsense and chaos. While his wit is fundamentally serious, Ramón was often amused by the irrationality and disorder of life. He expressed his amusement in aphorisms that he called *greguerías*. The *greguería*, according to him, resulted from combining humorous remarks with striking metaphors ("Humorismo+metáfora=greguería").[16] Thus, while Ramón wrote primarily novels and plays, his art is essentially lyrical. More than any particular work by Ramón, it is his innovative wit that revitalized Spanish letters. His escape from logic, which anticipated the surrealists' fondness for *le hasard*, the sheer gaiety of his free association of disparate objects, and his irrepressible acceptance of life's most dismal moments restored lost confidence to writers who followed the Generation of '98. Yet Ramón's humor is neither empty nor blind; it is, as Rodolfo Cardona reminds us, "preceded by the knowledge of death."[17] The heroes of Ramón's novels *La mujer de ámbar* and *El hombre perdido* are, like Camus's stranger, lost in a meaningless world. But Ramón's rebellious attitude of nonconformity disarms the gloomiest foretellers of doomsday. "El humor," he remarked, "ha acabado con el miedo . . . cosa importantísima, porque . . . el miedo es el peor consejero de la vida" [Humor has done away with fear . . . which is very important, because . . . fear is life's worst counselor].[18]

The breaking up of traditional ideas and values was, for Ramón Gómez de la Serna, a challenge that offered him limitless possibilities for literary frolic and experiment. Assuming that the game is deadly and that life is meaningless, he nevertheless portrayed a chaotic world with sharp and perceptive humor. Another writer who responded creatively to chaos was Camilo José Cela, who viewed Spain in one of her darkest hours. In the years following the Spanish Civil War, Cela encountered a derelict society, riven by fratricide and the enormous waste of human life. His portrayal of agony and degradation, like Ramón's encounter with chaos, is sometimes amusing. Cela's notion that humor is "tanto lanza como escudo" [as much a sword as a shield][19] identifies him as a writer who, like Ramón, found humor the only remaining defense against disorder and decay.

The *humour noir* of Quevedo and Goya, the comic despair of Cervantes, and the corrosive wit of Baroja all reappear in Cela's portrayal of the violence that lies beneath the surface of modern life. Through his novels and short stories wander an endless number of swiftly drawn but faceless characters—victims of the extreme poverty, ignorance, injustice, and passion that shriveled Spanish life just after the Civil War. Some of these victims—for example, Pascual Duarte and Mrs. Caldwell—emerge as protagonists in the novels named after them. Others appear only momentarily as part of a grotesque panorama of social disintegration: From the collection of stories entitled *Esas nubes que pasan*, there is Joaquín Bonhome, "con su pata de palo de pino, que sangraba resina" [with his leg of pine wood, which oozed resin], and his wife, Menchu, "con su ojo de cristal que manaba un agüilla amarillita y pegajosa" [with her glass eye which oozed yellowish matter],[20] and Menchu's brother, Fermín, a female impersonator whose unpopular role in life makes him a convenient scapegoat to blame for the murder in "El misterioso asesinato en la rue Blanchard." There is Picatel—lame, albino, disfigured by smallpox—who gets revenge by stabbing his enemy's flock of sheep, one by one, with his pocket knife in "La naranja es fruta de invierno" [The orange is a winter fruit]. Cela's gallery of characters in *La colmena* includes doña Rosa; while having a drink in her café, one can feel under the table the letters spelling "Here lie the mortal remains of . . . ," for some of the marble tabletops are tombstones turned upside down. The only real value left in Cela's world is the author's unmistakable smile at, yet sympathy for, the wretched deformity that is mankind.

An apparently inexhaustible reservoir of psychic energy, Spanish humor has traditionally been a source of stoical tenacity and resistance. Though this humor is often amusing, it is fundamentally an admission of despair. From the harsh laughter of the picaresque to Goya's chilling *humour noir*, Lorca expresses the full gamut of Spanish humor. Gómez de la Serna's somber whimsy, as well as the comic futility of Cervantes and of the Generation of '98, is reflected in Lorca's works. For Lorca, humor is a mask that hides the sinister face of reality. If we are to understand the face, we must examine the mask closely, for there is strong evidence that, in Lorca's art as well as in much of modern art, face and mask have become one.

1. Lyric Poetry

Yo	[I
voy llorando por la calle	wander the street
grotesco y sin solución	anxious and weeping
con tristeza de Cyrano	with the sadness of Cyrano
y de Quijote	and of Quijote]

These lines,[1] written in December, 1918, and thus among the earliest that Lorca wrote, reveal the young poet's understanding of himself as a man wearing a comic mask. Like don Quijote, his most desperate moments appear sadly comic. So, too, in Lorca's art, frolic and dance of death, gaiety and despair are often indistinguishable, making us aware of the uncanny similarity of these two moods. Lorca's identification with Cyrano confirms the ambiguity of his self-image, for Cyrano is often regarded as a French Quijote. Yet the mention of Rostand's comic hero adds an extra turn of the screw: unlike don Quijote, Cyrano was from the beginning aware of his pose, so that his mental anguish was not a final, crushing realization but a day-to-day awakening to the futility of life.

Lorca's identification with a dramatic character like Cyrano is significant, for it is in dramatic form that his comic spirit is most fully expressed —perhaps because, as Henri Louis Bergson remarks, only the human is comic: "Un paysage pourra être beau, gracieux, sublime, insignifiant ou laid; il ne sera jamais risible" [A landscape can be beautiful, graceful, sublime, trivial or ugly; it can never be comic].[2] Yet Lorca's comic spirit is also apparent in his lyric poetry; his poems are full of dialogues and characters conceived in dramatic form. Occasionally, situations in which there are no active characters are handled in a theatrical or visually dramatic manner. Many of the brief dialogues and personages that appear in his lyric works are humorous, indicating Lorca's natural proclivity for creating comic characters and scenes. Thus, while Lorca's verse is, for the most part, not amusing, it reveals the diversity of his comic spirit. From reading Lorca's poems it also becomes apparent that he began to conceive of comic characters and situations from the beginning of his career.

In his first book, *Libro de poemas*, Lorca began learning his craft by writing fables. Though he did not cultivate the genre assiduously, he resorted repeatedly to the animal metaphor, amused by the implied resemblance, both physical and behavioral, between animals and humans. The characters of "Los encuentros de un caracol aventurero" are two "ranas viejas" [old frogs] and a snail, described as a "pacífico burgués" [stolid bourgeois]. The two frogs are beggars who pass judgment on art: "Estos cantos modernos—murmuraba una de ellas [one of them murmured]—son inútiles" [These modern verses . . . are useless], a satiric allusion to those who reject modern poetry. The frogs also comment upon religion, which they profess but do not believe. Caricatures of hypocrites anxious to appear devout, the two frogs feign indignation when they learn that the snail neither prays nor believes in eternal life:

"Una hereje era tu abuela.	[Your grandmother was a heretic.
La verdad te la decimos	We tell you the truth.
nosotras. Creerás en ella,"	Believe it,"
dicen las ranas furiosas.	say the furious frogs.] (P. 177)

A similar caricature appears in the poem "El lagarto viejo," in which a lizard, with "aire muy triste / de viejo catedrático" [the sad air / of an old professor], reminds the poet of an aging pedant. The lizard, addressed respectfully as "don Lagarto," is a figure comparable to the dignified but mistreated schoolmaster, don Martín, in *Doña Rosita la soltera*. Like don Martín, don Lagarto is the traditional stereotype of the schoolteacher too inept to be an artist. In spite of his "talante correcto / y su cuello planchado" [correct bearing / and starched collar], don Lagarto blinks his eyes, "esos ojos marchitos de artista fracasado" [those tired eyes of a disappointed artist].

The fable, with its comparison between animal and human behavior, has always been a genre preferred by poets with a didactic or critical bent. While Lorca did not write fables for the purpose of social commentary, "Los encuentros de un caracol" [The adventures of a snail] is not without a moral. The poem, beginning with the presentation of the comic frogs and snail, soon takes on ominous meaning. An outcast ant who dares to differ from his fellows is slain by them. While the hypocritical frogs and stolid snail are amusing, the ants, caricatures of rigid conventionality, are not. Like the "ranas viejas," they fear the dissenter because his ideas differ from their own; in contrast to the harmless frogs, the ants attack their victim and leave him to die. While the fable begins with a comic scene, it concludes, as Roy Campbell notes, with a combination of "comic grotesqueness and a heart-rending pathos."[3] Thus, as in the later plays, Lorca introduces defeat and death by means of comic scenes and characters.

The fables of *Libro de poemas* are the poetic exercises of a young poet amusing himself by mocking the characters of the adult world—the teachers and the elderly—whom he confronted as a child. Lorca's friend Carlos Morla Lynch recalls that, even as an adult, the poet performed impromptu skits with this same "caricatura inofensiva . . . y humorismo irresistible" [harmless caricature . . . and irresistible humor].[4] Included in the repertoire that he improvised for his friends was a skit about a country priest at mass—"Su misa pueblerina de madrugada . . . con toses y carrasperas y puntapiés a gallos y gallinas inexistentes 'que han entrado en la capilla'" [A country mass at dawn . . . with coughs and sputterings and kicks aimed at nonexistent chickens that entered the chapel].[5] For Lorca, laughter—whether simple or complex, disarming or desperate— was an instinctive reaction to life. This is apparent in *Libro de poemas*, in which the poet expresses his sense of loss as his childhood and religious faith recede into the past. Unlike the fables, many poems in this early book are not amusing but present life as a grim joke.

"Pajarita de papel" [Paper bird] is one of these dark poems in which a child's toy, the "águila de niños" [child's eagle] that brings delight, becomes for the poet the forlorn and grotesque symbol of childhood illusion. The "pájaro *clown*" [the clown bird] inhabits a house of cards that symbolizes the blissful days of childhood. But the poet, having experienced the pains of growing up, knows that the toy, like childhood, is fragile and short-lived. As the paper bird sits before its house, it seems not a toy to the poet but a sinister cartoon, "ciega y sin alas / . . . el atleta grotesco que sonríe / ahorcado por un hilo" [blind and without wings / . . . the grotesque athlete that smiles / hung by a thread]. Though gaiety prevails as the children amuse themselves with the toy, for the poet this gaiety is hollow because it hides reality; childhood passes swiftly, "mientras ríen los niños, / y callan los papás" [while the children smile, / and the parents keep silent]. The poem concludes with a disturbing suggestion that parents, knowing the disillusionment to come, sit quietly by like silent accomplices.

The same indictment of a figure of authority is expressed in "Canción para la luna." Again the poet uses gallows humor to voice his despair at no longer being able to accept the religious beliefs he has been taught:

Jehová acostumbra	[Jehova is in the habit
sembrar su finca	of sowing his fields
con ojos muertos	with the dead eyes
y cabecitas	and little skulls
de su contrarias	of his military
milicias.	adversaries.] (P. 215)

In the final line, Lorca affirms his independence from religion with bitter sarcasm, adding parenthetically, "(Ya habréis notado que soy nihilista)" [(You will have noted that I'm a nihilist)].

"Elegía del silencio" also registers anger at an unreliable God. In a satiric but jaunty mood the poet implores a friend to take the following action:

Si Jehová se ha dormido	[If Jehova has gone to sleep
sube al trono brillante,	climb up on the shining throne,
quiébrale en su cabeza	break a burnt-out star
un lucero apagado	over his head

| y acaba seriamente | and put an end |
| con la música eterna. | to the eternal music.] (P. 219) |

These irreverent lines disguise youthful hostility toward the poet's spiritual father, who has left him alone and without comfort. His defiance becomes more brazen in "Prólogo," a monologue in which the poet addresses God with the petulance of an abandoned child:

Además, Satanás me quiere	[Besides, Satan loves me very
mucho,	much,
fue compañero mío	he was my companion
en un examen de	on a lusty spree,
lujuria, y el pícaro	and the rascal
buscará a Margarita	will look for Margarita
—me lo tiene ofrecido—	—He offered to do it for me—
. . . . . .	. . . . . .
Y entonces, ¡oh, Señor!,	And then, Oh, Lord,
seré tan rico	I will be as rich as you
o más que tú,	or more so,
porque el vacío	because emptiness
no puede compararse	cannot compare with
al vino	the wine
con que Satán obsequia	that Satan
a sus buenos amigos.	offers his good friends.
Licor hecho con llanto.	A liquor made with tears.] (P. 241)

Satirical commentary from the mouths of animals and mockery of the experiences and beliefs of childhood do not, at first glance, seem particularly menacing. It is important, however, to keep in mind that such satirical laughter conceals wounds that never entirely disappear from Lorca's psyche. The antiauthoritarian poems of *Libro de poemas* are amusing in their puerile challenge of the powers that restrain youth. This apparently harmless humor is repeated later in *Mariana Pineda*, in which two nuns, as ingenuous yet as perceptive as children, question the authorities' claim that the frail Mariana is a political threat. In the later plays, Lorca's protest against authority grows more aggressive and overt.

Just as caricature and *humour noir* express the young poet's disillusionment and dissatisfaction with authority, the fear of death is also concealed behind a variety of comic disguises. As in all Lorca's works, death haunts *Libro de poemas*. The figure of death, however, does not always appear as a fearful specter but sometimes masquerades as a kindly parent taking her children to a carnival, as in "Otro sueño":

y mi corazón da vueltas	[and my heart jumps
lleno de tedio,	full of boredom,
como un tiovivo en que la Muerte	like a merry-go-round on which Death
pasea a sus hijuelos.	gives her children a spin.] (P. 278)

In "La luna y la muerte" death appears as a bizarre, preposterous old woman:

Doña Muerte, arrugada,	[Lady Death, wrinkled,
pasea por sauzales	wanders through the willow groves
con su absurdo cortejo	with her absurd cortege
de ilusiones remotas.	of dim illusions.] (P. 265)

This representation of death in the guise of an absurd old crone is perhaps an early prototype of the crafty Mendiga, who appears in the third act of *Bodas de sangre*. Pointing the way to Novio, who is lost in the forest, the old woman is the personification of death, politely directing her victims down the last road they will follow.

The ominous humor of *Libro de poemas* expresses the adolescent's abrasive first contact with and defense against the realities of the adult world. In this early book, childhood has not entirely faded from Lorca's mind, yet his delight in the toys and fables of his past is fraught with apprehension and visions of death. Turning increasingly to the avant-garde, Lorca began to write freer, less serious verse; the frivolity of *Canciones*, his first avant-garde book, contrasts sharply with the somber *Libro de poemas*. The poet appears to have regained his sense of merriment and is at play with the words and images of his craft. Much of the verbal frolic of *Canciones* is devoted to the cultivation of images, one of the foremost concerns of avant-garde poets during the 1920's. Yet the book is not merely a Gongoristic exercise in image making, for Lorca is no longer concerned with aesthetic beauty. Humor is of central importance in *Canciones*. Breaking away from traditional forms, such as ballads and fables, Lorca now turns to children's songs and nursery rhymes. These verses add spontaneity and zest to the incongruous humor and delight in nonsense that characterize his outlook on life.

Frivolous and ironic poems dealing with the preoccupations of school children account for some of the gaiety of *Canciones*. Among the first in the book is the wry "La canción del colegial," dedicated to the most important days in the lives of school-age youngsters, Saturday and Sunday. In a similar mock-serious manner, a young man contemplates death in "Suicidio," as the poet suggests, "Quizá fué por no saberte / la Geometría" [Perhaps it was because of not knowing you / Geometry]. "Ribereñas" evokes the image of a young man trying without success to be serious:

Pero tus ojos... ¡Ah!	[But your eyes—Ah!
(balalín)	(balalín)
... perdona, tus ojeras...	—pardon, the dark circles under your eyes—
(balalán)	(balalán)
y esa rosa de oro	and that golden rose
(balalín)	(balalín)
y esa... no puedo, esa...	and that—I can't, that—
(balalán)	(balalán)
. . . .	. . . .
¡Oh tu encanto secreto!..., tu...	Oh your secret charm! your—
(balalín)	(balalín)
lín	lín
lín	lín
lín...)	lín—)
Dispensa.	Pardon.] (P. 387)

The fables that captured Lorca's imagination in *Libro de poemas* lose their didactic and satirical intent in *Canciones*. In this more innovative book, children's songs are merely fanciful evocations of the creatures of nature in such poems as "Caracola," "El lagarto está llorando," and "La canción del mariquita." The imagery of these modernized fables corresponds to Ramón Gómez de la Serna's formula for the *greguería*: "humorismo + metáfora." Both Lorca and Ramón were intrigued with animals, and some of their best images are humorous comparisons of animals with humans. Lorca's reference to lizards as aged creatures—"qué viejos son los lagartos"—parallels the *greguería* in which the cat "tiene desde joven los bigotes blancos" [has had a white mustache since childhood].[6] The mock-serious image of the ladybug, who "organiza / los bucles de su cabeza" [arranges / her curls], seems based on the same amusing comparison as in the *greguería*: "El león daría la mitad de su vida por un peine" [The lion would give half his life for a comb].[7]

Like the fables in *Canciones*, poems based on nursery rhymes retain only a suggestion of their traditional origin. "El niño mudo" is an example of a poem that begins in the traditional manner, by suggesting a narrative. The narration, however, is not continued but only serves as a topic around which the poet improvises new and capricious metaphors. The poem begins by relating that a child has lost his voice:

No la quiero para hablar	[I don't want it to speak with
me haré con ella un anillo	I'll make a ring with it
que llevará mi silencio	that my silence will wear
en su dedo pequeñito.	on its little finger.] (P. 404)

The gaiety of *Canciones* is sustained by such poems as "Tío-vivo," "Dos marinos en la Orilla," and "Canción tonta," which convey a carnival spirit of pleasure and nonsense. "Lunes, miércoles y viernes" is a kind of poetic prank: "La luna estaba de broma / diciendo que era una rosa" [The moon is joking / saying that she was a rose]. The reference to a severed head in "Canción inútil," in which the poet imagines himself "Labrando la bandeja / donde no irá mi cabeza" [Carving a tray / on which my head will not lie], foreshadows the mock-violent prose tales in *Narraciones*.

Erotic imagery is also presented in an amusing manner in *Canciones*. The voluptuous Leonarda of "En Málaga" is comic because her sensuality is described in religious terms. Referring to Leonarda's "carne pontifical y traje blanco" [pontifical flesh and white suit], Lorca achieves the effect of comic irreverence in much the same way that Federico Fellini does in his film *La dolce vita*, which portrays a seductive movie star in a severe black costume crowned with a priest's hat. But, like Fellini's Silvia, Leonarda is no nun. The location of her house, facing "a los tranvías y a los barcos" [the streetcars and ships], implies that Leonarda has numerous lovers. With her "culo / de Ceres in retórica de marmól" [rear / like Ceres' in a flourish of marble], Leonarda is an early version of the puppet heroine Rosita. In the later puppet farce Rosita is described as having a "culito como un queso" [little rear like a cheese]; like Leonarda, Rosita, too, has had many lovers. Thus, some of the comic details of "En Málaga" appear later in dramatic form in the *Retablillo de don Cristóbal*.

The poems of *Canciones* are ingenious and often amusing. Lorca appears to be engaged in witty games, taking liberties with rhyme, such as "Abejaruco. / Uco uco uco uco" in "Malestar y noche," and finding great delight in nonsense, as in "Canción tonta." Dedicating a series of "juegos" [games] to "la cabeza de Luis Buñuel" [the head of Luis Buñuel], Lorca seems to have recovered from his confrontation with harsh realities in *Libro de poemas*. But *Canciones* is not entirely without macabre moments. Death is not so prominent as in the first book; it appears, however, in a group of verses entitled "Nocturnos de la ventana." The poet, describing a young girl who has drowned, announces that he will pray for her:

Yo luego pondré a su lado	[And then I will place by her
las pequeñas calabazas	little pumpkins
para que se tenga a flote,	so that she remains afloat,
¡ay!, sobre la mar salada.	ay! upon the salty sea.] (P. 370)

This reference to death without grief or melancholy reflects the startling juxtaposition of whimsy and death found in the grim lullabies, or "nanas infantiles," which Lorca collected and discussed in an essay.

Canciones is a collection of ironic, sarcastic, and frivolous verses in which Lorca learned to manipulate striking imagery and new techniques of poetic expression. The jovial exuberance of the book results from a new literary iconoclasm which Lorca found, not in the highly distilled technique of Mallarmé, but in the humorous aesthetics of Gómez de la Serna's *greguerías*. Lorca was not solely dedicated to "dignifying" the purely metaphorical element of poetry[8] but instead sought a poetic idiom capable of expressing the witty and capricious, yet sardonic and macabre, thoughts inherent in his attitude toward life. Thus, it is mischief rather than dignity that best characterizes the poems of *Canciones*.

In his best-known book of poems, *Romancero gitano*, Lorca's imagination is drawn away from the child's realm of fables and fantasy toward the equally exotic world of gypsies. Lorca knew how to make this strange (for many Spaniards as well as the non-Spanish) subculture his own. By use of comic techniques that make alien behavior seem familiar, Lorca rendered the gypsy kingdom accessible to all. Like the poor everywhere, the gypsy society is a marginal one, lacking sufficient power and prestige to ensure immunity against brutal attacks from outside antagonists, such as the police. In "Romance de la guardia civil española" Lorca again resorts to caricature, satirizing the civil guard as repulsive and menacing creatures who lurk about at night:

Jorobados y nocturnos,	[Humpbacked and nocturnal,
por donde animan ordenan	wherever they go they cause
silencios de goma oscura	gum-shoe silence
y miedos de fina arena.	and fears like fine sand.] (P. 453)

In terms equivalent to those used by the black people of the South to satirize white Klan members, Lorca portrays the civil guards as comic grotesques whose minds are as deformed as their bodies. They take advantage of their position of authority to terrorize the gypsies. Discovering a fiesta in the gypsy quarter, complete with carousing, lights, and banners, the guards move in and sack the area. The gypsies, surprised by the onslaught, become the helpless victims of the brutal guards. The defensive humor of caricature is the gypsy's only means of expressing his protest and hatred of oppression by the civil guards.

In addition to the vicious caricatures in "Romance de la guardia civil," other comic characters, more amusing than hostile, appear throughout *Romancero*. "La monja gitana" describes a young gypsy whose suppressed desires contradict her religious vocation. In the character of the gypsy nun Lorca contrives an incongruous combination of traits, for, as J.-L. Schonberg points out: "Qu' il existe des religieuses Gitanes, Lorca, mieux que personne devait en douter. Une Gitane, même nonnaine, cultiverait ses vices et son tempérament; elle sauterait les murs du monastère plutôt que de s'atteindre à des travaux d'aigulle. Mais qui sait? . . . Il se peut fort bien . . . qu' elle calcule une fuite romantique" [Lorca, more than anyone, should doubt that there exist religious gypsy women. A gypsy girl, even a nun, would cultivate her vices and her spirit, would scale the cloister walls before submitting to doing needlework. But, who knows? . . . It may well be . . . that she is planning to escape to her lover].[9]

The contrast between the nun's chastity and the visions of handsome gypsy horsemen that run through her mind as she embroiders makes the frustrated gypsy nun a comic character. The church hovers as a kind of *éminence grise* in the background: "La iglesia gruñe a lo lejos / como un oso panza arriba" [The church growls in the distance / like a bear with a full stomach]. The comparison of the cupola and the sound of bells to the distant groaning of a fat bear not only serves as a backdrop to the poem, which is almost theatrical in its attention to visual and auditory details, but completes the comic burlesque as well. In "La monja gitana" sexual frustration is presented in a comic manner; Lorca again portrays frustration and isolation with comic irony in *Doña Rosita la soltera*. When the heroine contemplates marriage by proxy, her maid inquires, "¿Y por la noche, qué?" [And what happens at night?].

In one of the best-known poems of the *Romancero*, "La casada infiel," Lorca resolves an ironic situation with a subtle wit that displays his thorough understanding of the gypsy code of honor. Lorca's gypsy finds that he has been tricked by a country girl, as he explains abashedly in the opening lines of the poem:

Y que yo me la llevé al río	[I took her with me to the river
creyendo que era mozuela,	thinking she was single,
pero tenía marido.	but she was married.] (P. 434)

Trying to justify his behavior toward the girl, he adds that, thinking she was a virgin, he felt obliged to accept her attentions "casi por compromiso" [almost as a duty]. The gypsy's embarrassment becomes amusing; he relates as much of the encounter as his modesty will allow. But what Arturo Barea aptly terms his "ostentatious" masculine dignity stops him short of repeating their conversation:[10] "No quiero decir, por hombre, / las cosas que ella me dijo" [Being a man, I won't tell / the things she told me]. The gypsy's enjoyment of the episode is spoiled by the suspi-

cion that he has been the object of a joke, so he insults the girl by paying
her for her time:

La regalé un costurero	[I gave her a sewing basket
grande de raso pajizo,	with a straw-colored ribbon,
y no quise enamorarme	I didn't want to fall for her
porque teniendo marido	because, having a husband
me dijo que era mozuela.	she told me she was free.] (P. 436)

Lorca observed amusing ironies not only in the gypsy character and
his code of honor, but also in his sense of religious devotion. The puppetlike figures of saints in the trio of poems—"San Miguel," "San Rafael," and
"San Gabriel"—are presented by Lorca as comical when adorned in extravagant costumes by gypsies whose Christianity is tinged with supersti-
tion and folklore. San Miguel, decked out in lace and ribbons, presides
over the dawn from his niche. The traditionally manly saint appears to
Lorca to be uncomfortable in the effeminate garb: "Arcángel domesticado
. . . / finge una cólera dulce / de plumas y ruiseñores" [Harmless archan-
gel . . . / pretends in a sweet way, to be ferocious / with plumes and night-
ingales]. "San Rafael," an obscure poem that J.-L. Schonberg calls a "satire
obscène," has only four lines referring directly to the saint.[11] In "San
Gabriel" it is not the visual details of dress but the gypsies' childlike attitude toward the saint that amuses the poet. The figure of San Gabriel is
gaudily dressed as the procession bearing his statue moves through the
streets of Seville. Hoping the saint is so pleased with his finery that he will
do them favors, they remind him, "No olvides que los gitanos / te regala-
ron el traje" [Don't forget that the gypsies / gave you the finery]. While
these absurdly arrayed religious images appear comic, they have a strong
erotic appeal to the gypsy mind, in which pagan and Christian symbols in-
termingle. Thus, Lorca's caricature of the saints is, in these poems, sympathetic, for he acknowledges that they are sincerely worshipped by the
gypsy folk.

Another caricature in *Romancero* is the figure of the British consul in
"Preciosa y el aire." David Bary explains that the British eccentric, frequently found in diplomatic service, is a comic stereotype.[12] Observing
his odd behavior is something of a spectator sport for amused Spaniards.

Lorca's use of a comic figure in an otherwise gloomy poem leads Bary to question the "tragic" tone of "Preciosa y el aire." But the mood of impending doom is not impaired. As is more evident in Lorca's theater, the presence of a caricature in an ominous scene is typical of Lorca's art, in which humor and disaster coexist.

The sense of impending doom in the "Burla de don Pedro a caballo" is actually enhanced by the use of whimsical humor. The treacherous murder of the young knight is a historical theme, dramatized by Lope de Vega in his *comedia El caballero de Olmedo*. Lorca calls his own version of the legend a *burla*, or prank, a term that indicates his attitude toward death as revealed in the poem. The ballad begins as don Pedro, mounted on a fine horse, passes through town "en la busca / del pan y del beso" [in search / of food and the fair sex]. The cause of the knight's death is not explained, but the final lines jestingly relate that

Sobre la flor enfriada,	[Here lies don Pedro,
está don Pedro olvidado,	playing with frogs,
¡ay!, jugando con las ranas.	he is now forgotten.] (P. 463)

That death is presented as a *burla*, or joke, on the young noble conveys perhaps better than a serious statement the poet's realization that death is not only inevitable but also sly and mysterious. Although Lope dramatizes don Pedro's death with scenes alternately comic and tragic, the play ends on a note of gloom. But the whimsical, sardonic lines of the *burla* suggest that "this ironic treatment of the dead knight [is] original with Lorca."[13]

Death appears as a playful but fatal jest in "Burla de don Pedro a caballo"; in "Romance de la luna, luna" it masquerades as a seductive moon-woman. A gypsy boy whom she visits warns the moon-woman to leave before the gypsy troupe returns to camp. But she has taken a liking to the child. Decked out in an extravagant costume with a huge bustle, a "polisón de nardos," she beguiles the boy and wins power over him. He disappears with her, and when the gypsies return they discover that "por el cielo va la luna / con un niño de la mano" [through the sky the moon passes / holding a child by the hand]. This opening poem begins *Romancero* with the same whimsical presentation of death found in "Burla de don Pedro a caballo," the penultimate ballad of the book.

Of the eighteen poems in *Romancero*, half are comic or ironic. In most of these the play between naïve amusement and deep pessimism creates a tense situation, the outcome of which is made to seem surprising: an eccentric British consul appears just in time to save Preciosa from certain disaster; an innocent gypsy boy falls victim to an enchanting figure who dances about in an outlandish dress; without explanation, the virile don Pedro becomes a corpse, playing with frogs underground; the manly saints of Christendom seem ridiculous when dressed like dolls by superstitious gypsies. J.-L. Schonberg describes this book as a "guignolade," a puppet show; for, despite its dark themes of murder and martyrdom, *Romancero* conveys the mock-serious tone of an amusing charade. Lorca treats somber themes with "une énorme ironie prête à jongler avec la vie, l'amour, la morte, les pleurs, la religion, et les mots" [enormous irony, tending to play with life, love, death, tears, religion, and words].[14] Yet *Romancero* is one of Lorca's most characteristic works and represents the best of his lyric poetry in the folkloric vein. As he turned from the gypsy realm of *Romancero* to the modern scene, from lyric poetry to prose and drama, Lorca continued to express his thoughts with the same comic irony as in *Romancero*. The satire of cruelty and injustice, the disasters in a comic guise, and the ingenuous yet ominous characters of the ballads of *Romancero* are recognizable throughout most of Lorca's lyric and dramatic art.

Lorca's ironic humor appears incidentally in other lyric works, such as *Cantares populares* and *Diván del Tamarit*. A series of thirteen whimsical poems, *Cantares populares* consists of light-hearted verses written in traditional ballad form. One of the most interesting of these songs is the last, "Romance de don Boyso," in which a surprise ending is enhanced with comic irony. The ballad tells the story of don Boyso, who rides into Moorish lands "a buscar amiga" [to find a girl]. He finds a young Christian girl and takes her with him "por ver que decía" [to see what she'd say]. She tells him of her brother, whom she has missed while she has been held captive by the Moors. Finally don Boyso discloses his intentions and also the identity of the girl:

Abra la mi madre   [Mother, open
puertas de alegría,   the doors of joy,

| por traerla nuera | for a daughter-in-law |
| le traigo su hija. | I bring you your daughter.] (P. 666) |

This poem is not intended to arouse laughter, nor is it particularly amusing. Yet the revelation that the girl is don Boyso's sister comes as a surprise. Like much of modern humor, the humor of these lines lies in revealing the unexpected, "the absurd . . . the inexplicable, the nonsensical —in other words, the comic."[15] Another example of Lorca's liking for improbable and incongruous situations is found in the "Gacela de la huida," a poem included in *Diván del Tamarit*. The sinister delight expressed in this verse is reminiscent not only of the "Burla de don Pedro a caballo," but also of the *nanas infantiles*, or cradle songs, that Lorca collected.

No hay noche que, al dar un beso,	[There is never a night that, when kissing,
no sienta la sonrisa de las gentes sin rostro,	one doesn't feel the smiles of faceless people,
ni hay nadie que, al tocar un recién nacido,	nor is there anyone who touches a new-born child,
olvide las inmóviles calaveras de caballo.	who can forget the still skulls of horses.] (P. 565)

In his essay on cradle songs Lorca appears intrigued with certain lullabies "cuya severidad lírica es tan madura que más bien parece canto para morir que canto para el primer sueño" [whose lyrical austerity is so ancient that they seem songs lamenting death rather than putting an infant to sleep] (p. 103). The poet's liking for incongruity is reflected in the grim verses of "Gacela," in which the grotesque specter of death restrains even the joy that comes from touching the face of a beloved or the tiny form of a newborn child.

I have left until last *Poema del cante jondo*, for in it Lorca's comic spirit takes dramatic rather than lyric form. *Poema del cante jondo* closes with two satirical dialogues, "two fantasies of black humor,"[16] that are typical of Lorca's later dramatic works. The first is entitled "Escena del teniente colonel de la Guardia Civil." Like the bully don Cristóbal of Lorca's two puppet plays, the officer who is the main character is a comic type, a parody of an authoritarian figure. The principal difference between the puppet and the officer is that the latter is wearing a military uniform in which he struts about showing off his medals and ribbons. He takes pride in having once spoken to the archbishop, who, with "veinticuatro borlas moradas" [twenty-four purple academic tassels], wears even more elaborate decorations than the officer.

Suddenly the vision of Romeo and Juliet embracing appears before the officer. He hears the following verses, "Señor alcalde, sus niños / están mirando a la luna" [Mr. Mayor, your children / are moon watching], announcing the possibility that the mayor's daughters may be susceptible to love. The officer can only respond by caressing the barrel of his nearby gun and repeating three times that he is an officer of the guard.

Upon hearing the verses, the sergeant brings forth a gypsy whom he has arrested without cause: "Me lo encontré y lo he traído" [I met him and brought him in]. He interrogates him as if he were a criminal, but the gypsy is not intimidated. Instead he begins to enumerate the qualities that make him physically attractive, each one a blow to the officer. "Nubes y anillos en mi sangre" [clouds and rings in my blood], the gypsy announces while the officer cries out as if in pain. When the gypsy continues, "Y naranjas en la nieve" [oranges in the snow], the officer falls dead and his "alma de tabaco y café con leche" [coffee-and-tobacco soul] rises and departs through the window. The gypsy, however, is brought to justice for having so many charms and is beaten by four guards as the sketch ends with a poem entitled "Canción del gitano Apaleado."

This fanciful satire is evidence that, for Lorca, the bitter feud between the gypsy and his society could be portrayed as both genuinely comic and pathetic. As early as 1933 Octavio Ramírez noted the "rasgo, casi cómico, y bien peculiar a la raza" [almost comic streak, peculiar to them] that characterizes the gypsy hatred for the civil guard.[17] Lorca's absurd caricature of the officer expresses the defensive humor of the gypsy folk toward the police. Yet the notion that the gypsy's plight might be presented in a comic manner is shocking to Berenguer Carisomo,[18] who, like many of Lorca's critics, has defined the tragic mode so narrowly that it cannot adequately describe his art, in which the comic spirit plays a definitive role.

The second of the dialogues of *Poema del cante jondo* is an early example of Lorca's practice of inserting a comic moment into a foreboding scene. In "Diálogo del Amargo" the young gypsy, Amargo, meets his death in the same vaguely ominous way as don Pedro in *Romancero*. On his way to Granada, Amargo is offered a ride by a man whose three brothers sell knives. With the dry wit of country folk who want nothing to do with strangers, Amargo declines the offer, "because my feet don't hurt," a laconic remark that conceals his fear of imminent danger. But Amargo's wit is to no avail, and he does not intimidate the stranger. "Diálogo del Amargo," like the preceding "Escena del teniente colonel," ends with a song lamenting the gypsy's ill fate.

Lorca cannot, of course, be considered a comic poet; yet many of his poems are ironic and whimsical, and one of his books, *Canciones*, is almost entirely composed of literary antics. Only two of Lorca's major lyric works do not express his sense of humor or comic absurdity in some way. One that naturally does not is the elegy on the death of Ignacio Sánchez Mejías. Lorca had no need to dramatize the unmitigated grief of this poem with irony or to conceal death's palpable presence behind a comic guise. *Poeta en Nueva York* is the other of Lorca's major lyric works that does not express his comic spirit. That Lorca made his sojourn to New York, as Angel del Río has related, because of an emotional depression that plagued him is confirmed by the poet himself in letters to his friends (p. 1673). Both in a personal as well as in a literary sense, Lorca's experience in New York was a *saison en enfer* [season in hell] during which the poet, temporarily lacking the customary reserve of inner strength and poise that allowed him to deride hopelessness and horror, lost his ability to laugh at monsters. The grotesque images of *Poeta en Nueva York* show none of Lorca's previous delight in horror that he expresses, for example, in the prose *Narraciones*. Although, in the poems of New York, technological man seems to be more brutal than the primitive blacks of Harlem, this irony is conveyed only by visions of slaughter. The poet protests injustice and cruelty; he can, however, no longer relish the ridiculous image of his enemies that he had previously created with the grotesque caricatures of the civil guards and in the religious satire of his early poems and prose. The extreme desolation of *Poeta en Nueva York*, unbroken by any vestige of humor, is clearly the result of a collapse of the poet's psychological defenses.

With the exception, then, of Lorca's famous elegy and *Poeta en Nueva*

York, both written while he was in a state of emotional shock, Lorca's lyric poetry reveals the various kinds of humor that make up his comic outlook. Though not a writer of social protest in the restricted sense of political propaganda, Lorca denounces the savage violence of the civil guards by means of satirical caricatures. He recalls his adolescent religious crisis in grim comic verse. Amused and delighted by the creatures of fable, as in *Canciones*, he expresses despair by means of whimsical ambiguous humor. Amusement at ominous events is particularly characteristic of Lorca's comic spirit. Vicente Aleixandre had this combination of opposing moods in mind when he described Lorca as "disipador de tristezas, hechicero de la alegría, conjurador del gozo de la vida . . . capaz de toda la alegría del Universo; pero su sima profunda . . . no era la de la alegría" [one who banishes melancholy, casts spells of happiness, a conjuror of love of life . . . capable of all the joy in the world; but his profound depths . . . are not ones of joy] (pp. 1830–1831).

While Lorca's humor runs its full gamut in his lyric poetry, it becomes more important in his theater, for most of his plays are tragicomedies and farces in which humor is the principal means of expression. The incidental comic scenes and characters that appear in his lyric poetry are developed more fully in his plays. If the wide range of Lorca's humor is suggested in his poems, his comic outlook becomes central to the meaning of his dramatic art.

2. Tragicomedies and Farces

Lorca's first two plays, *El maleficio de la mariposa* and *Mariana Pineda*, are hardly more than lyrical presentations of dramatic characters. Neither of the two verse plays was successful: *El maleficio* was discontinued after only two performances, while *Mariana Pineda* was received more politely for a week's run in both Madrid and Barcelona. If Lorca, as a beginning playwright, had not yet learned to integrate lyrical elements into dramatic form, his natural proclivity for comic techniques helped him to expand his poetic dialogues into full-fledged theater. The comic characters and satiric and whimsical verses of his lyric works reappear in Lorca's plays to dramatize themes of unfulfillment and death.

The emergence of dramatic scenes from Lorca's lyric poetry is nowhere more apparent than in his first play, *El maleficio*. The fable was conceived as a dialogue in verse, one of several that Lorca wrote, two of which appeared in *Libro de poemas*. Gregorio Martínez Sierra, the director of the avant-garde Teatro Eslava in Madrid, was so impressed by Lorca's recitation of the dialogue that he promised to stage the piece if the poet would prepare a version for the theater. Lorca was aware that the work was premature, but the opportunity to have a play staged at the Teatro Eslava was too good to pass up.[1] Thus, Lorca saw his first play produced on March 22, 1920, not quite a year after he had arrived from Granada to take up residence for the first time in Madrid.

Reading *El maleficio* now, one may well wonder what attracted Martínez Sierra's interest in a play whose characters are cockroaches, a butterfly, and a scorpion. To understand this, it is helpful to remember that the
theater in Spain, as in most of Europe, had been for the first two decades
of the twentieth century so dominated by realism that drawing-room comedy and bourgeois tragedy monopolized the Spanish stage. Only ten years
before, Maurice Maeterlinck had challenged the durable realistic theater
with his poetic dramas. In 1908 his *L'Oiseau bleu* offered an imaginative
alternative to the well-worn bourgeois comedies of the day. Although
Chantecler failed on the French stage in 1910, Rostand followed Maeterlinck's example of writing fables in an effort to escape the threadbare conventions of realism.

In Spain, Martínez Sierra had, as translator and producer of the works
of Maeterlinck, been one of those most responsible for introducing the
Belgian dramatist to the Spanish public. Maeterlinck was read not only
by modernist poets and playwrights but also by younger Spanish writers,
such as Lorca. There are many traces of Maeterlinckian fantasy and mystery in Lorca's first play. The music accompanying *El maleficio* was by De-
bussy, whose opera *Pelléas et Mélisande* was inspired by Maeterlinck's
play. Thus, it may have been the symbolist tones of *El maleficio* that Martínez Sierra admired, for it was he who chose its title, which reflects the
ethereal, enigmatic dramas of Maeterlinck. Yet this title does not accurately suit the character of Lorca's piece.[2] In spite of its symbolist overtones,
the caricature and burlesque of *El maleficio* distinguish it from the rather
sentimental plays of Maeterlinck and their Spanish modernist counterparts.
Lacking the optimism, for example, of *L'Oiseau Bleu*, the insect characters
of *El Maleficio* fail in their quest for happiness. Parody of human behavior in *El maleficio* sets it apart from symbolist theater and defines it as a
peculiarly Lorquian work. In the prologue Lorca terms his dramatized
fable a "comedia rota," a disturbed or broken comedy, which accurately
describes its mixture of whimsy and despair.

In *Maleficio*, as in Lorca's earlier poetic fables, animals serve as a comic
guise for the burlesque of human behavior. Instead of implying that humans often act like insects, as Karel Čapek suggests in *The Insect Play*
(1923), Lorca views small creatures of nature with wonder and delight.
He achieves an amusing contrast between the human and the insect world

by reducing the scale of time: the oldest insect has lived for six years, while another complains of being old at the age of only two months. The illusion of tiny size was enhanced by sets depicting giant flower stalks and plants that dwarfed the human figures on the stage. This Lilliputian framework provided the adolescent playwright a setting sufficiently remote from the real world so that he could safely parody religious and social ideas, which in their human context seemed to him ridiculous.

The hero of the fable is an idealistic poet-roach, Curianito, who falls in love with a white butterfly. Among the comic characters in the piece is the poet's mother. She discovers that Silvia, the lady roach, who is enchanted with Curianito, is also rich. Like the greedy mother of Belisa, anxious to marry her daughter to the rich old bachelor in *El amor de don Perlimplín*, the mother of the poet-roach vows to force her son into marriage with Silvia if necessary. The villain of the piece is Alacranito the scorpion, who is a drunkard and a glutton. Alacranito is a *leñador*, a woodcutter; like the woodcutters who speak of knives and blades in the third act of *Bodas de sangre*, he is a sinister creature. But Alacranito is also a buffoon. Like Cristóbal of Lorca's puppet farces, his threats and his attempts to bully others are merely comic. He is also somewhat lascivious; caught spying on the romantic young Silvia, who "en su clase de insecto repugnante es encantadora" [as a repugnant insect is, in her way, enchanting] (p. 676), he greets her with a comic flourish. Winking at Curianito maliciously, Alacranito asks the two roaches if he is interrupting their plans to build a nest. When he is rebuffed by Curianito and Silvia, the scorpion retorts, "La *alistogracia* también tiene sus pesares" [The *alistogracia* also has its sorrows] (p. 691). *Alistogracia* is a pun on *aristocracia*, and expresses the tipsy clown's opinion that these two roaches may be lively and elegant (*listo con gracia*), but they are also snobs and thus belong to the *alistogracia*.

The comic cruelty of Alacranito becomes grotesque when he horrifies the other roaches by boasting of having eaten a worm. But he passed over the worm's offspring, explaining, "Y no me comí al nene por estar en lactancia. / Y a mí me gustan grandes" [I didn't eat the baby because it was still nursing. / I like larger ones] (p. 693). The final scene of Act I ends with both comedy and despair: Alacranito, "tumbado panza arriba en el prado" [passed out on his back in the meadow], sings of good things to eat, while the poet-roach, who has discovered he is in love, sits on a stone and begins to sob.

Act II opens with a scene laden with religious satire. One of the roaches, Curianita Santa, is a caricature of the *beatas*, women whose constant presence at church makes them appear more devout than most but whose devotion is often superficial. Repeating the commands of Gran Cucaracho, Curianita Santa is like the children of a currently popular comic strip who speak with mock reverence of the Great Pumpkin. As the saintly roach tries to proselytize her neighbors, the ensuing conversation becomes an amusing parody of a religious debate:

> *Curianita 1ª*:   ¿Es que el Gran Cucaracho no comía, comadre?
>   (*Con sorna*) Pues, decidle a un hambriento esas frases.
>
> *Curianita Santa*:   El hambre es un demonio con antenas de fuego a quien hay que alejar...
>
> *Curianita 1ª*:   ¿Comiendo, eh?
>
> *Curianita Santa*:   Orando.
>
> [*Curianita 1ª*:   You mean the Great Cockroach didn't eat, comrade?
>   (*Scornfully*) Well, tell that to someone who's hungry.
>
> *Curianita Santa*:   Hunger is a demon with fiery antennae whom we must avoid by—
>
> *Curianita 1ª*:   Eating, eh?
>
> *Curianita Santa*:   Praying.] (P. 703)

The mixture of tragedy and farce that ends the first act of the fable is repeated in Act II. The white butterfly, who represents love and death, lies wounded, lamenting its fate in a poetic monologue. As the stricken creature finishes its lament, the scorpion approaches, sniffing fresh meat: "(*por la derecha*) asoma la graciosísima pinza de Alacranito" [(*from the right*) Alacranito's graceful pincher begins to feel about] (p. 709). He makes threatening moves toward the butterfly but is chased off by the roaches who guard the fallen beauty. Singing vicious little verses, Alacranito abruptly changes the pathos of the scene to comic burlesque as he gleefully licks his chops over the butterfly, a tempting morsel. Unable to approach the butterfly, the gluttonous scorpion heads home, muttering to himself about his dinner: "Ya me voy a mi cueva / a comerme diez moscas" [I'm going to my den now / to eat ten flies]. Although the published text is unfinished, the melancholy fable ends when the butterfly recovers and flies away, leaving behind the sad poet, who soon dies.

Audiences in Madrid, accustomed to Benavente's sophisticated dukes and duchesses, whose witty repartee filled the theaters of the 1920's, were vociferously unreceptive to such fare as *El maleficio*. Lorca must have known that his efforts to revive theater while avoiding the predictable comedy of manners would fail. In the prologue to the piece, he entreats the public before it has heard the play,

¿Por qué os causan repugnancia algunos insectos limpios y brillantes
que se mueven graciosamente entre las hierbas? ¿Y por qué a
vosotros . . . llenos de pecados y de vicios incurables, os inspiran
asco los buenos gusanos que se pasean tranquilamente por el pradera
. . . ? Tal vez os riáis al oir hablar a estos insectos como hombrecitos,
como adolescentes.

[Why do a few clean and shiny insects moving about gracefully in
the grass revolt you? And why are you . . . yourselves full of
incurable vices and sins, nauseated by the good worms passing
peacefully by in the meadow . . . ? Perhaps you'll laugh when you
hear these insects speak like little men, like adolescents.] (P. 670)

This defensive introduction indicates that Lorca had in mind a new kind of theater that would challenge a complacent audience. Satirical caricatures, grotesque jokes about eating flies and worms, and the comic contrast between human and insect behavior were merely the techniques by which he could both entertain and jolt an unsuspecting public.

Lorca's second play, *Mariana Pineda*, is more conventional than *El maleficio*. Yet it, too, is a melancholy tale of love and death presented in a whimsical way. Just as *El maleficio* is a dramatized fable, *Mariana Pineda* is, as Sumner M. Greenfield points out, a "dramatization of a children's song."[3] The play is based on a historical event but is stylized so that history is ignored and the piece takes on the quality of some of the *nanas infantiles*, or cradle songs, in which the theme of death is treated as a kind of sinister farce.

The theme of Mariana's martyrdom is presented not as harsh reality but as a legend recalled nostalgically by a group of little girls singing in the street. Their song, a popular ballad, recounts the tale of that "día tan triste en Granada" [day, so sad, in Granada] when the young widow, Mariana, was beheaded for not informing the police of the whereabouts of her liberal friends, particularly their leader Pedro, whom Mariana loved. The first scene of the play establishes the foreboding fact that Mariana is embroidering a flag for the liberals who are clandestinely preparing a revolt against the government.

In the second scene, comic relief counters the foreboding mood. This scene is much like the playful meeting in *Doña Rosita* between the heroine and two of her friends who come to visit. Mariana's visitor, her friend Amparo, jokes with Clavela the maid and makes a pun on her name, for a *clavela* is a carnation, one of Lorca's most frequent symbols of sensuality. Amparo greets Clavela by asking her, "¿Qué tal su esposo el clavel?" [How is your husband "el clavel"? (masculine form of the name)]. Clavela responds flatly, "Marchito" [Faded]. Amparo laughs, advising her "¡Paciencia! ¡Pero clavel que no huele, / se corta de la maceta!" [Patience! But a carnation with no smell, / gets pulled from the vase] (pp. 785–786).

Impending doom dominates Act II. Mariana's possible escape from her tormentors becomes increasingly difficult, and she is finally arrested. In Act III the inexorable approach of Mariana's destruction is again interrupted by comic relief. In the convent where she is being held prisoner, Mariana is an object of much interest to the nuns. Like wide-eyed children, they discuss the reason for her arrest. Since Mariana has not committed a crime, the nuns assume she must be a Mason, for Masons were traditionally liberal and therefore suspect in nineteenth-century Spain. The nuns' ingenuous humor underscores the injustice of Mariana's arrest:

Novicia 2ª: Dicen que es masona.	[*Novicia 2ª*: They say she's a mason.

Novicia 1ª: ¿Qué es esto?	*Novicia 1ª*: What's that?
Novicia 2ª: ¡Pues... no sé!	*Novicia 2ª*: Well, I don't know!
Novicia 1ª: ¿Porqué está presa?	*Novicia 1ª*: Why is she a prisoner?
Novicia 2ª: Porque no quiere al rey.	*Novicia 2ª*: Because she doesn't like the king.
Novicia 1ª: ¿Qué más da? . . .	*Novicia 1ª*: So what? . . .
Novicia 2ª: ¡Ni a la reina!	*Novicia 2ª*: Nor the queen!
Novicia 1ª: Yo tampoco los quiero.	*Novicia 1ª*: I don't like them either.] (Pp. 862–863)

The nuns take turns spying on Mariana through a keyhole. The Mother Superior surprises them, scolds them, and sends them away. As soon as they are out of sight the dignified head of the convent puts her eye to the keyhole. When Mariana approaches the door, the embarrassed Mother Superior jumps back, alarmed at the prospect of being discovered spying on her charge.

Whimsical humor in *Mariana Pineda*, however, is not confined to incidental scenes; it is repeated in the more crucial moments that forecast the heroine's death. At the end of the first act, Mariana's two children have found the flag their mother is sewing for the rebels. With the exuberance of children at play, the two wrap themselves in the flag and pretend that they are corpses at a funeral:

Tilín, tilán; abuela,	[Tilín, talán, grandmother,
dile al curita nuestro	tell our priest
que traiga bandoleras	to bring banners
y flores de romero.	and wild flowers.
. . . . .	. . . . . .
Ya vienen los obispos	Now the bishops are coming
decían *ure memento*,	they were saying *ure memento*

| y cerraban los ojos | and were closing their eyes |
| poniéndose muy serios. | becoming very serious.] (P. 817) |

This scene, though it provides comic relief, is not incidental. It introduces the central theme of Mariana's martyrdom by presenting a comic version of death. In the context of a children's game, death loses its impact and becomes unreal. Like a merry account of a sad tale, the manner of presentation precludes our taking death entirely seriously and, indeed, makes it appear amusing.

A similar scene in which Mariana's small son and daughter again sing a song of death is repeated in the second *estampa*, or act. They demand that Clavela recite the ballad of the duke of Lucena as the price for going to bed. The two children know the story so well that they sing with innocent delight the account of a girl who embroiders a flag for the duke, soon to be killed in battle:

Pos las calles de Córdoba	[Throughout the streets of Cordova
lo llevan a enterrar,	they carry him away to be buried,
muy vestido de fraile	in his priest's habit
en caja de coral.	and coral coffin.] (P. 823)

Like the handsome knight of Olmedo in Lorca's poem "Burla de don Pedro a caballo" (see chap. 1), who suddenly became a corpse "jugando con las ranas" [playing with the frogs], the duke of Lucena is accompanied to his grave by a green finch that sings while perched on his coffin:

La albahaca y los claveles	[Sweet basil and carnations
sobre la caja van,	lie upon the coffin,
y un verderol antiguo	and the traditional greenfinch
cantando el pío pa.	sings his chirping song.]

Mariana stands in the doorway listening to these gay but strangely mournful verses, which remind her of the ominous presence of death.

The atmosphere of whimsy is sustained in the play not only by children's songs and games that introduce, punctuate, and terminate the work, but also by the creation of simplified dramatic characters. Though the characters are drawn from the historical personages who participated in the heroine's demise, Lorca has not psychologically defined any character other than the protagonist. The secondary figures are distinguishable only as "good guys" or villains. Mariana is an admirable characterization, yet she remains a childlike figure, speaking of her own death as a presence that "sentada en la fuente / toca una blanda vihuela" [seated at the fountain / plays a mellow guitar]. She refuses to believe that her lover has fled to England and will not return to rescue her. The bearer of this cruel news is the gardener, one of the stock comic servants imported from the commedia dell'arte into the early *entremeses* of Torres Naharo.[4] In *Mariana Pineda* the gardener retains his traditional comic mask. His name is "Alegrito," and he is a pleasant chap who "ríe constantemente con una sonrisa suave y sana" [laughs constantly with a soft, cheerful smile] (p. 867). Yet it is, ironically, this comic figure who informs Mariana of her death sentence.

Lorca's manner of staging *Mariana Pineda* also contributes to the contrived artificiality of the play. While the suspense of Pedro's escape from government forces is genuine, and the pathos of Mariana's downfall is authentic, the play is presented as a series of *estampas*, or static prints, much like a puppet play contained within a frame, or *retablo*. The stage is described in the prologue as being enclosed in a frame, "como una vieja estampa iluminada en azul, verde, amarillo, rosa y celeste, sobre un fondo de paredes negras. Una de las casas que se vean estará pintada con escenas marinas y guirnaldas de frutas" [like an old print lighted in colors of blue, green, yellow, pink, and sky-blue on a background of dark walls. One of the houses that is visible is painted with beach scenes and garlands of fruit]. The sets, painted by Salvador Dalí, were not funereal but lively, enhancing the visual appeal of a period play. The final scene, in which the heroine is led offstage to her death, is not accompanied by weeping and lamentation but by a repetition of the opening ballad, this time sung by a chorus of young boys. Church bells toll while a light, "maravillosa y delirante" [marvelous, delirious] (p. 891), creates what appears to be the beginning of a dream rather than martyrdom. Consciously artificial, *Mariana Pineda* remains, like Lorca's early fables, the creation of a child's world, a kind of serious farce.

That this ingenuous vision was precisely Lorca's intention is clear from the remarks he made to a fellow playwright, Manuel Machado, in which he explained his conception of the play:

> Hoy no se puede hacer en serio *pastiche*, es decir, un drama del pasado. Yo veía dos maneras para realizar mi intento: una, tratando el tema con truculencias y manchones de cartel callejero (pero esto lo hace insuperablemente don Ramón [del Valle-Inclán]), y otra, la que he seguido, que responde a una visión nocturna, lunar e infantil.

> [Today you can't do a serious *pastiche*, that is, a traditional play. I saw two ways of achieving my purpose: one, treating the theme savagely, with painted cardboard characters (but don Ramón [del Valle-Inclán] does this incomparably), and the other, which I have followed, which corresponds to a dreamlike, somewhat moon-struck, childlike vision.] (P. 122)

Admitting that *Mariana Pineda* was not an avant-garde piece, Lorca at the same time insisted, "no es tampoco la usadera" [nor is it the ordinary piece]. It is easy to agree with him that *Mariana Pineda* is unique. The central theme is presented in an entirely ambiguous way: little girls and boys play at death, while martyrdom is accompanied not by a funeral dirge but by children's songs. It is characteristic of Lorca's mind that he treated the cruel injustice of Mariana's martyrdom in this whimsical manner. Perhaps he could best accept death by reducing it to the level of a sinister game.

FARCES

Lorca's laughter at danger and death changes from the eerie whimsy of *Mariana Pineda* into the more freewheeling slapstick humor of farce in *La zapatera* and *Don Perlimplín*. Farce is of special importance in Lorca's dramatic art. The laughingstocks, base jokes, and low humor of traditional comic theater were intended merely to entertain, but Lorca, along with other modern playwrights, adapted these techniques to portray serious, even tragic, situations.

As a writer of farce, Lorca could draw upon a rich tradition. Farces had been written in Spain from the late fifteenth and early sixteenth centuries, when the founders of Spanish drama—Gil Vicente, Juan del Encina, and Torres Naharro—began to steer the theater away from its purely liturgical function. Juan del Encina included in his *Cancionero* of 1496 several rustic, bawdy skits called carnival eclogues. Gil Vicente, a Portuguese poet who also wrote in Spanish, penned numerous comedies and farces. Among them are three *Autos* satirizing figures of authority in which indignant kings and clerics protest their arrival into hell. Torres Naharro, who contributed the earliest dramatic criticism to Spanish literature, also wrote scathing satires. In one of these, *Comedia Tinelaria*, servants of the mess hall (*tinelo*) lambast a corrupt society; another, *Comedia Soldadesca*, is a burlesque of the military profession. Both Juan del Encina and Torres Naharro had lived for extended periods in Italy; both borrowed stock comic types and situations from the commedia dell'arte.

By the mid-sixteenth century, Spanish farce had been considerably refined by Lope de Rueda, whose short comic sketches, or *pasos*, were no longer based on crude erotic jokes and foul language but on more subtle delineation of comic characters and situations.[5] Some of the *pasos* (scenes to pass the time) were entr'actes or *entremeses*, comic skits interspersed between the acts of a full-length play. Some were independent playlets. Lope de Rueda's masterpiece is *Las aceitunas*, a one-act comic skit with the theme of "don't count your chickens before they hatch," in which a husband quarrels with his wife about the value their olive crop will have when, within thirty years, it matures.

With Cervantes's eight *entremeses*, published a year before he died (1615), the Spanish farce rose to its highest level of artistry. Cervantes made of the Spanish farce, or *entremés*, a fully developed literary genre in which stock comic types become credible human beings and comic situations express a wide range of humor. If *El rufián viudo* and *El juez de los divorcios* are filled with grotesque humor and physical violence, *El retablo de las maravillas* is a hilarious yet complex satire of human vanity. Of all Cervantes's plays, only his *entremeses* can be considered worthy of the talent that produced the *Novelas ejemplares* and *Don Quijote*. As in the famous novel, the humor of his *entremeses* is slapstick, yet it is also capable of revealing cruelty and fear in a subtle manner.

Cervantes, one of the greatest humorists of all time,[6] was of lifelong interest to Lorca. In 1923 the young poet adapted one of Cervantes's *entremeses, Los dos habladores,* for puppets and, accompanying the piece with music from Stravinsky's "Story of a Soldier," included it on a program with two other puppet plays. Ten years later, when Lorca became director of the traveling theater La Barraca, Cervantes's *entremeses* formed part of the company's repertoire. It is not surprising, then, that Lorca's farce *La zapatera prodigiosa* bears many close resemblances to the *entremeses* and particularly reflects Cervantes's complex comic spirit.

La zapatera is composed almost entirely of techniques borrowed from the early *entremeses*. The extravagant prologue to the piece, in which the author begs the spectators' attention and attempts to prepare them for the absurdities of farce, parallels the explanatory monologues used in the one-act *pasos* of the seventeenth century. These monologues did not introduce the skit but frequently interrupted the action to explain some detail or deceit that was to follow. The explanatory prologue was also frequently used in puppet theater to introduce the characters and the situation to the audience.

The theme of *La zapatera*—the young girl married to an old man—is one of the oldest in farce. It seemed especially intriguing to Lorca, for he used it in three of his farces: *La zapatera, Los títeres de cachiporra,* and *El amor de don Perlimplín.* Previous works in which this theme appears— Cervantes's *El juez de los divorcios*[7] and Alarcón's *Sombrero de tres picos*[8] —have been cited as sources of *La zapatera.* Lorca's treatment of the theme, however, is unlike either of these two works. The crucial question of *La zapatera* is not so much the young wife's honor but her fate at the hands of angry villagers, some of whom would like to kill her.

The characters of *La zapatera* are all stereotypes and are designated, as in ancient farce, by generic rather than proper names. Just as Lorca identifies the village women merely by different colored dresses, two of the *zapatera*'s young admirers—the boy with the sash and the boy with the hat—are distinguishable only by their costumes. The two aging don Juans—the mayor and the puppetlike don Mirlo—are descendants of Pantalone, a stock figure of commedia dell'arte skits who represented lechery and avarice.[9] The *zapatera*'s husband is a sympathetic figure but, dressed in his red velvet suit with large silver buttons and short pants, he too is comic, a "leve caricatura cerventina" [light caricature in the style of Cervantes], as Lorca described him years later in an interview (p. 133).

The mischievous wife is also a comic type. Flirting with the young men of the village, the *zapatera* infuriates her neighbors. But the independent young wife is not cowed by her enemies. She bravely faces her tormentors and dares the mayor to make good his threat to put her in jail. When she at last admits that her old husband is indeed the man she loved, she appears to have matured. This maturity is only temporary, however, for the *zapatera's* character does not evolve, as some critics suggest.[10] To interpret her personality as one that changes is to invest the comic type with subtleties of character that the *zapatera* does not possess, since her role as the saucy, discontented housewife is reasserted at the end of the farce.

In *La zapatera* Lorca seems to have mastered all the traditional tricks of farce. Much of the merriment is provided by the young wife's antics, such as teasing her husband and spinning his chair about. Rapid conversation, as Gustave Lanson points out, is one of the essentials of farce, and the *zapatera* is almost never silent.[11] She begins the play by interrupting the prologue in her impatience to appear in public view. Chattering and defiant throughout, she ends the play by resuming her bantering insults as if her life had never been in danger at all.

The farcical tone of the play is enhanced by mime and gesture, the primary agents of slapstick. Lorca's use of physical animation, such as in the closing scene of Act I in which the village women run about the stage shouting and encircling the *zapatera*, creates the general noise and commotion characteristic of slapstick. The physical abuse in *La zapatera* is not as violent as the knocks and blows delivered in traditional farce, such as in Cervantes's *entremeses*. Lorca, however, called the piece a "farsa violenta," for the threat of physical violence, if only suggested, is important because it allows the possibility of tragedy to develop. As the villagers sing songs about the *zapatera* and the mayor threatens to jail her, dramatic tension and suspense increase.

To rescue his heroine Lorca resorts to disguise and fantasy, standard comic devices favored often by Cervantes in both his great novel and *El retablo de las maravillas*. The *zapatera's* tormentors are momentarily diverted as they hear the tinny blast of an out-of-tune horn. A puppeteer has just arrived and the villagers all gather to watch the puppet show. But the puppets enact a version of the *zapatera's* own predicament, and her neighbors are reminded of her brazen behavior. Like don Quijote, who, incited by the violence he watched on Master Pedro's puppet stage, drew his sword and slew the wooden dolls, the villagers react violently to the make-believe. The *zapatera* sobs aloud at the melodrama, while her neighbors, identifying her with the puppet villain, gather in a hostile crowd outside her house. She is saved from the vengeance of her neighbors only by the puppeteer, who, discarding his disguise, turns out to be her husband, the *zapatero*. Tragedy is thus averted, and the crowd's desire to rid their village of the suspicious *zapatera* is thwarted.

In the honor tragedies of the golden age, wives suspected of dishonor were nearly always killed. Although the *zapatera* has a close call, Lorca casts the question of her honor in a comic light. Her flirtations with young men and with don Mirlo are not shocking but comic. The suspicious neighbors who hate the *zapatera's* boldness and disdain for what they consider proper behavior are chased away by the *zapatero*, who calls them "grandísimas embusteras, mentirosas, mal nacidas" [the biggest liars, deceivers, trash] (p. 972). Their obsession with the *zapatera's* honor is revealed to be absurd, for the heroine is finally vindicated. In the last scene, the *zapatera* begins again to abuse the husband who saved her life, and thus the farce ends with one of the best jokes of the play.

While Lorca's heroine is innocent, she barely escapes disaster. Only after a long conversation with the puppeteer, in which the young wife admits to loving her absent husband and advises the puppeteer to return to his wife, does she discover that her salvation is at hand. Characteristically juxtaposing tragedy and farce, Lorca reaches a comic resolution to the question of honor in *La zapatera*. This tension between tragedy and farce is resolved in pathos in all his other plays. In *Don Perlimplín*, for example, buffoonery gradually turns into self-sacrifice and death. In *La zapatera* Lorca masters the techniques of farce and uses them to burlesque the traditional theme of honor. *Don Perlimplín* is another version of this theme in which Lorca probes more deeply into the mind of his central character.

Don Perlimplín is one of Lorca's most genuinely amusing plays. All the techniques of farce are present in the prologue and the three scenes that comprise this piece, which Lorca called an "aleluya erótica" [erotic lace-paper valentine]. The theme used is the standard comic conflict of the old man married to a young wife. The setting is extravagant, and the costumes, complete with lace and overdecorated wigs, mock the stiff dignity of an eighteenth-century drawing room. The characters are again stock figures of comedy—the greedy matron anxious to make a wealthy match for her daughter, the faithful servant, Marcolfa, and the voluptuous, nubile Belisa. Don Perlimplín, the old man who marries Belisa, is also a comic type and is made to appear ridiculous in the first half of the farce.

The entire matter of Perlimplín's marriage is seen as a joke played on the old man by conniving women. Marcolfa convinces him that she will not live forever and that he must find a wife to care for him. She tells him what to say when he approaches his prospective bride. Perlimplín has so little enthusiasm for the project that when he meets Belisa he can only repeat what he has been told to say. He naïvely admits to Belisa, "Hemos decidido que me quiero casar" [We've decided that I want to marry] (p. 983). The old man's fears of marriage are based on the childhood memory of a woman who strangled her husband. This gruesome image is comic in *Don Perlimplín*, for the old man is absurdly fearful. In *Yerma* this same image becomes a horrible and tragic reality.

Perlimplín's fears are overshadowed by the hilarious mother of Belisa. The matron appears, dressed in "una gran peluca dieciochesca llena de pájaros, cintas y abalorios" [a huge eighteenth-century wig, decorated with birds, ribbons, and sequins] (p. 984). She tries to hide her exuberance over Perlimplín's wealth under a comic veneer of modesty. She orders Belisa out of the room while she discusses the marriage arrangement with Perlimplín because "no está bien que una doncella oiga ciertas conversaciones" [a young girl shouldn't hear certain conversations]. Her attempts to flatter Perlimplín exceed the boundaries of reason: "Siempre dije a mi pobre hija que usted tiene la gracia y modales de aquella gran señora que fue su madre, a la cual no tuve la dicha de conocer" [I always told my poor daughter that you have the grace and manners of that great lady, your mother, whom I never had the pleasure of meeting] (p. 984). When the marriage is agreed upon, she informs Belisa that Perlimplín will be "un encantador marido" [an enchanting husband] (p. 985). The comic irony of this statement contrasts with Perlimplín's consternation as he wails, "¡Ay, Marcolfa, Marcolfa! ¿En qué mundo me vas a meter?" [What have you gotten me into?] (p. 986). But the matter is settled, and Marcolfa laughs as the curtain closes on Perlimplín's helpless protests.

The farcical expository action of the prologue is followed by the hilarious presentation of the wedding night, which comprises scene one. Belisa's ample sensuality engulfs the timid Perlimplín and he is terrified. The sparse dialogue between the trembling Perlimplín and his bored bride illustrates Lorca's consummate handling of understatement and comic irony:

Perlimplín:	¿Te molesto?	[*Perlimplín*:	Do I bother you?
Belisa:	¿Cómo es posible?	*Belisa*:	How could that be?
Perlimplín:	¿Tienes sueño?	*Perlimplín*:	Are you sleepy?
Belisa:	¿Sueño?	*Belisa*:	Sleepy?] (P. 989)

Subtle use of voice intonation produces another comic contrast:

Perlimplín (*en voz baja*): Belisa.   [*Perlimplín* (*whispering*): Belisa.

Belisa (*en voz alta*): ¿Qué, hijito?   *Belisa* (*aloud*): What, dear?

Perlimplín (*en voz baja*): He   *Perlimplín* (*whispering*): I've
   apagado la luz.   turned out the light.

Belisa (*guasona*): Ya lo veo.   *Belisa* (*jokingly*): So I see.

Perlimplín (*en voz mucho más*   *Perlimplín* (*in much lower*
   baja): Belisa ...   *tones*): Belisa—

Belisa (*en voz alta*): ¿Qué,   *Belisa* (*aloud*): What, dear?
   encanto?

Perlimplín: ¡Te adoro!   *Perlimplín*: I adore you!] (P. 993)

At this point two sprites pull a curtain across the darkened stage. Their comic dialogue forms an interlude in the action, indicating the passage of time. The two sprites, similar to the young boy who befriends the *zapatera* and also to the puckish Mosquito of *Tragicomedia de don Cristóbal*, chatter and laugh at the characters of the farce. One makes a joke of Belisa's overwhelming sensuality, recalling that her perfume was so strong that it anesthetized him: "me quedé dormido y desperté entre los garros de sus gatos" [I fell asleep and woke up between the cat's claws] (p. 995). The other sprite reminds the audience that Perlimplín on his wedding night is as frightened as a newborn duckling.

This merry interlude is a device used to introduce the fact that Belisa has deceived her husband on their first night. The number of lovers she has already entertained is indicated by five doors that stand open at the back of the stage. When the curtain around the marriage bed is drawn, we see Perlimplín, crowned with a huge pair of gilded horns, sitting by the calm Belisa. However absurd he appears, Perlimplín is also pathetic, for he confesses to Belisa that he truly loves her. The ambiguous mixture of tragedy and farce is intensified when, at the end of the scene, Perlimplín sings a strange song of love and death and declares that for the first time in his life he is happy.

With the final lines of scene one, it becomes clear that Lorca, having begun the piece with a stock comic character, has decided to invest the ridiculous Perlimplín with human qualities worthy of serious consideration. Up to now a puppetlike laughingstock, Perlimplín assumes the complexity of an agonized hero who begins to suffer an identity crisis. Like the humorist who, as Pirandello observed,[12] dismantles the soul's illusions in order to lay bare its workings, Lorca gradually penetrates the mind of Perlimplín. He dramatizes not only the way love has transformed the old man but also the humiliation it brings him. As Pirandello does in *Pensaci, Giacomino!* Lorca reveals that the old man, for whom books had always been enough, possesses a complex mind and is capable of playing a role quite opposite that of the laughingstock.

In the second scene the ridiculous Perlimplín has assumed a strange aura of composure. He has already begun to carry out an elaborate scheme that will end in his death. He has sent Belisa erotic letters she believes are from a young lover but that Perlimplín himself has written. He encourages her excitement and is eager to discuss the letters with her. He titillates her curiosity by telling her that he sees the young man passing in the street below. Belisa rushes to the window and, of course, sees no one, but Perlimplín explains that the young man has just turned a corner and that she will see him later. His attempts to arouse Belisa in this way are both pathetic and grotesque, for in Perlimplín's mind he no longer exists as an old man: "Ya estoy fuera del mundo y de la moral ridícula de este mundo" [I am now beyond the world and its ridiculous morality]. Perlimplín has already begun to assume the role of Belisa's young lover. In his own mind he is now capable of being loved by Belisa; therefore, he seems immune to the kind of moral outrage Marcolfa feels when she learns that Perlimplín is encouraging Belisa's fondness for her handsome suitor. Marcolfa is so shocked by Perlimplín's lack of concern for his honor that she quits his service in a huff of righteous indignation.

The action culminates when Belisa arrives in the garden. Splendidly arrayed, she awaits the appearance of her lover. But it is Perlimplín who comes forth from the darkness. He tells Belisa that he plans to kill her lover so that the handsome young fellow can never be unfaithful to her. He explains to the horrified Belisa that "el te querrá con el amor infinito de los difuntos y yo quedaré libre de esta oscura pesadilla de tu cuerpo grandioso . . . ¡¡¡que nunca podría descifrar!!!" [he will love you with the infinite love of the dead and I will be free of this nightmare of your over-powering body . . . which I would never figure out!] (p. 1015). As Perlimplín disappears, Belisa cries that she will kill him if he harms her lover. Suddenly a figure wrapped in a red cape emerges from among the trees. Belisa, seeing that the man is wounded, thinks it is her lover and runs to him. The man in the cape tells her that he has just been stabbed by her husband. Now Belisa recognizes the man in the cape. It is Perlimplín, who, still playing the part of the lover, tells Belisa that as her husband stabbed him he shouted, "¡Belisa ya tiene un alma!" [Now Belisa has a soul!] (p. 1016).

While Perlimplín enacts his sad charade, the bewildered Belisa is still concerned with the young lover who she thinks has disappeared. The pathos of the dying Perlimplín, explaining to Belisa, "Yo soy mi alma y tu eres tu cuerpo. . . . Déjame en este último instante, puesto que tanto me has querido, morir abrazado a él" [I am my soul and you are your body. . . . Let me, in this last moment, since you've loved me so much, die embracing it], contrasts with her total stupefaction. "¿Por qué me has engañado?" [Why have you deceived me?] demands Belisa. Faced with events beyond her grasp and thus, for her, absurd, she cries, "Nunca creí que fuese tan complicado" [I never thought you were so complicated]. This understatement, expressing Belisa's complete confusion, is sadly comic. Thus, the dramatic impact of this farce is ambiguous, for, although the old man's sacrifice is moving, Belisa's muddled horror is amusing. While she admits to Marcolfa that she loved Perlimplín, Belisa's first concern is for her young lover, and she asks desperately, "Dios mío; ¿dónde está?" [My God, where is he?].

Lorca's use of complex humor in the portrayal of farcical types is consistent with Pirandello's theory of humor. "Every feeling, thought, and idea which arises in the humorist splits itself into contraries," the Italian author explained.[13] And Lorca must have had much the same conception of humor when he created the figure of Perlimplín, who appears at once both noble and absurd. Lorca knew and admired the plays of Pirandello;[14] and he found, as the Italian playwright did, that humor could be a means of exploring the contradictions of the human personality. Lorca's treatment of dual identity in *Don Perlimplín* recalls Pirandello's dramatization of the same theme in *Così è (se vi pare)*, written in 1916. The identity of Signora Ponza is, like that of Perlimplín, defined according to different points of view. Like Perlimplín, Signora Ponza recognizes the multiple facets of her being as she announces in the final scene that she is both "la figlia della Signora Frola . . . el la seconda moglie del Signor Ponza" [the daughter of Signora Frola . . . and the second wife of Signor Ponza].[15] Perlimplín resembles the Signora in becoming a human puppet, willingly sacrificing his own identity in order to gain love.

Another Pirandellian character who is similar to Perlimplín is the pedant, Professor Toti of *Pensaci, Giacomino!* Both Toti and Perlimplín have denied themselves love until late in life. Both marry young women and shock the conventional sense of propriety by not feeling ashamed at the dishonor they bring to themselves. Just as Belisa is blatantly unfaithful, Toti's young wife has a child by her lover Giacomino. Perlimplín is indifferent when Marcolfa accuses him, "¡Usted mismo fomente en su mujer el peor de los pecados!" [You yourself bring out the worst sins in your wife!]; Toti is also undismayed by what others think. He goes so far as to persuade young Giacomino to ignore the scandal caused by the unusual *ménage à trois* and to be glad that his child can have a respectable name and a good home. In each of these plays, what begins as a burlesque of honor and virtue is transformed into a serious appraisal of the value of love. Lorca, like Pirandello, uses burlesque, defiant humor, and surprise to reveal the character of a comic martyr capable of defying accepted morality for the sake of love. Thus, Pirandello's definition of humor as the spirit "which disassembles the machine of each image"[16] describes the complex comic spirit of *Don Perlimplín*, in which Lorca reveals the incongruities of his hero's personality by means of laughter and ridicule.

On one level *Don Perlimplín* is a comic dramatization of the need for love. This need produces contradictory behavior in an old man who has fallen in love, and Lorca both laughs at and approves of his protagonist's blissful discovery. On another level *Don Perlimplín* can be considered a parody of the theme of honor as it was portrayed in the Spanish drama of the golden age. And, as a parody, Lorca's farce is closely related to the *esperpentos* of Valle-Inclán, which contribute much to the importance of farce as a dramatic form. In the best known of the *esperpentos, Los cuernos de don Friolera* (1921), Valle-Inclán has, like Lorca, ridiculed the traditional Spanish theme of honor.

Both Lorca and Valle-Inclán find in traditional farce a point of departure for a modern burlesque of the honor theme. They begin their plays with stock comic characters as protagonists: both Friolera and Perlimplín are stereotypes of the fiftyish husband deceived by a young wife. Friolera is described as being a puppet; like Perlimplín he is easily manipulated by others. Just as Marcolfa tells Perlimplín that he must marry, Friolera dutifully follows his officers' orders to shoot his unfaithful wife. It is at this point, when they accede to the demands made upon them, that the two comic figures transcend the limits of traditional laughingstocks and begin to suffer. As Ricardo Gullón points out, "the conception of character as a multiple being is basic to the *esperpento*,"[17] and Valle's puppet-hero, like Perlimplín, assumes a poignancy not ordinarily contained within the ancient comic type. Perlimplín becomes unexpectedly complex and even noble, sacrificing his life to win a moment of Belisa's love. Friolera also gains an added dimension—that of humility. He attempts to shoot his wife, but his aim is bad and he misses, killing his innocent daughter instead. Overcome with remorse and guilt, the puppet begs to be sent away to a hospital. Thus, the husband, the Calderonian figure of authority and the defender of honor, becomes in these two modern farces a pathetic clown.

The parody of the traditional notion of honor extends not only to the principal character, the husband, but also to the traditional solution to the dilemma of dishonor. In such golden age masterpieces as Pedro Calderón's *El médico de su honra*, the wife is regrettably killed by the self-righteous husband. Lorca and Valle-Inclán have subverted this vindication of the traditional honor code, for their victim is not the wife but the husband himself. Perlimplín rises above and actually flouts the conventional conception of honor. When the shocked Marcolfa threatens to quit because of the old man's indifference to his wife's escapades, he sings, "¡Don Perlimplín no tiene honor! ¡No tiene honor!" (p. 1010). When Friolera's attempt to avenge his honor in the traditional manner is thwarted, the poor puppet is emotionally undone by his mistake. Thus, the traditional conception of honor based on vengeance is portrayed by both Lorca and Valle-Inclán as being horrible and absurd.

By presenting the traditional honor theme not in the tragic mode, as Calderón had done in his honor tragedies, but in the insolent manner of farce, Lorca derides the traditional interpretation of the honor code by suggesting that it is ruthless and cruel. Nor does he justify violence in the service of honor as portrayed in traditional farce. Retribution appears odious to Valle's puppet-hero and does not even occur to Perlimplín. Following the example of the *esperpentos*, Lorca created what may be called an "honor farce" that distorts the traditional concept of honor.

In his first series of dramatic experiments, Lorca mastered the techniques of traditional comedy and farce. In *El maleficio* and *Mariana Pineda* he became adept at puns, comic relief, and caricature. In *La zapatera* he learned to handle witty repartee. While acquiring the skills of a comic dramatist, Lorca expressed his own comic spirit by introducing themes of disaster by means of farcical and whimsical scenes. In *Don Perlimplín* Lorca achieved consummate mastery in expressing despair with techniques of farce. As Marie Laffranque suggests, *Don Perlimplín* represents a new stage in Lorca's development as a dramatist.[18] In this play Lorca produced for the first time forceful dramatic impact with his disturbing mixture of tragedy and farce.

If Lorca expressed his comic attitude with traditional dramatic forms in his early tragicomedies and farces, he soon found new possibilities in experimenting with avant-garde styles. In his cinematic skits, prose tales, and a full-length play—*Así que pasen cinco años*—Lorca discovered a natural affinity between his own disturbing humor and the chaotic language of surrealism.

3. Avant-garde Prose and Plays

More than any other Spanish playwright of his time, Lorca valued his dramatic heritage. We have seen how, in his tragicomedies and farces, he stylized traditional comic characters and situations and adapted the age-old themes and antics of farce. Yet Lorca's works are unquestionably modern and cannot be fully understood apart from the avant-garde art of his day. Jorge Guillén recalls that Lorca turned to the avant-garde to avoid being cast in the mold of the "gypsy poet."[1] It was not in Lorca's nature, however, to assume literary affectations. If he learned the idiom of the avant-garde, it was because there was in it something that corresponded to his own artistic temperament. The abrasive, satiric wit and the bitter *humour noir* cherished by surrealists are evident in the earliest stages of Lorca's art.

Lorca's interest in the avant-garde, particularly in surrealism, was neither short-lived nor insignificant, as some critics have suggested.[2] His most intense period of experimentation seems to have occurred from 1925 to 1930. During these years he produced a series of eight prose tales, grouped together under the title of *Narraciones*, and four cinematic skits. This period of apprenticeship culminated in two major surrealist achievements: *Poeta en Nueva York* and *Así que pasen cinco años*. If these two works are unlike anything Lorca had ever written, the grim humor of the surrealist play, *Así que pasen cinco años*, is entirely consistent with Lorca's comic spirit. The verbal caper, mischievous humor, and grotesquerie that began to emerge in his lyric poetry become the predominant means of expression in his experimental tales and skits.

In his first published work, the travelogue *Impresiones y paisajes* (1918), Lorca records his recollections of Spain with the same irreverent humor later adopted by surrealists in their revolt against artistic and social conventions. Seeing different regions of his country for the first time on student excursions, the young poet was particularly impressed by a Carthusian monastery, which seemed to him a kind of burial ground for the living. "¡Qué angustia tan dolorosa estos sepulcros de hombres que se mueven como muñecos en un teatro de tormentos!" [How painful and sad are these tombs of men who move about like dolls in a stormy play!] (p. 1545). He reacted to this funereal scene with characteristic ambivalence: "¡Qué carcajadas de risa y llanto dará el corazón!" [What guffaws of laughter and tears the heart will give!]. And he appreciated the irony of those who seek silence and solitude only to encounter alone the passions they sought to escape: "¡Enorme pesadilla la de estos hombres que huyen de las asechanzas de la carne y entran en el silencio y la soledad, que son los grandes afrodisíacos!" [The enormous nightmare of these men who shrink from the delights of the flesh that lie in wait for them and enter into silence and solitude, the greatest aphrodisiacs!] (p. 1546). But the Monastery at Silos appeared even more comical to the adolescent poet.

Mealtime at the Monasterio de Silos takes on the appearance of a farce. The solemnity of those present—the monks, the abbot, and the young friar reciting Scripture—seem decidedly droll to Lorca, who records the scene with a comic dramatist's eye for caricature and ridiculous gesture. As the meal begins, a monk arrives late. "Se arrodilla ante el abad con las manos sobre el pecho y con gesto lastimoso de pobre hombre inclina la cabeza. El superior lo bendice descuidadamente, así como el que da un manotazo al aire, y entonces el desdichado vejete se retira a comer" [He kneels before the abbot with his hands on his chest and, with the pitiful gesture of a wretched man, bows his head. The superior blesses him absent-mindedly, like one who gives a flick of the hand in the air, and the unhappy old fellow withdraws to eat] (p. 1560).

During the meal a recitation is delivered by the young friar, an emaciated figure "con color de ictericia, la cabeza larga, desproporcionada" [with the color of jaundice, a disproportionately large head] (p. 1560). This pathetic young man climbs to the white pulpit, crosses himself, and, "abriendo el libro venerable" [opening the venerable book], begins to read:

Es la historia de un antiguo padre de la Iglesia lo que cuenta el
libro.... La eterna tentación del demonio en los anacoretas.
... Lucha cruenta con el enemigo invisible que ellos creen del
exterior sin notar que está escondido muy hondo en el corazón.
... y son monstruos verdes de ojos amarillos, lo ve bajo el lecho,
y son serpientes de fuego con cabeza de ratón, y son lagartos
gelatinosos y horribles los que contempla en sus pesadillas. Una
vida de martirios espantosos.

[It is the story of an old church father that the book narrates....
The eternal temptation by the devil of the penitents.... The cruel
fight with the invisible enemy that they believe lives outside themselves without seeing that he is hidden deeply within their hearts....
green monsters with yellow eyes, he sees under the bed; fiery serpents
with rats' heads, gelatinous and horrible lizards are what he sees
in his nightmares. A life of frightful sufferings.]

The reading was, Lorca remembers, a deplorable performance. Pronouncing words with great difficulty, pausing at the wrong places, the young friar had the added handicap of a high-pitched voice, a voice "de niño en escuela pueblerina" [of a country schoolboy]. His brothers, however, seemed not to notice.

La trágica vida del santo desquiciado e histérico no hacía mella en los
espíritus de los monjes. La habrían oído tantas veces que había llegado
a serles indiferente. Los monjes comían con gran apetito, alguno se

apipaba de lo lindo. . . . Entre el odioso sonsonete de la lectura se oía
el choque de los tenedores contra los platos.

[The tragic life of the shattered and hysterical saint had no effect on
the monks' spirits. They had heard it so often that it had become
stale to them. The monks ate with large appetites. . . . The sound of
forks on plates mingled with the hateful drone of the reading.]
(P. 1561)

Lorca's satire of the church was so bitter that an uncensored version of
Impresiones y paisajes has never been published.[3]

Obvious delight in monsters and the portrayal of the holy brothers and
their false piety as ridiculous, together with the use of terms like *gela-
tinoso*, all betray the poet's acquaintance with the precursor of surrealism,
Le Comte de Lautréamont. In "Monasterio de Silos" he refers to the "loco
y fantástico conde de Lautréamont" (p. 1559), and throughout *Impresiones y paisajes* he seems amused by the same grotesquerie cultivated by
Lautréamont in his strange tales, *Les Chants de Maldoror.*

In a passage of the travelogue entitled "Canéfora de la pesadilla," Lorca
depicts a bawdy house in the Albaicín, the old Moorish quarter of Granada, whose decaying patio is "empedrado con musgo" [encrusted with
moss]. Under the "carcomidas balaustradas" [worm-eaten balustrades]
hangs a "Cristo espantoso con faldas de bailarina" [frightful Christ with
ballerina skirts] (p. 1569). This juxtaposition of holiness and depravity
suggested by a figure of Christ dressed in tattered ballerina skirts recalls
the three doll-like figures of the saints described in *Romancero gitano*;
it is also similar to Lautréamont's account in the third canto of *Les Chants*
of a convent that has become a house of prostitution.

In the narrations of both poets there is an attempt to exaggerate sca-
brous material for shock value. Lorca's observations are neither as exten-
sive nor as defiling as Lautréamont's, yet he displays the same liking for
the grotesque in his portrayal of a degraded female character: "Tenía un
vientre muy abultado, como de eterno embarazo; . . . sobre sus pómulos
una pupa amarillenta mostraba toda su maloliente carroña, y un ojo horrible derramaba lágrimas sobre ella, que la figura atroz limpiaba con su
manaza . . . y se cree oler a azufre" [Her stomach was swollen, as if in
perpetual pregnancy; . . . a yellowish sore showed its putrid flesh on her

cheekbone, and tears from her terrible eye flowed over it, which the frightful creature wiped with her paw . . . and the odor of sulphur seemed to be in the air] (p. 1569). The *canéfora* is certainly one of the poet's most vivid characters. Lorca remarks that she reminds him of Goya's figures; she is also similar to Lautréamont's prostitute who "se relevait tremblante, couverte de blessures" [appeared shivering, covered with sores].[4]

Like curious adolescents, both Lorca and Lautréamont are intrigued by depravity. Lorca, noting the sounds emanating from the brothel, recalls hearing laughter, "y entre palmas sexuales y ayes dolorosos una voz aguardentosa cantaba obscenidades" [amid the sounds of hands slapping flesh and painful groans a drunken voice was singing obscenities] (p. 1570). Lorca, though fascinated by obscenity, does not cultivate it as diligently as Lautréamont. Restrained when compared to Lautréamont, Lorca nevertheless exhibits a fondness for grotesquerie and vicious humor that is unmistakable in his earliest works.

Lorca's interest in Lautréamont was shared by Salvador Dalí, whom he met while living at the Residencia de Estudiantes in Madrid. During the years of Lorca's surrealist experiments, his association with Dalí was constant. The friendship with Dalí is important as a measure of Lorca's knowledge of avant-garde aesthetics. The two young Spaniards shared not only a fascination with Lautréamont but also the anti-intellectual view of art held later by surrealists. With derisive humor they labeled those artists whom they considered passé as either unreceptive to new ideas or untalented. Their association resulted in artistic collaboration when, in 1927, Dalí designed the sets for the Barcelona production of *Mariana Pineda*. Lorca's knowledge of the illogic of dream imagery must have been enriched by Dalí, who by 1926 had read Freud's *Interpretation of Dreams* —one of the works that inspired the surrealists' interest in the subconscious mind. By 1927 the young painter had completed the canvas entitled *La sangre es más dulce que la miel* [Blood is sweeter than honey], which was full of the strange imagery and distortions characteristic of surrealist art.

Another member of Lorca's group of friends at the Residencia in Madrid was Luis Buñuel. Even though Buñuel is reported to have scorned the poetry of Lorca and other "perros andaluces" [Andalusian dogs][5] who did not devote themselves exclusively to the avant-garde, Buñuel's influence at the Residencia was significant. He managed to add film screenings to the activities available to students; thus, Lorca became acquainted with the American film comedies of Buster Keaton and Charlie Chaplin. The madcap humor of these slapstick comedies is easily distorted into the violent and nonsensical imagery of surrealism. The cinema, as Yves Duplessis has so aptly remarked, is humor's "chosen territory."[6] Some of the artistic devices most cherished by surrealists—grotesquerie, absurd antics, and the clash between unrelated objects—were presented in the American comedies on a scale undreamed of even by surrealists themselves.

Lorca's close friendships thus included Buñuel, who left for Paris in 1925 to work under the film maker Jean Epstein, and Dalí, who departed for Paris in 1929 to become the most flamboyant surrealist of them all. In 1928 Dalí and Buñuel collaborated on the first surrealist film, *Un Chien andalou*; in 1930 Buñuel, with less help from Dalí, scandalized the public with *L'âge d'or*. It is with these works in mind that Lorca's *Narraciones* must be considered, for its jolting imagery and caustic humor correspond closely to his friends' surrealist scenarios.

Lorca began publishing *Narraciones* in 1927. The tales were not conceived as a collection but were written for various occasions and published over a period of years. The first to appear, "Santa Lucía y San Lázaro," is the longest and most interesting of the group. "Historia de este gallo," the most traditional of the tales, was written as an introduction to the literary magazine *El gallo*, which Lorca helped to edit, and appeared in its first issue in 1928. "Suicidio en Alejandría" and "Nadadora sumergida" were also written in 1928. The two tales of sadism, "Degollación del Bautista" and "Degollación de los inocentes," were also written in 1928; the former was published in 1930. "Amantes asesinados por una perdiz" and "La gallina," the least interesting of the tales, were written at undetermined dates and published posthumously. None of the pieces have plots, but are, like *Chien andalou*, "un long montage" of images,[7] some of which are unified by a central theme. Almost all of the tales in *Narraciones* reveal the destructive and brutal humor in which both Lautréamont and the surrealists delighted.

Some of Lorca's most savage religious satire is contained in "Santa Lucía y San Lázaro." André Breton explained that laughter frees man from all that is false and pompous and that by laughing at serious things man "se refuse à se laisser entamer, à se laisser imposer la souffrance par les réalités extérieures" [refuses to allow himself to be dominated, to allow suffering to be imposed on him by exterior reality].[8] The antireligious humor of "Santa Lucía y San Lázaro" expresses the poet's refusal to remain pious before the images of the church. Seeing the image of Santa Lucía in a painting, Lorca lets his imagination begin to play: "Ella demostró en la plaza pública, ante el asombro del pueblo, que mil hombres y cincuenta pares de bueyes no pueden con la palomilla luminosa del Espíritu Santo. . . . Nuestro señor, seguramente, estaba sentado con cetro y corona sobre su cintura" [She revealed in the public square, before the astonishment of the townspeople, that a thousand pairs of oxen have no power with the luminous little dove of the Holy Spirit. . . . Our Lord, surely, was seated with crown and scepter, upon her waist] (p. 14). The mischievous irreverence of this sketch is further apparent in the distortion of church symbols: "En una de las puertas de salida estaba colgado el esquelto de un pez antiguo; en otra, el esqueleto de un serafín" [In one of the doorways was hung the skeleton of an ancient fish; in the other, the skeleton of a seraphim] (p. 16). Three years later Buñuel used a similar image in *L'âge d'or* depicting four archbishops as skeletons still draped in capes and crowned with miters.

The *Narraciones* stories are similar to the verses of *Canciones*, literary games in which the poet amuses himself with verbal play. In "Santa Lucía y San Lázaro" the figure of Santa Lucía inspires the poet to display his virtuosity in contriving images. Informing the reader that "Pude componer . . . ocho naturalezas muertas con los ojos de Santa Lucía" [I could compose . . . eight still lifes with the eyes of Santa Lucía] (p. 17), he proceeds to develop a series of images based on the free association of eyes with improbable objects.

Another of the prose sketches, "Suicidio en Alejandría," is a lively piece of badinage in which prose commentary is interspersed with pairs of numbers. Characteristic of Lorca's frequent juxtaposition of gaiety and disaster, this jaunty piece is a tale of suicide. The opening lines tell of carnage and butchery, but such horrors are impossible to take seriously when immediately followed by inane comments: "Cuando pusieron la cabeza cortada sobre la mesa del despacho, se rompieron todas las cristales. 'Será necesario calmar a esas rosas' dijo la anciana." [When they put the severed head on the office table, all the glass broke. "It will be necessary to calm those roses," said the old lady.] Midway through "Suicidio en Alejandría" Lorca seems to tire of this game: "Adios. ¡Socorro! Amor, amor mío. Ya morimos juntos. ¡Ay! Terminad vosotros por caridad este poema" [Good-bye. Help! Love, my love. Now we will die together. Ay! For pity's sake end this poem] (p. 32).

Lorca sent copies of "Suicidio en Alejandría" and "Nadadora sumergida" to his friend Sebastian Gasch, explaining that the two prose sketches "responden a mi nueva manera *espiritualista,* emoción pura . . . desligada del control lógico pero . . . con una tremenda lógica poética. No es surrealismo, ¡ojo!, la conciencia más clara los ilumina. . . . Naturalmente están en prosa porque el verso es una ligadura que no resisten" [correspond to my new *spiritualist* manner, pure emotion . . . out of logic's control, but . . . with a tremendous poetic logic. Careful, it is not surrealism; the clearest conscious mind illuminates them. . . . Naturally they are in prose because verse is too tight a binding for them] (p. 1654). While rejecting automatic writing, Lorca experimented in "Nadadora sumergida" with other surrealist techniques, such as the humor of non sequitur, in which nonsense is cultivated for its own sake. "Nadadora sumergida" is a delightful parody of newspaper gossip columns. Subtitled "Pequeño homenaje a un cronista de salones" [Brief homage to a gossip columnist], it is a satirical sketch in which Lorca "se ríe de las gacetillas mundanas cuyo mérito es no tener . . . ningún sentido fuera de su admirable tontería" [laughs at the trivial news briefs whose primary value is not to have . . . any meaning whatever outside their admirable nonsense].[9] Unrelated remarks are strung together without unifying elements, such as plot or theme, to lend continuity:

> Madame Barthou hacía irresistible la noche con sus enfermos diamantes del Cairo, y el traje violeta de Olga Montcha acusaba, cada minuto más palpable, su amor por el muerto zar.
>
> Margarita Gross y la españolísima Lola Cabeza de Vaca llevaban contadas más de mil olas sin ningún resultado.

[Mme. Barthou made the night irresistible with her sick diamonds from Cairo, and the violet dress of Olga Montcha denounced, more palpably each minute, her love for the dead czar.

Margarita Gross and the very Spanish Lola Cabeza de Vaca had counted more than a thousand ocean waves without getting any results.] (P. 33)

In "Nadadora sumergida," trivia, miscellaneous remarks, and death notices are run together to parody the style of newspaper columns in which there is no change of tone to differentiate inanity from items of more substance. Interspersed with nonsense and parody are the following comments: "Desde entonces dejé la literatura vieja que yo había cultivado con gran éxito. Es preciso romperlo todo para que las dogmas se purifiquen y las normas tengan nuevo temblor" [Since then I left the old literature that I had cultivated with great success. It is necessary to break with everything so that dogmas may be purified and standards be newly shaken] (p. 34). Such remarks reveal that, while the *Narraciones* tales were frivolous literary games, Lorca recognized the value of experimentation.

The most amusing work in the *Narraciones* is "Historia de este gallo," a witty piece of caricature and burlesque that Lorca wrote to introduce his literary magazine, *Gallo*. Satirizing the lethargic atmosphere of Granada, Lorca creates the curious figure of the aging don Alhambro, who has a vision of how he can best stir Granada from its stupor. Images of Carlos Tercero "en cuarenta planos diferentes, rodearon a don Alhambro con el ritmo y la locura de los espejos rotos. 'Bee, bee, funda un periódico'—balaban aristocráticamente los borregos magníficos del perfil de Carlos" [in forty different planes surrounded don Alhambro with the rhythm and the madness of broken mirrors. "Baa, Baa, set up a newspaper"—bleated aristocratically the magnificent curls of Carlos in profile]. The old man searches in vain to find a rooster as a mascot for his paper, only to be told, " 'Ya nos lo hemos comido' y veía notar en los ojos del que hablaba una cresta diminuta" ["We have eaten it already," and he noted in the speaker's eyes a tiny crest] (Pp. 21–22).

"Historia de este gallo" is not written in the same style as the other prose tales. Its imagery is easily recognizable, and the narration follows an orderly sequence. It is also well-meaning and lacks the vicious sarcasm of the early surrealist films. Lorca ridicules the factionalism and triviality of Granadine society in a harmless manner when he begins by relating that "en aquella época venturosa Granada estaba dividida por dos grandes escuelas de bordado. De una parte, las monjas del Beaterio de Santo Domingo. De la otra, la eminente Paquita Raya. . . . Todas las personas morenas eran partidarios de Paquita. Todas las rubias, castañas y un pequeño núcleo de albinas, partidarias de las monjas" [in that adventurous era Granada was divided into two schools of embroidery. On the one hand were the nuns of the Devout Sisters of Santo Domingo. On the other, Paquita Raya. . . . The brunettes were on Paquita's side. Blondes, and a small group of albinos, were on the nuns' side.] (p. 23).

The harmless merriment of "Historia de este gallo" contrasts sharply with the cruelty and sadism of the two *Narraciones* tales entitled "Degollación del Bautista" and "Degollación de los inocentes." These two pieces are examples of Lorca's manner of referring to ominous or terrifying events in a whimsical manner. Like Lautréamont's scenes of torture and tearing flesh in *Maldoror* and the opening shots of a razor slicing a girl's eyeball in *Un Chien andalou*, Lorca's variations on the theme of decapitation are trumped-up savagery designed to be the ultimate shockers. Variations of atrocities are treated as sinister games. The beheading of the saint in "Degollación del Bautista" is seen as a spectator sport, on the same level as a soccer match. The beheading was horrible, relates the poet in mock exhilaration "pero maravillosamente desarrollada. El cuchillo era prodigioso" [but marvelously carried out. The knife was prodigious]. And, after all, "la carne es siempre panza de rana" [flesh is always like a frog's belly]. Like a Doctor Caligari horror film, there is grim pleasure in the careful planning of a horrid deed. "Hay que ir contra la carne . . . para que el horror mueva su bosque intravenoso. El especialista de la degollación es enemigo de las esmeraldas. . . . No conoce el chicle pero conoce el cuello tiernísimo de la perdiz viva" [You have to go against the flesh . . . for horror to stir its intravenous forest. The specialist in beheadings is the enemy of emeralds. . . . He doesn't know what chewing gum is but he does know the very tender neck of the love partridge] (p. 28).

Verbal play begins "Degollación de los inocentes" on a note of nonsense: "Tris tras. Zig zag, rig rag, milg malg." The mock-savagery of this tale is directed against animals—the "ruiseñor con dos patitas rojas" [nightingale with two little red feet]—and children. A list of names of small boys about to become victims is followed by the word "Inocentes." The tone of the sketch is lighthearted: "Dicen que se está inventado la navaja eléctrica para reanimar la operación" [They say that they are inventing an electric blade that will revitalize the operation]. The poet is self-consciously aware of his game—"Sangre. Con toda la fuerza de su g." Yet the image of a nightmarish society, such as that depicted in *Poeta en Nueva York*, in which the weak and helpless are devoured, looms in the back of the poet's mind: "Si meditamos y somos llenos de piedad verdadera daremos la degollación como una de las grandes obras de misericordia" [If we meditate and are filled with pity, we will administer beheadings as one of the greatest acts of mercy] (p. 30). The two tales of decapitation are comic sketches on the theme of brutality; the same images and themes assume profound tones of agony in the poems of New York.

The infantile sadism of the "degollaciones" tales has its counterpart in the slapstick comedies that were being made during the 1920's by Charlie Chaplin, Harold Lloyd, and Buster Keaton. In these film farces human beings were little more than objects in the rapid development of comic gags. One of the most popular comics of the day was W. C. Fields, whose humor was so aggressive that audiences finally began staying away from his films.[10] Georges de Coulteray, in his study of sadism in the movies, reminds us of the veritable "hurricane of custard pies," people falling from cliffs and windows, terrorized heroines tied to railroad tracks, and comic heroes who met repeated disasters.[11] In his prose sketches Lorca is more aware of the seriousness underlying the antics of farce than were the silent film clowns. One of these, however, the deadpan Buster Keaton, seemed to personify the kind of humor most characteristic of Lorca's comic spirit. Thus, it is no surprise that Keaton inspired Lorca to write a cinematic skit, *El paseo de Buster Keaton*; for, no matter how vigorous his physical antics, Keaton's impassive face was the epitome of the serious clown.

The film comedies that Lorca saw during his student days were the basis for the film scenario *El paseo de Buster Keaton*, which was written in 1925. All the elements of farce are present in *El paseo*, yet violence lies close beneath the surface of frivolity. In the opening scene Buster kills his children. He counts their four bodies, then pedals off on his bike dreaming of love. Such cruelty is not to be taken seriously, however, for Buster's weapon is only a wooden knife. This is the same kind of gratuitous violence Buñuel used in the fantastic love scene of *L'âge d'or*, in which the ecstatic young woman exclaims to her lover, "What joy! What joy! To have murdered our children!"[12] Yet the presence of violence becomes more ominous when Buster passes by a Negro who squats on a pile of old tires and oil drums eating a straw hat. Buster does not seem concerned with this image of poverty and degradation, for he pedals on, and his bicycle is described as being "empapada de inocencia" [imbued with innocence] (p. 894). Recalling Lorca's sympathetic portrayal of degraded blacks in *Poeta en Nueva York*, one may easily interpret *El paseo* as a protest against the mechanical quality that life and death assume in a technological society.[13] This conclusion, however, seems based on hindsight, because it is the poet's delight in the techniques of the cinema rather than his anger or protest that prevails in this early skit. Dialogue is entirely secondary to the action, which is composed of visual stunts.

The visual play in *El paseo* is merely an extension of the verbal frolic of *Narraciones*. Unusual camera angles and the speed of a bicycle are used, as in the early film comedies, to create a zany and chaotic effect in which anything can happen. As Buster wheels past on the "turbulent trajectory"[14] typical of his fast-moving antics, Lorca views the scene with the eye of a film director, noting that "el paisaje se achica entre las ruedas de la máquina" [the landscape recedes behind the bicycle wheels]. When Buster finds himself in a garden with a young girl, more visual pranks are played. Four angels with "alas de gasa celeste" [wings of sheerest gauze]

—perhaps symbolizing Buster's euphoria—dance among the flowers; they are accompanied by young girls playing the piano "como si montaran en bicicleta" [as if they were riding a bicycle] (p. 895), an image possibly inspired by the player pianos popular in that day. An amorous figure, a girl with the head of a nightingale, rides her bicycle up to Buster and immediately faints. The final frame, or sequence of images, in the piece depicts Buster bending over to kiss the girl while the gleaming stars of police badges twinkle over the horizon. Thus, *El paseo*, begun with a disturbing scene of violence, ends on a note of farce. The clown gets the girl; and the comic chase, one of the standard antics of American film comedies, is suggested by the distant presence of the cops.

Though Lorca's next two cinematic skits, *La doncella, el marinero y el estudiante* and *Quimera*, are not as innovative as *El paseo*, they nevertheless are strangely disconcerting sketches. As in *El paseo*, the tone of farce predominates, but the fear of the passage of time is present and foreshadows the full treatment of this theme in *Así que pasen cinco años*. The young girl of *La doncella* resembles the gypsy nun of *Romancero*, who embroiders while dreaming of gallant young men. She symbolizes all women, answering to each of the names the old woman calls her— María, Rosa Trinidad, Segismunda. The girl eagerly embroiders her linens with all the letters of the alphabet so that her lover may call her by any name he likes. A sailor who comes her way admires her beauty, but the wishes of both the sailor and the girl are subject to approval by their superiors—the sailor's captain and the girl's mother—so they come to no agreement. The sailor is followed by a student who also admires the *doncella*, but love is once more denied. The piece ends with the poet describing the *doncella* as a siren who, standing on her balcony, "piensa dar un salto desde la letra Z y lanzarse al abismo" [thinks of jumping off the letter Z and throwing herself into the abyss] (p. 903).

Quimera presents the well-worn situation of farce, the domestic quarrel. The struggle seems to be between the harried husband Enrique, who is leaving on a trip, and his six children, who quarrel about the gifts they want him to bring them when he returns. A doddering old servant, called simply "Viejo," reminds Enrique that time passes: "Peor es que todo ande y que el río suene" [The worst thing is that everything goes on and that the river rushes] (p. 906). But Enrique, worried that he may miss his train, retorts, "Lo peor del mundo es un criado viejo" [The worst thing in the world is an old servant], and departs to the sound of shrieking children who by now are bursting into tears over their dilemma of what to ask their father to bring them.

The last of Lorca's short scenarios, "A Trip to the Moon,"[15] was written while Lorca was in New York and reveals the poet's interest in the various devices of the cinema—fade-in, fade-out, and multiple exposure. "A Trip to the Moon" is composed of agonizing images of the cruelty, sexual suffering, and identity crisis of a small boy wearing a harlequin suit. Although the piece begins, as in "Suicidio en Alejandría," with an innocuous play on the numbers thirteen and twenty-two, the succeeding frames are an excruciating series of images. The central theme is the trauma of a boy punished for undefined sexual exploits. Images such as the hand squeezing a fish until it dies, which appears in Dalí's autobiography, and the nude figure with protruding veins and tendons, are frankly Daliesque. Unlike the mummery of *Narraciones*, in which the poet can hardly conceal his amusement, "A Trip to the Moon" resembles the shrill horror of the poems of New York—except for the last scene. In the final moments of the film-script a young man and a girl paint a mustache on a corpse (the boy's father?) and kiss "amid great bursts of laughter." "A Trip to the Moon" is Lorca's most violent and most sexually overt work. That it closes with grim *humour noir* only enhances the terror of the piece, at the same time evoking the uneasy feeling that the experience portrayed has all been a horrible joke. This savage glee at the death of a person who is treated not as a human being but as an object also describes the final scene of *Así que pasen cinco años*.

Just as suffering and death are treated with painful and sardonic humor in *Narraciones*, life is seen as a cruel game in *Así que pasen cinco años*. This tragic farce is the result of five years of experimentation with surrealist techniques and the devices of silent film comedy. In *Así que pasen*, Lorca achieves maximum liberation from traditional dramatic forms; yet, as a mixture of tragedy and farce it is characteristic of Lorca's comic spirit. Even though Arturo Berenguer Carisomo insists that "Lorca sin España, sin su raza y su tradición carece en absoluto de sentido" [Lorca, without Spain, his race and his tradition is absolutely meaningless],[16]

Así que pasen is an entirely lucid treatment of the central themes of Lorca's art—sexual frustration and death.

The theme of sexual frustration is given dramatic urgency in *Así que pasen* by constant reference to time. Although the hour remains six o'clock throughout the play, time runs out on the youth who is the central character. Aware that without love he will perish, El joven earnestly pursues romantic love, but, instead of finding it, falls prey to doubt, childish nostalgia, and fear of death. The harder he searches for affection, the further it recedes from him. His is the ironic failure of loving either prematurely or too late. La mecanógrafa, who seems fond of him, is certain that love will come and does not mind waiting for it, exclaiming, "Qué hermoso es esperar con seguridad el momento de ser amada" [How beautiful it is to confidently await the moment of being loved] (p. 1117). But waiting proves fatal to the young man. An uncertain and rather childish fellow, he waits too long. His pursuit is finally ended by death, which haunts him throughout the play.

Así que pasen is most accurately described by Marie Laffranque, who labels it an "allégorie du temps perdu" [an allegory of lost time].[17] As in medieval morality drama, the characters of Lorca's play are symbolic. All have generic names except for the servant Juan, whose name is so common that it lends him no personal identity. Lorca's protagonist, like those of morality plays, is engaged in a life-or-death struggle. Yet elements of farce are inserted in a dreamlike manner into the piece, so that the result is a parade of comic and fantastic characters through a surrealistic tale of desperation and death.

As R. G. Knight suggests, *Así que pasen* portrays a character in various stages of breakdown, suffering from inertia, vacillation, and despair.[18] El joven is an infantile young man, apprehensive and fastidious, who is introduced in the first scene as a ridiculous worrier who often gets up at midnight to pull weeds in his garden because, as he insists, "No quiero hierbas en mi casa ni muebles rotos" [I don't want weeds in my house, nor broken furniture] (p. 1047). According to Rafael Martínez Nadal, weeds signify death in Lorca's metaphorical language.[19] Thus, the young man's compulsion to pull weeds, repeated in the final act, can be seen as a death-wish that accompanies him from the outset.

Lorca's hero resembles the prim cyclist in the early scenes of *Un Chien andalou*, who is also fastidious and infantile. In *Chien andalou*, the cyclist's suit is laid out before him on a bed, symbolizing his alienation from himself. In *Así que pasen*, El Joven's clothes are also laid out on the bed (p. 1133), suggesting that he, too, is alienated and confused. Like the cyclist, El joven is a "good little boy . . . but no longer a child."[20] He is still preoccupied, however, with the things of childhood. Asking his servant the whereabouts of the small bed in which he slept as a boy, the young man seems irritated when he is told that it was given away long ago. Clearly, El joven's concern for his clothes and objects long outgrown represents his desire to withdraw from the world, a desire in constant conflict with his pursuit of love.

El joven is tormented by childhood fears of mutilation and death. A vision that disturbs him is that of a child and one of his playmates who appears as a large blue cat. The vision is an ominous one. The cat has been stoned by other children and is wounded. Finally a large hand pushes the animal out through a door. The general tone of the encounter, however, is amusing and whimsical. When the cat informs the child that she is a "gata" and not a "gato," he offers to catch her a rat but only if she will limit herself to eating "una patita, porque estás enferma" [a little foot, because you're sick]. The child tells the cat of his nightmares, some of which are sinister—"un hombre con martillo iba clavando estrellas de papel sobre mi caja" [a man with a hammer was nailing paper stars on my coffin]—and others, merely amusing, such as his fear of being eaten by the lizard family:

Niño: Vienen a comernos.

Gata: ¿Quién?

Niño: El lagarto y la lagarta,
con sus hijitos pequeños, que son muchos.

Gata: ¿Y qué nos comen?

Niño: La cara
con los dedos
y la cuca.

Gata:　(*Ofendida.*)
　　　　Yo no tengo cuca.

Niño:　(*Enérgico.*)
　　　　¡Gata!,
　　　　te comerán las patitas y el bigote.
　　　　Vámonos; de casa en casa
　　　　llegaremos donde pacen
　　　　las caballitos del agua.

[*Niño*:　They're coming to eat us up.

Gata:　Who?

Niño:　Mr. and Mrs. Lizard,
　　　　and their little children, who are numerous.

Gata:　And what are they going to eat?

Niño:　Our faces
　　　　our fingers
　　　　and our rears.

Gata:　(*Offended.*) I don't have a rear.

Niño:　(*With enthusiasm.*)
　　　　Cat!
　　　　They'll eat your little paws and your whiskers.
　　　　Let's go; from house to house
　　　　we'll find a place
　　　　where little sea horses graze.] (P. 1066)

In this dramatic sequence, as in Lorca's sinister lyric poems based on
nursery rhymes, death looms largest when it threatens innocent children
at play.

The central figure of *Así que pasen* represents a personality in decay;
the other characters of the play are also symbolic. Some represent various
facets of the young man's personality: El viejo embodies the fears of old

age and death that torment him; Amigo primero is the ladies' man El joven would like to be; Amigo segundo is the adolescent he has yet to outgrow. Others—La novia and her friend the rugby player, who engage in a sort of sexual display together—symbolize the sexual vigor and attraction that the young man appears to lack.

Although the prudish youth is, at times, a ridiculous figure, he is also pathetic, for he is taunted throughout the play by those whom he encounters. His suffering begins in the first act. When he admits that he has waited five years for his fiancée, El viejo, as if daring the youth to live more fully, asks, "¿No se atreve usted a huir?, ¿a volar?, ¿a ensanchar su amor por todo el cielo?" [Don't you dare to escape? To fly off? To spread your love through the sky?] (p. 1049). El joven, revealing his passive and fearful nature, covers his face with his hands, replying, "¡La quiero demasiado!" [I love her too much!].

The young man's only pleasant moments occur when he is visited by his two friends. Amigo primero is a don juan type who tries to convince El joven that waiting five years for any woman is a waste of time. The young man, justifying himself, explains that "esperando, el nudo se deshace y la fruta madura" [Waiting, the knot unravels and the fruit ripens]. But Amigo, continuing the pun, quips, "Yo prefiero comerla verde, o mejor todavía, me gusta cortar su flor para ponerla en mi solapa" [I prefer to eat it green, or still better, I like to cut the flower and put it in my lapel] (p. 1072). The second friend, outlandishly garbed in a white suit with large blue buttons, white gloves and shoes, and a vest and tie of frilly lace, is a childish figure, perhaps androgynous, for Lorca notes that this role could be played by a woman as well as by a young boy. Amigo segundo echoes El joven's fears of old age and death. Announcing that he hopes to be buried in a child's coffin, he drops off to sleep. Amigo segundo closes the first act singing the following verses, which ominously reveal the young man's death wish:

Yo vuelvo por mis alas	[I'll return for my wings
dejadme volver.	let me return.
Quiero morirme siendo ayer.	I want to die being yesterday.
Quiero morirme siendo amanecer.	I want to die being dawn.] (P. 1077)

Act II opens in La novia's bedroom. Decorated with tasseled curtains, walls painted with doves and cherubs, and a large bed "llena de colgaduras y plumajes" [full of trappings and plumes], this setting recalls the hilarious decor of Belisa's bedroom in *Don Perlimplín*.[21] The exaggerated *mise en scène* is also an example of the kind of burlesque achieved in *Doña Rosita la soltera*, in which costumes and sets parody the elaborate fashions of the early 1900's. Her hair done in long curls, La novia of *Así que pasen* bounces out of bed arrayed in a splendid lace gown with a train and bright red swags of ribbons. Her lover, the rugby player, has driven up outside in his car and is honking the horn. La novia runs to the balcony and calls for him to come up. The rugby player, symbolic of the arch-*macho*, utters not a word in the play, but only smokes and embraces the girl. He stands in silence as she clings to him, chattering uninterruptedly of her passion. She lights his cigars, embraces him, and leans against the silent athlete as if she were making love to a large, stuffed doll. At last she sends him out when El joven, who has waited five years for her, finally arrives to claim his love.

Like don Perlimplín, El joven finds that he has been betrayed. As in the earlier play, the scene in which the hero realizes the futility of his hopes is presented with such exaggeration that the effect of this cruel moment is comic. La novia scolds the maid, instructing her to fling over the balcony the bouquet the young man has brought her. She also informs her aged father that she will not marry her fiancé. Mocking El joven, she asks disdainfully, as if trying to remember: "¿Y tu no eras más alto? . . . ¿No tenías una sonrisa violenta? . . . ¿Y no jugabas tú el rugby?" [Weren't you taller? . . . Didn't you have a cruel smile? . . . And didn't you play rugby?] (p. 1093). She also remarks that his hand is "una mano de cera cortada" [a severed hand of wax]. This image parallels the phallic significance of the severed hand in *Un Chien andalou*.[22] (Lorca's preoccupation with severed hands is also seen in one of his drawings, entitled *Manos cortadas*.) If we interpret the hand according to Carl Jung,[23] the "mano de cera cortada" becomes a phallic symbol, and La novia thus refers to the failure of the young man's sexual drive.

When El joven tells La novia that he has dreamed of her, she dismisses him abruptly, insisting, "Aquí no se sueña. Yo no quiero soñar" [No dreaming here. I don't want to dream] (p. 1094), as if dreaming were a kiss of death. Later she tells her father that she does not like the young man because he talks too much (p. 1089). She prefers the virile rugby player, who is dumb but sexually attractive.

La novia's father is a caricature of authority rendered helpless by senility, reminding us of Lorca's aversion to the aged.[24] Much like doña Rosita's uncle, an amateur botanist, La novia's father is a myopic old man whose hobby is astronomy.[25] Dressed in a white wig, black suit, and white gloves, he squints through a pair of field glasses hanging from a cord about his neck. He complains that he will not be able to view the lunar eclipse he has long anticipated because when he becomes upset, "Se me sube la sangre a los ojos y no veo" [My blood rises to my eyes and I can't see] (p. 1089). Trying desperately to persuade his daughter to fulfill her promise, he raises his hand to strike her but turns away wailing: "Todos contra mí. Ahora empezará el eclipse. . . . Lo he estado esperando mucho tiempo. Y ahora yo no lo veo" [All against me. Now the eclipse will begin. . . . I have waited for it a long time. And now I won't see it] (p. 1090).

The amusing burlesque of the first and second acts becomes a comedy of despair in Act III, in which a series of farcical figures—Harlequin, a sequined clown with a powdered head resembling a skull, and the extravagant Máscara—introduce the theme of death that brings the young man's doom. In the commedia dell'arte, Harlequin was the chief of the zanni, or comic types. A quick-witted prankster, he was not so dangerous as he was amoral.[26] His parti-colored suit, which attracted painters of the 1920's, such as Picasso and Dalí, is symbolic of ambiguity. Harlequin thus represents the coexistence of opposite forces—comedy and tragedy, life and death. In Así que pasen Harlequin sings of the struggle between "ayer y mañana" [yesterday and tomorrow] (p. 1108). He has two masks—one is smiling, the other, a sleeping face—that he interchanges as he repeats verses underlining the passive personality of El joven: "Nadie puede abrir semillas / en el corazón del sueño" [Nobody can sprout seeds / in the depths of sleep]. He is comical as he plays a white violin with two golden strings, yet strangely malicious as he teases a young girl who sings of her lover in the opening scene of Act III.

A clown, who joins Harlequin's antics, is also a curiously frightening figure. Though his suit is sequin covered, his head is powdered and gives "una sensación de calavera" [the feeling of being a skull] (p. 1111). Lorca's description of a clown's head that looks like a skull parallels medieval depictions of death as a comic character. Hans Holbein rendered the figure of death draped in a jester's suit in his fifteenth-century series of prints entitled *Dance of Death*.[27] The clown in *Así que pasen* is the same kind of fearsome fool who cavorts about, laughing and singing, yet who is also sinister. The sequence between the clown and Harlequin is equivalent to the medieval danse macabre, for these two characters drive the young girl to tears and torment El joven to the brink of desperation.

In *Así que pasen* Lorca uses bizarre costumes, much as Federico Fellini has done in his films, to enhance the fantastic, dreamlike, and nightmarish effects of certain characters. Following the capers of the clown and Harlequin, La mecanógrafa, wearing a tennis frock with a long cape and beret, appears, accompanied by an exotic figure simply called Máscara. Máscara's costume is described in detail:

> un traje 1900 con larga cola amarillo rabioso, pelo de seda amarillo, cayendo como un manto, y máscara blanca de yeso; guantes hasta el codo, del mismo color. Lleva sombrero amarillo y todo el pecho sembrado con lentejuelas de oro. El efecto de este personaje debe ser el de una llamarada sobre el fondo de azules lunares y troncos nocturnos. Habla con un leve acento italiano.
> [a 1900's costume with a train of screaming yellow, hair of yellow silk, falling like a mantle, and a white plaster mask. Elbow-length gloves of the same color. She wears a yellow hat and her bodice is embroidered in yellow sequins. The effect of this character should be that of a flash of light upon a background of blue moonlight and dark tree trunks. She speaks with a slight Italian accent.] (P. 1115)

Máscara, dressed in gold, comes onstage laughing. She would seem to represent the bright light of love; instead, she tells a tale of alternating disdain and longing that echoes El joven's own experience. The extravagant Máscara, now abandoned and alone, relates her own version of frustration. Yet she tells her sad story effusively, much in the manner of the gossip-column nonsense that Lorca parodied in "Nadadora sumergida." Fragments of information and unidentified names are thrown together in dazzling confusion. Laughter is combined with tears as Máscara and the stenographer repeat the lines exchanged by El joven and the old man in the first scene:

Mecanógrafa:	¡De pequeña yo guardaba los dulces para comerlos después!	[Mecanógrafa:	When I was a little girl I saved the sweets to eat last!
Máscara:	¡Ja, ja, ja! ¿verdad? Saben mejor.	Máscara:	Ha, ha, ha, really? They taste better.]
			(P. 1117)

Thus, the experience of El joven, who once rejected the love that he now needs so desperately, is briefly reenacted, this time by female characters.

This whimsical interlude is interrupted by Harlequin and the clown, who playfully contrive to have the young man meet La mecanógrafa. Again the youth is the victim of a cruel joke. La mecanógrafa seems fond of him and voices his own desire as she repeats, "Quiero vivir" [I want to live]. Life and love are tantalizingly close, as El joven begs her to follow him. But the moment slips by and La mecanógrafa pronounces the fatal word, "¡Espera!" [Wait!] (p. 1123). Reminding El joven that he abandoned her when she proclaimed her love for him in the past, she now treats him with the same disinterest he displayed toward her in Act I. El viejo, who represents the denial of life, has been watching this scene. Seeing the young man drop his head in his hands as he loses his last hope, the old man is elated and whispers, "Bravo" (p. 1129). The clown and Harlequin also seem pleased, as if with a malicious prank. The clown directs the bewildered hero offstage to the left; the grinning Harlequin repeats "por allí" [that way], and bows to the right. The scene ends with the strange music of Harlequin's two-stringed violin.

Así que pasen concludes with the motif of the cruel game. Three jugadores, or card players, come to El joven's house. While waiting for their host, who is to be their victim, the players plan their method of attack. Laughing, they are confident of success. The young man is the inevitable loser because, as they explain, "Ni a la otra ni a la señorita mecanógrafa

se les occurrirá venir por aquí hasta que pasen cinco años, si es que vienen" [It will not occur to her or to the typist to come here until five years
pass, if they come at all] (p. 1137). Soon El joven appears and the fatal
game begins. He resists, realizing he has already lost. He tries to gain
time, but eventually he must make the final play. He lays down his last
card as an ace of hearts lights up on the library shelves. One of the players shoots it down, and the young man clasps his chest. Clearly, he is
dying, yet the gamblers amuse themselves with a pun. When one of them
directs the other to cut, presumably referring to the deck of cards, the first
player pulls out a pair of scissors and cuts the air with them. The players
then leave, and the young man dies alone. As in the poem "Burla de don
Pedro a caballo," his death appears more pathetic because it is presented
as a mischievous prank.

Precisely because of its disturbing comic mood, *Así que pasen* is one of
Lorca's most characteristic works. As in his early fables and farces, comic
figures caper in an atmosphere of impending doom. The most forceful impact of the play comes with the sense of the absurdity of life in which
man is a victim, both of time and of his own *abulia*, or lack of will. The
protagonist's most arduous struggles are ridiculous; his desperate efforts to
live fully are futile since he faces inevitable yet unexpected disaster. This
absurdity is vividly conveyed by the cinematic techniques of *Así que
pasen* in which characters arbitrarily appear, exit, and exchange meaningless words:

Viejo:	Si él tiene veinte años puede tener veinte lunas.
Mecanógrafa (*Lírica*):	Veinte rosas, veinte nortes de nieve.
Joven (*Irritado*):	Calla.
[*Viejo*:	If he is twenty years old he can as well be twenty moons old.
Mecanógrafa (*Lyrically*):	Twenty roses, twenty snowy winds.
Joven (*Irritated*):	Hush.] (P. 1126)

The old man and La mecanógrafa amuse themselves by inventing lyrical
images for "años" similar to the series of images for eyes that Lorca enu-

merates in "Santa Lucía y San Lázaro" (p. 17). The words have no meaning in themselves and give the effect of nonsense. Their psychological impact on El joven, however, is clearly negative. He becomes impatient with
the old man and the stenographer whose frivolous diversion seems to
mock the gravity of his predicament.

The atmosphere of farce is created by the appearance of fantastic characters, such as the blue cat and the manikin, who speak as ordinary humans, and the foolish antics of the clown and Harlequin. El joven is ridiculed by this pair of jesters in Act III when they block his path as he tries
to cross the stage:

> Arlequín: Dice que va a su casa.
>
> Payaso: (*Dando una bofetada de circo al Arlequín*)
> ¡Toma casa!
>
> Arlequín: (*Cae al suelo, gritando*) ¡Ay, que me duele,
> que me duele!
>
> [Harlequin: He says he's going home.
>
> Clown: (*Giving a ridiculous wallop to Harlequin*) Take that!
>
> Harlequin: (*Falls to the ground, moaning*) Oh, I'm hurt, I'm hurt!]
> (P. 1119)

The preposterous costumes of La mecanógrafa and Máscara also seem to
mock El joven's anguish. In the presence of such outlandish figures he is
upstaged, and his sorrow and frustration seem sadly irrelevant. His last
attempt to gain love is accompanied by ridiculous squeaky sounds produced by a two-stringed violin, and his death is caused by tricksters who
take delight in the merry chase after their victim. *Así que pasen* is Lorca's
most innovative full-length play; because of its sardonic humor, it is surely
one of his most disquieting.

Any discussion of Lorca's experimental work must now take into account *El público*. Although this piece is incomplete and fragmentary, we
know enough about it[28] to affirm that Lorca's social attitudes and ideas
about the theater were more advanced than those of many avant-garde

artists of his day. As long as the complete text of *El público* remains unpublished, it is impossible to estimate its artistic value. Yet, a brief study of the two published fragments, supplemented by details from Martínez Nadal's more finished version, reveals a side of Lorca's artistic temperament that had only begun to develop: the impatience of an aggressive modern playwright fed up with recalcitrant, unimaginative audiences who refused to tolerate in the theater any play that did not adhere to moral and artistic conventions.

The draft of *El público* owned by Martínez Nadal consists of five scenes; two of these, full of copyist's errors, are included in the Aguilar edition of Lorca's *Obras completas*. The action of the play centers on a main character, a theater director, who has cast a young boy in the heroine's role for a performance of *Romeo and Juliet*. When the members of the audience discover that the passion enacted on the stage is genuine and that the role of Juliet is played by a fifteen-year-old youth, they destroy the stage, murder the two actors, and threaten to lynch the director. While the audience avenges its outraged sense of morality, a group of students discusses what has happened. The students are revolted by the angry spectators, who "enarbolaron los cuchillos y los bastones porque la letra era más fuerte que ellos y la doctrina cuando se desata su caballera puede atropellar sin miedo a las verdades más inocentes" [bristle with knives and sticks because ideas are stronger than they are and dogma, when it goes unchecked, can trample the most innocent truths] (p. 1166). Representing enlightened tolerance, the students ridicule the irate public: "Un espectador no debe formar nunca parte del drama. Cuando la gente va al acuárium no asesina a las serpientes del mar . . . sino que resbala sobre los cristales sus ojos y aprende" [A spectator should never become part of the play. When people go to the aquarium they don't kill the sea serpents . . . they watch them swim about the tank and learn about them] (p. 1165). If this ironic remark is amusing, the humor of *El público* is often more vicious.

The critical satire of *El público* is aimed not only at conventional sexual mores but at social institutions as well. Martínez Nadal confirms the playwright's attitude of impatience with restrictions imposed by an exhausted morality: "Ante el sufrimiento, la sangre y la muerte del hombre, los preceptos morales se desvanecen en nada" [In the face of suffering, blood and death, moral principles dissolve].[29] Lorca's irritation with inflexible traditions is also obvious in his parody of religious figures in *El público*. In addition to the main action by the public and the commentary on it by students, a third scenario is presented: a male nurse and two thieves surround a "desnudo" who lies on an upright bed, which suggests a cross. The nude, described as a "desnudo rojo" in the manuscript owned by Martínez Nadal, represents Christianity lying moribund and helpless in the face of brutality, hypocrisy, and injustice. As the public destroys the stage, the thieves chant, "Santo. Santo. Santo." The nude repeats Christ's words, "Padre, en tus manos encomiendo mi espíritu" [Father, into your hands I commend my spirit] (p. 1164). Yet these traditionally sacred words appear ridiculous; not only are they out of context, but also the nurse corrects the dying man—"Te has adelantado dos minutos" [You're two minutes early]—for being out of step with the play. The hollow dignity of the religious figure is emphasized when the prompter appears and announces that "se había perdido la barba de José de Arimatea" [Joseph of Arimathea's beard is lost] (p. 1162).

In *El público* Lorca satirizes not only a vacant religious institution but also other traditional figures of authority, such as professors. The violence inflicted by the public provokes malicious glee on the part of the students. Their crude jokes indicate the extent of their disdain:

> *Estudiante 4°*: La primera bomba de la revolución barrió la cabeza del profesor de Retórica.
>
> *Estudiante 2°*: Con alegría para su mujer, que ahora trabajará tanto que tendrá que ponerse dos grifos en las tetas.
>
> [*Estudiante 4°*: The first bomb of the revolution swept off the head of the Rhetoric Professor.
>
> *Estudiante 2°*: Good riddance for his wife, who will work so hard now that she'll have to put two faucets on her teats] (P. 1157)

Unlike the enraged public, the students are not disturbed by the exchange of a young boy for a woman in the role of Juliet but appear tolerant of the various forms of human passion. With the attitude of today's

youth, who—along with a desire for political, economic, and social re-
form—seek the relaxation of strict sexual codes, the students insist on
freedom in its widest sense: one of them asks, "¿Y si quiero enamorarme
de ti?" [And if I want to fall in love with you?] to which his classmate
responds, "... yo te dejo" [... I'll let you] (p. 1167).

The demand for moral tolerance is inextricably linked with the demand
that the audience accept the playwright's illusion, however scandalous it
may seem. The students debate the dramatist's right to use whatever
dramatic distortions he wishes:

> *Muchacho 1°*: Aquí está la gran equivocación de todos y por eso
> el teatro agoniza: el público no debe atravesar las sedas y los car-
> tones que el poeta levanta en su dormitorio. Romeo puede ser un...
> grano de sal y Julieta ser un mapa. ¿Qué le importa esto al público?

> [*Muchacho 1°*: Here is everyone's big mistake and the reason
> why the theater is suffering: the public shouldn't cross over the silk
> and cardboard sets that the poet puts up in his inner sanctum.
> Romeo can be a grain of salt and Juliet a map. What difference
> does it make to the public?] (P. 1160)

While the public must "willingly suspend its disbelief" in order for the
theater to function, the theme of artistic freedom in *El público* is neither
more nor less important than moral tolerance.[30] Indeed, the crisis, or
"revolution," brought about in the play is not caused by the public's anger
at new dramatic techniques, for they are unconcerned with the mechanics
of art. Rather, the public is incensed when it learns that Juliet is not a
girl and that the love between the protagonists is genuine. As Martínez
Nadal points out, Lorca could easily have concealed the theme of unconventional love within the safe confines of puppet theater. But instead
he chose to treat the theme openly, to dramatize in *El público* "lo que
pasa todos los días" [what happens every day]. Lorca's use of the theater
as a forum in which he could challenge conventional moral codes, as well
as his demand for dramatic freedom, are affirmed by his *port-parole*
[character who speaks for the author], the director, who asserts, "Hay que
destruir el teatro o hay que vivir en el teatro" [We have to destroy the
theater or live in it].[31] Thus, Lorca presented his conception of theater

not as a museum but as living art, in which a society's darkest secrets must be brought to light.

El público is in every way a revolutionary work. Lorca was, of course, aware that the theme of the play was inflammatory. When he finished reading it to a group of friends, they remained silent and dumbfounded. Martínez Nadal reports that Lorca accepted philosophically his friends' silence and confusion, confiding to him that "no se han enterado de nada o se han asustado, y lo comprendo. La obra es muy difícil y por el momento irrepresentable, tienen razón. Pero dentro de diez o veinte años será un exitazo; ya lo verás" [they have either not understood anything or have been frightened, and I understand. The work is very difficult and for the moment, unpresentable; they're right. But within ten or twenty years it will be a smash hit; you'll see].[32] Lorca's confidence in *El público* and his staunch defense of it seem proof that he knew instinctively the direction that modern theater would take. Indeed, he was leading the way toward the Theater of the Absurd, in which all social attitudes, including man's view of himself, would be challenged and ridiculed.

El público is, at the same time, Lorca's most didactic play. It is not, of course, a special pleading for perversion but rather a desperate cry for compassion. As Lázaro Carreter has pointed out, Lorca attempted in all his plays "más de educar que de enseñar, de afinar y refinar los espíritus" [More to educate than to teach, to polish and refine the spirit].[33] Lorca's savage burlesque of the typical theater audience represents the protest of an artist against a public unwilling even to consider new forms of expression. The bold trickery by the director, who substitutes the boy in the role of Juliet, mocks the sense of propriety of a culture incapable of dealing with deviations from the norm except by violent reprisal. Finally, the disdainful jokes of students who view the public's venomous reaction as a kind of vestigial barbarity represent the humor of futility, in which laughter that could as easily turn to weeping is much more heroic than tears.

Within the privacy of experimentation Lorca confronted the terrifying disorder and violence of his thoughts more straightforwardly than he had yet done in his traditional works. The undaunted, childlike heroines of his successful plays, *La zapatera* and *Mariana Pineda*, are replaced in the experimental works by the melancholy fools, Buster Keaton and El joven, who make their uncertain, often ludicrous way through a chaotic dream world. The violent language of surrealism afforded Lorca the opportunity to satirize conventional attitudes and institutions more directly than he had done before. In *Narraciones* he laughs sardonically at decayed religious tradition and takes sadistic glee in the shocking effects of brutality and the rending of flesh. In "A Trip to the Moon" the poet laughs at guilt-ridden attitudes toward sex. His previous obsession with the fear of death is revealed in *Así que pasen* to be a fear of life as well. In *El público* Lorca gives dramatic form to his preoccupation with homosexuality. This uninhibited dramatization of a disordered world was possible only in the context of a literary game and could best be expressed by the contorted imagery and the dark humor of surrealism.

Escape from conventional moral and literary restraints was not the only value that Lorca discovered in surrealist humor. As John B. Trend has perceptively remarked, Lorca was a poet whose "strongest impressions were visual";[34] thus, the pictorial quality of surrealism, as well as its iconoclasm, appealed to Lorca. In the paintings of Dalí and Max Ernst and in the films of Buñuel and Dalí, surrealism had established a new bond between poetry and the visual arts. Indeed, as Anna Balakian reminds us, "The concepts of Lautréamont and Rimbaud were to be illustrated in art before they reached their maturation in poetry."[35] With the development of such cinematic techniques as the fade-in, the flashback, and the double exposure, the creation of shocking caricatures, nonsensical images, and grotesquerie entered a new realm of possibility. And in *El paseo, Así que pasen,* and "A Trip to the Moon," Lorca exploits all of these techniques. The visualization of startling and grotesque images represents perhaps the most important contribution of surrealism to Lorca's art. For, although he exhausts the chaotic rhetoric of surrealism in the poems of New York, caricatures and grotesque figures continue to appear in dramatic form, particularly in his last two plays.

4. Puppet Farces

By 1931 Lorca had concluded his experimentation with surrealism, yet he had not exhausted his interest in comic violence. While surrealist films and painting, together with American silent comedies, provided him with visual imagery that paralleled his own dark comic spirit, there was still another source of violent humor that intrigued Lorca—puppet theater. It is not surprising that, having learned the language of the avant-garde, Lorca returned to the infantile world of puppets. For in puppet theater he encountered one of the oldest and certainly one of the most violent traditions of slapstick comedy.

Lorca is not the only serious modern playwright to draw inspiration from puppet theater. Some of the most original minds that have written for the stage—Alfred Jarry, Jean Cocteau, Luigi Pirandello, and Spanish dramatists Valle-Inclán and Jacinto Grau—have dramatized their vision of the world by relating human experience to the theater of the Grand Guignol. A brief preview of the significance of puppets in the works of some of these dramatists may provide insight into the appeal of primitive make-believe to the serious playwright and thus allow a better understanding of Lorca's recurrent interest in puppetry.

Alfred Jarry created an upheaval in French theater in 1896 when he resorted to the conventions of puppet theater in *Ubu roi*. For Jarry, only the exaggerations of puppetry could adequately suggest the unlimited dimensions of human greed, stupidity, and viciousness personified in the ridiculous figure of Ubu. Jarry directed that the play be staged as a *guignol,* or puppet show, with the use of a single stage set, placards to indicate scene changes, and human actors mimicking the stiff movements of wooden dolls.[1] Ubu, like the bullies of puppet plays, carries a cane, the equivalent of the bully's slapstick. A spoof of the military officer, Ubu is a captain of the Polish Dragoons but nevertheless wears a bowler hat. When he kills his trusting king, Wenceslaus, he takes over the throne, squashes the crown over his bowler, and sallies forth to liquidate the nobility and to collect personally the double taxes he has levied upon the peasants. Clearly, as Wallace Fowlie comments,[2] Jarry intended to assault and shock a conventional bourgeois public by abolishing the polite vocabulary and dialogue of realism and by reducing dramatic action to its most elemental form of fisticuffs and insults. The devices of puppet theater, such as rigidity of character and physical and verbal abuse, provided Jarry with a convenient means for presenting an unrestrained portrayal of villainy.

Perhaps the most direct inheritors of *Ubu roi* are the dramatists of the Theater of the Absurd, such as Ionesco and Genet, to whom we shall return in chapter six. In Spain the theater of Jarry has its direct equivalent in the bitter farces of Valle-Inclán. Just as Jarry mocked theatrical and social institutions by techniques of the *guignolade,* Valle-Inclán satirized the Spanish military and monarchy within the puppet arena. Valle-Inclán wrote at least eight farces to be enacted by one-dimensional figures that he termed "siluetas" and "marionetas." In two of his best dramatic works, the *esperpento Los cuernos de don Friolera* and *Farsa y licencia de la reina castiza,* the puppetlike characters remain wooden and ridiculous throughout, thus heightening the satirical impact of these two plays.

The similarity between Valle-Inclán's puppet don Friolera and Lorca's don Perlimplín has been mentioned in chapter two. Friolera, like Jarry's Ubu, is a military officer in a wild burlesque of official codes of behavior. The despotic and corrupt Ubu has a manner of speaking all his own. Valle-Inclán also delighted in ridiculing pompous and brutal military types. In *Don Friolera* the absurd figure of don Lauro Rovirosa, a bald lieutenant, pronounces pedantic judgments while his glass eye rolls about in his head.

Valle's *Farsa y licencia de la reina castiza,* a savage parody of a nineteenth-century Spanish monarch, is another example of the satirical use of puppetry. The work is described as a "farsa para muñecos" [farce for dolls], and, as in *Ubu roi*, the sets are deliberately askew. King Ubu's hilarious yet degrading references to his wife are echoed in Valle's description of the Spanish queen, whose overblown shape suggests a "hiperbólico acordeón" [overblown accordion]. As in Jarry's farce, the puppets of *La reina castiza* are incarnations of vice: just as Jarry depicts Mother Ubu greedily robbing graves in search of gold, the Spanish queen is portrayed as a depraved and giddy creature who cannot resist writing indiscreet letters to her lovers. Thus, for Valle-Inclán, as well as for Jarry, puppetry was a technique by which the deceptions of a corrupt society were stripped away to reveal its fundamental crudity and baseness.

During the 1920's Italian dramatists gave another meaning to the analogy between puppet and human behavior. The writers of the *teatro del grottesco* frequently dramatized the helplessness of man by use of puppets. In *Marionette, che passione!* Rosso di San Secondo's characters suffer, yet remain mechanical creatures entirely at the mercy of overwhelming passions. Most of Pirandello's dramatis personae—Enrico IV, the six characters in search of an author, the writer reduced to a puppet by success in *Quando si è Qualcuno*—are all creatures imprisoned. Ciampa, in *Il Berretto a sonagli*, despairs of a life manipulated by forces out of man's reach when he exclaims, "Pupi siamo... Lo spirito divino entra in noi e si fa pupo. Pupo io, pupo lei, pupi tutti" [We are puppets—the divine spirit enters us and makes us puppets. I'm a puppet, so are you, we're all puppets].[3] The puppet analogy was one of the favorite motifs of Massino Bontempelli, a writer influenced by Pirandello. In *Siepe a nordovest* (1923), Bontempelli reversed the roles of puppet and man and portrayed humans performing for the amusement of puppets. In *Nostra Dea* Bontempelli's heroine is an automaton without a personality of her own. A similar heroine in *Minnie, la candida* is also a mechanical creature who cannot distinguish between men and puppets. Finally, Ugo Falena suggests in *Il raggio di luna* that the puppet's wooden existence is, compared to the vicissitudes of human life, not so bad after all. Having been humans for a brief time, Falena's marionettes prefer their more controlled and more durable state.

The parallel between human limitations and the restricted life of a doll enacted on the stage of the Italian *teatro del grottesco* is carried one step further by the Spanish playwright Jacinto Grau. The puppets in his *El señor del Pigmalión* are autonomous creatures who finally gain control over their helpless creator. Pigmalión creates a set of mechanical dolls but, through his fondness for them, soon becomes a puppet in the hands of his creatures. The dolls hate Pigmalión and escape from their boxes, their metal parts clicking loudly. The comedy assumes a somber tone when the dolls shoot Pigmalión and then stand on his chest to take his pulse. Pigmalión is left in the care of the moron-puppet, Juan, who bashes in his creator's skull, repeating, "Cu cu, cu cu."

Puppet theater has thus provided a rich vein of innovative techniques for modern dramatists. The comparison of humans with wooden figures not only suggests the futility of human effort, as in Grau's play, but also provides limitless possibilities for satire of the rank primitiveness of so-called civilized man, as in the farces of Jarry and Valle-Inclán. Lorca, too, was intrigued with puppet theater. His childhood delight in marionettes became an artistic preoccupation in 1923 when the young playwright, collaborating with the composer Manuel de Falla, staged a series of puppet plays for a group of friends. The program included Cervantes's *entremés Los dos habladores*, the medieval mystery *Los reyes magos*, and an original play now lost, *La niña que riega la albahaca*. Later, in 1928, Lorca wrote *La tragicomedia de don Cristóbal*, a puppet farce that probably served as a preliminary sketch for *Don Perlimplín*. In 1931, having concluded a prolonged period of experimentation with avant-garde forms, Lorca returned to the puppet medium and completed the final version of *Retablillo de don Cristóbal*.

Pointing to the many similarities between Lorca's puppet farces and *Don Perlimplín*, critics have generally considered the puppet pieces improvisations upon the theme of the *mal mariada* that culminated in the more serious *Don Perlimplín*. Puppetry was indeed an experimental medium in which Lorca worked out techniques used later on a larger scale. Since marionette theater originated from and developed along the same lines, indeed reproducing the same characters as the commedia dell'arte,[4] it is not surprising that Lorca's puppet skits resemble his plays inspired by traditional farce, *La zapatera prodigiosa* and *Don Perlimplín*. Yet traces of Lorca's experiments with puppet theater are apparent not only in his experimental works, but in his mature dramas as well. Several critics—J.-L. Schonberg,[5] William I. Oliver,[6] Guillermo de Torre,[7] and François Nourissier[8]—have pointed to Lorca's puppet plays as the source of his mature works. But so far the implications of this idea have not been examined.

Lorca's return to puppetry with the completion of *Retablillo* in 1931 and his continuing interest in staging his puppet works, both in Argentina in 1934 and in Madrid at the Lyceum Club in 1935, suggest that puppetry was not merely a childhood pastime or an adolescent workshop, but a lifelong preoccupation. There are in puppet farce, as in surrealism, elements characteristic of Lorca's own artistic temperament. The violence, elemental characterizations, and erotic tensions with which Lorca amused himself in the puppet medium are the same techniques with which he constructed both his surrealist experiments and his dramatic masterpieces. Like other modern playwrights, Lorca sought to revitalize the modern stage by returning to the primitive, uninhibited, freewheeling tradition of puppet theater.

Rather than serving as a guise for social satire, as in the works of Jarry and Valle-Inclán, puppet farce offered Lorca a way out of the clichés of realism and an escape from his own tendency toward excessive lyricism in the theater. At first glance, Lorca's puppet pieces seem ingenuous, even nostalgic representations in which the young playwright bids farewell to the toy personages of his childhood playlets. A brief consideration of the prologues to these farces, however, reveals a more serious intent. The puckish figure of Mosquito announces at the beginning of *Tragicomedia de don Cristóbal*:

> Yo y mi compañía venimos del teatro de los burgueses, del
> teatro de los condes y de los marqueses, un teatro de oro
> y cristales, donde los hombres van a dormirse y las
> señoras . . . a dormirse también. Y mi compañía estábamos
> encerrados . . . y huimos por esos campos en busca de la
> gente sencilla, para mostrarles las cosas, las cosillas,
> y las cositillas del mundo.

> [My company and I come from bourgeois theater, from the theater
> of counts and marquises, a theater of crystal and gold, where the
> men go to sleep and the ladies . . . also go to sleep. We felt trapped

... and we fled through these fields in search of simple folk, to show
them things, the little inconspicuous things of the world.] (Pp. 723–
724)

This is the kind of special pleading for the public's attention with which
Lorca also introduced his first play, *El maleficio*, wherein he begged the
public's indulgence. Such prologues were a warning to the public that
what might appear to be a childish spectacle should be understood instead as an effort to depart from the conventional realism of the day. In
the prologue to his first puppet farce, Lorca frankly admitted his desire
to escape the polite or bourgeois theater with its bland characters and
unimaginative dialogue. Like Antonin Artaud, who sought cruelty in the
theater as a means of shocking the audience into an increased awareness
of life, Lorca believed that theater should not lull spectators to sleep but
should awaken them to realities they had not yet begun to consider.

As he matured, Lorca repeatedly reaffirmed his conception of theater
as a violent experience in which the spectator would confront the unexpected. The best example of his administering shocks to his audience is,
of course, in *El público*, a play which is actually a form of combat between the dramatist and his public. In the prologue to *Retablillo de don
Cristóbal*, Lorca again, now less aggressively than in *El público*, demands
the spectator's tolerance. The director politely speaks of his confidence
that the spectator will listen to whatever is presented before him: "... si
un pájaro mueve un ala, que también la oigamos, y si una hormiguita
mueve la patita, que también lo oigamos" [... if a bird moves a wing, we
hear it, and if an ant moves a leg, we also hear it] (p. 1019). Lorca knew
that his search for fresh dramatic forms led away from bourgeois drama
toward a revival of a more primitive, violent theater. That this was to be
the direction his dramatic art would take is clear in the prologues to his
first play and to his puppet farces. Discussing his work with repertory theater in an interview in 1934, Lorca analyzed his public:

Hay un sólo público que hemos podido comprobar que no nos es adicto:
el intermedio, la burguesía, frívola, materializada. Nuestro público, los
verdaderos captadores del arte teatral, están en los dos extremos: las
clases cultas ... y el pueblo, el pueblo más pobre y más rudo ... fértil
a todos los estremecimientos del dolor y a todos los giros de la gracia.

[There is only one public that we have been able to prove is not
carried away with us: the middle brow, the bourgeois, frivolous, ma-
terialistic. Our public, those who are really hooked on dramatic art, are
of two extremes: the educated . . . and the humble, the poor, simple
folk, . . . receptive to all the shivers of pain and to all the graceful
flourishes.] (Pp. 1748–1749)

Lorca's commentary upon the success of his repertory group, La Barraca,
applies as well to the appeal of his own dramatic art. Thus, Lorca's search
for fresh dramatic expression and his own proclivity for violent spectacle
led him repeatedly to the puppet farce.

Lorca's two puppet farces are much alike. They share the same central
characters—Rosita and Cristóbal—some of the same jokes and dialogue,
and the theme of Rosita's marriage to the bully Cristóbal. In *Tragicomedia*, the earlier of the two pieces, the action is narrated by Mosquito, a
puckish figure, "mitad duende, mitad martinico, mitad insecto" [half spirit,
half sprite, half insect] (p. 723). He is a mischievous sprite who comments on and laughs at the other characters and their actions. He appears
only to speak to the audience or to encourage the puppets in a whimsical,
mocking tone.

In the ancient commedia dell'arte one of the best sources of jokes was
language—the use and misuse of words and the bizarre pronunciation of
foreign terms. This is the kind of simple laughter Lorca provokes in
Tragicomedia. Though Rosita's father insists she must marry Cristóbal,
she loves only Cocoliche, who wants to marry her but who has no money.
Cocoliche tells Rosita that he will write to Paris for a baby, but Rosita
says she does not want a baby who sounds like the French "con el chau,
chau, chau" [with the chau, chau, chau] (p. 730). There are other jokes
based on language, such as puns and plays on words. Comic effect is also
achieved by a shoemaker called Cansa-Almas, who stutters. Lorca, however, does not use dialect or jargon, as Cervantes does in one of his *entremeses*. Lorca's adaptation of popular humor is intended for a cultivated
audience, and jokes based on language are less frequent than comic situations and the ridiculous antics of the puppets.

The broad humor of Lorca's *Tragicomedia* is based on the old tricks of
the commedia—such as the lovers' quarrel, the use of disguise, obscenity,

and double entendre. Cocoliche, Rosita's lover, and Currito, one of her admirers, manage to enter Rosita's room secretly. Rosita hides them in the clothes closet, where they listen to the bells ringing out the news of Rosita's marriage to the rich Cristóbal. Now husband and wife, Rosita and Cristóbal return to the room, presumably to be alone, but noises from the closet arouse Cristóbal's suspicion. Rosita talks nervously about the stars, hoping to distract her jealous spouse. The bully, however, discovers the hidden puppets and flies into a rage. He sees Rosita and Cocoliche embrace and is literally undone by the sight. His mechanical springs begin to grind and, clutching his fat belly, he falls to the floor and dies.

The last scene is the funniest of the farce. The puppets toss Cristóbal into a coffin decorated with radishes and peppers, while a cortege of wooden figures plays a funeral march on toy whistles and a horn. Rosita cries a moment for Cristóbal, then embraces Cocoliche as the funeral turns into a celebration. Mosquito announces joyously:

Vamos a enterrar	[We are going to bury
al gran ganapán.	the great glutton.
Cristobita borracho	Drunken Cristobita
que no volverá.	will return no more.] (P. 780)

The second farce, *Retablillo de don Cristóbal*, is an amusing though more self-conscious piece. It remained unfinished until 1931, by which time Lorca had become a successful poet and dramatist whose artistic horizons had been considerably extended by his ventures into the literature of the avant-garde. Thus, his second puppet farce reveals the technical problems with which he struggled in his experimental works. Like Jacinto Grau in *El señor del Pigmalión*, Lorca, both in *El público* and in *Retablillo*, is preoccupied with the autonomy of dramatic characters. *Retablillo* begins with a debate between a poet and the director of the farce, who argue about the characterization of Cristóbal. The poet would like to humanize Cristóbal's bully image and pleads for the director to give the puppet a chance to prove his potential for being good. But the director insists that the traditionally ferocious Cristóbal be left as he is. Resisting the temptation to complicate the ancient comic type, the director demands of the poet, "¿Quién es usted para terminar con esta ley de maldad?" [Who are you to terminate this law of evil?]. William I. Oliver sees the poet as a "comic self-parody" of Lorca's own poetic nature, who would convert Cristóbal into a polite and sensitive character.[9]

The director prevails and calls for the puppets to come onstage and begin the play. The puppets, however, are uninterested and reluctant. Rosita says she is putting on her shoes, but sounds of snoring are heard offstage. Cristóbal, too, stalls for time, giving an obscene excuse—"Es que estoy meando" [I'm peeing]—for delay. Next, Cristóbal begins to dispute his role with the director. He has been cast as a doctor, but the bully resists: "Yo no soy un médico. Vamos al toro" [I'm not a doctor. I'm going to the bullfight] (p. 1023). He finally cooperates when the director tells him he will need money if he wishes to get married.

When the action at last begins, it concentrates on the wedding negotiations, this time handled by Rosita's mother, and on the postmarriage scene, during which Rosita produces five babies in mechanical, rapid succession. Rosita's mother insists that the babies are all her son-in-law's, but Cristóbal suspects that he may have been betrayed and begins to quarrel with her. The director, perhaps seeing no other way of ending the quarrel, gathers the puppets into his hands and terminates the play with a final speech praising the vitality of the puppet tradition.

For all their charm, the importance of these ingenuous puppet plays lies not so much in the works themselves as in what they tell us about Lorca's mature works. As William I. Oliver points out, it was in *Retablillo* "that Lorca declared his discovery of the mode of characterization, the approach to dramatic action and the control of dramatic dialogue that was to distinguish his masterpieces as something unique in modern drama."[10]

The dramatic characterizations of Lorca's mature dramas resemble the characters of the puppet farces in that they remain uncomplicated and somewhat elemental. Critics have often commented upon the lack of psychological definition in Lorca's plays. Alfredo de la Guardia remarks that Lorca's dramatis personae are symbolic, simplified figures;[11] William I. Oliver recalls the puppetlike quality of *Mariana Pineda*;[12] and the playwright's brother speaks of the "anonymous beings" of *Bodas de sangre*.[13] That Lorca is quite capable of drawing complex characters is evident in his study of the aging cuckold, don Perlimplín. Yet he seems more interested in simply outlining than in probing into dramatic characters; and the stock comic type, infinitely refined, recurs throughout his plays. The bully Cristóbal, who threatens to eat Rosita up (p. 767), is merely another version of the mock-ferocious villain Alacranito, who longs to take a bite of the insects in *El maleficio*. Later, in his masterpiece, *La casa de Bernarda Alba*, Lorca again creates a symbol of ferocity in the overpowering figure of Bernarda. As she shrieks for vengeance—"Matadla, Matadla" [Kill her, kill her]—at the woman who has had an illegitimate child, traces of the puppet-bully's fury flare up in Bernarda's character. She symbolizes the wooden inhumanity of an outraged society whose demands, like those of don Cristóbal, have been circumvented.

The puppet Rosita, married unwillingly to the rich Cristóbal, is another comic character who reappears in modified forms throughout Lorca's plays. Rosita is a comic version of Lorca's imprisoned heroines, who are compelled to risk disaster in order to satisfy their own passions. Rosita sings of her desire to marry in *Tragicomedia*, but, like the comic Novia of *Así que pasen* and the tormented bride of *Bodas de sangre*, she finds herself cornered into marrying someone she does not love. She protests her father's arrangement of her marriage to Cristóbal: "Dispone de mi mano y yo no tengo más remedio que aguantarme porque lo manda la ley. También la ley podía haberse estado en su casa" [Give me away and I have no other recourse than to bear with it, because that's the law. The law could've stayed home] (p. 733). In much the same way that Adela in *La casa de Bernarda Alba* struggles against her mother's decree of an eight-year mourning period, Rosita laments her father's power over her life: "Pienso que este luto me ha cogido en la peor época de mi vida para pasarlo" [I think that this mourning has happened to me at the worst possible time for it to happen] (p. 1466). The puppet heroine tries to assert her will: "Pues no quiero, no quiero, ¡ea! Y lo que es mi mano, de ninguna manera me la quitas. Yo tenía novio. . . . ¡Y tiro el collar!" [Well, I don't want to, I don't want to! And you're not giving away my hand in marriage. I had a boyfriend. . . . And I'm throwing away the collar you had around my neck!] (p. 732). Adela rebels against authority with equal vigor: "Esto hago yo con la vara de la dominadora" [This is what I'm doing with the tyrant's cane] (p. 1529). The puppet Rosita and the rebellious Adela are characters conceived along the same lines; both represent passionate disregard for authority. Their fate, of course, differs according to the action of the plot, whether farcical or serious. Rosita finally wins her lover because the puppet bully cracks apart and dies. Adela, who intends to live as Pepe's lover, kills herself when she believes Pepe has been shot.

The characters in *Tragicomedia* who represent authority—Rosita's father and Cristóbal—are miniatures of the overpowering Bernarda Alba, an epitome of the snarling tyrant. When Rosita protests her marriage to Cristóbal and her father tells her that she will have to obey, he gives the same reason that Bernarda repeats when she demands that her daughters observe an eight-year period of mourning: because it has been so in the past. "A bordar ya callar" [Sew and keep quiet], he shouts; "Tú harás caso de todo como hice yo caso de mi papá cuando me casó con tu mamá" [You'll do everything I tell you as I did what my father told me when he married me to your mother] (p. 733). If Rosita's father gives commands in much the same way as Bernarda, Cristóbal views his neighbors with the same hostility Bernarda displays toward the women of her village. Cristóbal announces his view that "no hay más de dos caminos a seguir con los hombres: o no conocerlos . . . ¡o quitarlos de en medio!" [there are only two ways to deal with men: either don't know any . . . or get them out of the way!] (p. 734). He does not wish to have guests at his wedding. When he insists that Rosita send away those guests who have come, he seems a prototype of the surly Bernarda, who shouts to the villagers as they leave her house: "¡Andar a vuestras casas a criticar todo lo que habéis visto! ¡Ojalá tardéis muchos años en pasar el arco de mi puerta!" [Go home and criticize all you've seen here! I hope you're a long time in coming back!] (p. 1450).

To suggest that some of the heroines of Lorca's mature plays derive from his puppet figures is not to diminish in any way their dramatic value. Indeed, their single-minded passions only intensify the dramatic conflict they must endure. As A. A. Parker has indicated in his enlightening study of Spanish drama of the golden age, action has traditionally prevailed over psychological refinement of character in the Spanish theater. Characterization was not the primary concern of playwrights such as Lope, Tirso de Molina, and Calderón.[14] Lorca, continuing this tradition, was drawn to puppet theater as an experimental medium—not because he lacked the talent for psychological discourse but because he, like the great Spanish dramatists of the past, was more interested in dramatic action. For this purpose, the puppet arena provided limitless possibilities.

The violence of *Tragicomedia* and *Retablillo* is enacted by dolls upon a tiny scale and is thus rendered harmless. No spectator will weep when the despairing Rosita vows to poison herself with "sublimado corrosivo" [corrosive sublimate]. Cristóbal's death scene, complete with toy mourners and a coffin draped in vegetables, can only inspire delight. Yet here the dramatist is working out in farce the violent themes of suicide, murder, and martyrdom that rend the heroines of his mature plays.

The theme of sacrifice is one Lorca frequently dramatized. The spinster doña Rosita is no less a martyr than the famous Mariana Pineda, for she, too, voluntarily surrenders her happiness and freedom to wait for her departed lover. Don Prelimplín sacrifices his life not only to win a moment of Belisa's love but also in order that Belisa may know love's deepest meaning. It is significant that the theme of sacrifice in Lorca's theater first appears in comic form. In the final scene of *Tragicomedia* Rosita sees herself as a diminutive Mariana Pineda who marches off to her sad fate: "¡Todo se ha perdido! ¡Todo! Voy al suplicio como Marianita Pineda. Ella tuvo una gargantilla de hierro en sus bodas con la muerte y yo tendré un collar . . . un collar de don Cristobita *[llora y canta]*" [All is lost! All! I'll go to the scaffold like Mariana Pineda. She wore an iron collar at her wedding with death and I'll have on a collar . . . don Cristobita's collar (she cries and sings)] (p. 762). The hilarious melodrama in which Rosita embraces her lover is described as "un idilio estilo dúo de ópera" [an idyll in the style of an operatic duet] (p. 777). Rosita is willing to die so that Cocoliche may escape from the clutches of the jealous Cristóbal: "Vete a tu casa; ahora, yo moriré" [Go home; now I can die]. In *Bodas de sangre* the bride uses similar words, hoping to save Leonardo from being hunted by her husband: "¡Huye! Es justo que yo aquí muera" [Run! It is fitting that I die here] (p. 1260). Thus, with similar shreds of dialogue, Lorca extends the theme of sacrifice from puppet farce to tragedy.

The fear of violent death that recurs almost obsessively throughout Lorca's lyric and dramatic works is expressed in terms of farce as well as in pathos and tragedy. In *Tragicomedia* disaster is foreshadowed, much as in *Bodas de sangre*, by visions of knives. Cocoliche is frightened by a dream in which Rosita appears dressed in mourning "con una corona de nardos sobre la cabeza y un puñal de plata en la mano" [with a crown of spikenards on her head and a silver knife in her hand] (p. 754). Finally, Currito takes out his knife and tries to stab Cristóbal. In the final lament of *Bodas de sangre*, with the repeated use of the diminutive *cuchillito*, death again appears reduced to the small, intimate scale to which it is confined in the puppet plays:

Madre: Se mataron los dos hombres del amor. Con un cuchillo Con un cuchillito que apenas cabe en la mano.	[*Madre*: Two men in love killed each other. With a knife With a little knife that barely fits in the hand.] (P. 1272)

Of all the forms of violent death, murder seems most prominent in Lorca's mind. A long line of homicide victims, including Antoñito el Camborio and other gypsies, *Yerma's* Juan, and Leonardo and his rival in *Bodas de sangre*, meet their dark fate in his lyric and dramatic works. We have noted how death is often presented in a mock-serious manner in poems, such as "Burla de don Pedro," and in the guise of comic figures, such as the clown and the jokesters of *Así que pasen*. The death of Cristóbal becomes a celebration in *Tragicomedia* when Rosita weeps a moment for her fallen husband, then embraces her dear Cocoliche. In *Retablillo* Cristobál becomes infuriated when he discovers that Rosita has had five babies. He vents his anger upon Rosita's mother and kills her; she falls flat but is promptly resurrected and renews the fight.

Not only murder but also physical abuse of all sorts abounds in Lorca's puppet farces. The marionette theater is, like many of the American film comedies, a rowdy world in which bodies are knocked about and heads are pounded. The slapstick antics of don Cristóbal are free of the more unsettling humor of surrealism. In his prose tales and skits Lorca imitated the exaggerated but disturbing scenes of torture and sadism that he encountered in passages of Lautréamont and in surrealist films; this sinister humor, however, is absent from his ingenuous puppet pieces. The doll-like small boy and his cat have an amusing conversation in *Así que pasen*, but the interlude becomes poignant when the children kill the cat and the boy dies as well. No such sentiment complicates Lorca's puppet plays. The victims of Cristóbal's club either retort by making fun of him, as Rosita's lovers do in *Tragicomedia*, or soon revive, as Rosita's mother does in *Retablillo*.

There is, however, a strong erotic current beneath the slapstick violence endured by Lorca's puppets. Particularly in *Retablillo*, obscene little verses contribute bawdy humor to the farce. In *Retablillo* Cristóbal appears in the role of a doctor who makes sure his patients have money before he treats them. When a patient sings brazenly of the places he has hidden his riches—

debajo del chalequito	[beneath my little jacket
seis duritos y tres duritos,	six little dollars and three little
y en el ojito	dollars,
del culito	and in the little eye
tengo un rollito	of my little hole
con veinte duritos	I have a little roll
	of twenty little dollars]—

Cristóbal agrees to cure him and gives him a blow with his club (p. 1027).

The marriage negotiations between Cristóbal and Rosita's mother are spiced with erotic verses and obscene insults. In order to entice the bully to pay her what she wants in exchange for Rosita, the greedy matron sings the following verse, which could easily come from the mouth of Juan Ruiz de Alarcón's *alcahueta*:

Yo soy la madre de doña Rosita	[I am Doña Rosita's mother
y quiero que se case,	and I want her to marry,
porque ya tiene dos pechitos	because she has little breasts
como dos naranjitas,	like two little oranges,
y un culito	and a little rear
como un quesito	like a little cheese
. . . . . .	. . . . . .
Y es lo que yo digo:	And here's what I say:
le hace falta un marido,	she needs a husband,
y si fuera posible, dos.	and if it were possible, two.
Ja, ja, ja, ja, ja.	Ha, ha, ha, ha, ha.] (P. 1029)

When Cristóbal balks at having to pay what the lewd old lady asks, the two exchange lusty insults.

Before the wedding negotiations, Rosita's voice is heard offstage singing a ribald song:

pero yo quisiera estar:	[but I want to be:
en el diván	on the divan
con Juan,	with Juan,
en el colchón	on the bed
con Ramón,	with Ramón,
en el canapé	on the sofa
con José,	with José,
. . . . . .	. . . . . .
en el suelo	on the floor
con el que yo quiero.	with the one I want.] (P. 1032)

The nubile Rosita also sings another verse revealing her limitless capacity for love:

¿Qué quieres?	[What do you want?
Me quiero casar	I want to marry
con un becerro nonato,	a young bull,
con un caimán,	a crocodile,
con un borriquito,	a young donkey,
con un general,	a general,
que para el caso	any of them will do
lo mismo me da.	I don't care which.] (P. 1035)

This verse recalls the student's question, "¿Y si yo quiero enamorarme de un cocodrilo?" [And if I wanted to love a crocodile?] (p. 1167) in *El público*, implying that love should be acceptable in all its forms.

After the wedding, however, Rosita becomes frightened of the ferocious Cristóbal, who smacks his lips:

> *Rosita*: ¡Ay!, Cristóbal. Tengo miedo.
> ¿Qué me vas a hacer?
>
> *Cristóbal*: Te haré muuuuuuuuuu.

> *Rosita*: ¡Ay!, no me asustarás.
> ¿A las doce de la noche que me harás?
>
> *Cristóbal*: Te haré aaaaaaaaaa.
>
> *Rosita*: ¡Ay!, no me asustarás.
> ¿A las tres de la mañana qué me harás?
>
> *Cristóbal*: Te haré piiiii.
>
> *Rosita*: Y entonces verás
> cómo mi urraquita se pone a volar.
>
> [*Rosita*: Oh! Cristóbal. I'm scared.
> What are you going to do to me?
>
> *Cristóbal*: I'm going to muuuuuuuuuu.
>
> *Rosita*: Oh! Don't frighten me.
> At midnight what will you do to me?
>
> *Cristóbal*: I'm going to aaaaaaaaaa.
>
> *Rosita*: Oh! Don't frighten me.
> At three in the morning what will you do to me?
>
> *Cristóbal*: I'm going to piiiii.
>
> *Rosita*: And then you'll see
> how my little crow can fly.] (Pp. 1037–1038)

The innocent charm that Lorca mentions in the prologue to *Retablillo* as one of the values of puppet theater is enlivened by bawdy jokes, such as those found in primitive farce and medieval satires. Erotic humor also heightens dramatic tension in Lorca's serious plays. The maid teases the bridegroom in the second act of *Bodas de sangre* with suggestive allusions to his wedding night, reminding him that she has left food out for him if he feels the need of sustenance at midnight. The aggressive and erotic remarks of the wise old crones in *Yerma* are, like Cristóbal's threats to Rosita, intended to shock, and indeed they have the desired effect upon the frantic heroine. La Poncia makes Bernarda's daughters laugh as she recalls in Act II the humorous moments of her courtship.

Lorca's puppet farces influenced not only his portrayal of dramatic characters, his handling of violent action, and his use of comic relief in the serious dramas; they also provided one of his most frequently used techniques of *mise en scène*. As the word *retablillo* indicates, the puppet farces were staged within a frame, or small enclosed arena. The action was created and contained within the miniature scale imposed by the frame. On the full-sized stage Lorca also made use of frames as a means of enhancing the pictorial values of his serious plays. *Mariana Pineda* is presented in three *estampas*, or prints, and *Don Perlimplín* is conceived as an "aleluya erótica en cuatro cuadros"—a decorated valentine in four sections. In his mature dramas, such as *Doña Rosita la soltera*, Lorca conceived of the frame as a technique that intensifies the static quality of dramatic action. *Doña Rosita* is described as a poem "dividido en varios jardines" [divided into several gardens], a subtitle that underlines the central impact of the play: the terrible stillness of a life in which nothing at all happens. Though Lorca's greatest play, *Bernarda Alba*, is described only as a "documental fotográfico," it too is conceived as a study of a stagnant, lifeless community. The stark white walls of Bernarda's house serve as a frame that contains and contrasts with the dark figures of the tyrant and her daughters dressed in black. Thus, Lorca enlarged the frame of puppet farce and dramatized within it the more restrained, stylized stiffness of his most serious plays.

Lorca turned to puppet theater as a source of technical innovation as did other modern dramatists, such as Jarry and Valle-Inclán. They all hoped to escape from the respectable bourgeois drama of the day and return to a freer, more primitive style of theater. Like Jacinto Grau, Lorca sought solutions to problems of characterization by manipulating puppet types already endowed with definite, indeed historical, comic traits. As he did in surrealism and in American film comedy, Lorca found in puppet theater a means of dramatizing his own chaotic, anarchic, and violent vision of the world.

William I. Oliver suggests that, as a proving ground for an apprentice playwright, the puppet theater did not serve Lorca well—that manipulation of wooden dolls did not adequately prepare him to create "the full-blown drama of living actors."[15] Yet it is that very woodenness of character that seems to draw Lorca to puppet theater and that also identifies his full-scale dramatic personages. One of the most delightful comic moments in *Tragicomedia* is Cristóbal's death. As his springs whirl and the bully falls dead, the puppets are amazed and a bit frightened to find that, instead of blood, sawdust is coming out of Cristóbal's navel. "¿Sabes una cosa?" [Know something?] demands the intrepid Cocoliche, who has just discovered his rival's secret: "¡Cristobita no era una persona!" [Cristobita wasn't a person!] (p. 779). This diagnosis is confirmed by Rosita's father, who pronounces the cause of Cristóbal's death: "Ha estallado" (He exploded].

The wooden, mechanical creature who dies of the pressure of fury upon his inner springs is closely akin to the distraught heroines of Lorca's serious plays, whose frustrations lead them to violent death. On a tiny scale Rosita and Cristóbal suffer desire, fear, defiance, sacrifice, and martyrdom —the same turbulent passions that rend Lorca's tragic heroines. Lorca first dramatized these passions and the characters who suffer them in comic form; the techniques with which they are portrayed in the farces— physical and verbal abuse, obscene humor, and supreme ferocity—are the same devices he later used to represent the characters and conflicts of his tragedies. Similarities of characterization and dialogue indicate that Lorca's handling of tragic action grew out of his experiments with puppet farce. His experience with presenting suffering and death in a comic manner helped to shape his conception of tragic conflict. In this way he came to represent agony as a mixture of tragedy and farce.

5. Master Plays

It would be strange indeed if one of the most basic characteristics of Lorca's art—his comic spirit—were not present in his mature and most important dramatic works, *Bodas de sangre, Yerma, Doña Rosita la soltera,* and *La casa de Bernarda Alba.* Yet so much has been written about Lorca's tragic vision that humor in these plays has been largely overlooked. Berenguer Carisomo[1] and Pedro Laín Entralgo[2] describe Lorca's folk dramas in terms of classical tragedy. Because they deal with a rural society, *Bodas, Yerma,* and *Bernarda Alba* do retain an aura of myth. The dramatic symbolism of these plays is drawn from nature and is woven into the story so that the forces of nature, or fate, seem close to, if not responsible for, the action. Other critics, including Alfredo de la Guardia[3] and Monalisa Lina Pérez Marchand,[4] take the opposite view and maintain that Lorca's folk plays are not tragic in any traditional sense. Appearing to agree with this view, William I. Oliver identifies the mythical content of these dramas as part of the spectacle Lorca created rather than the source of inevitable tragedy, taking the dramatist to task for his "short shrifting of the tragic statement."[5] Going further, Juan Guerrero Zamora suggests that Lorca did not understand the tragic mode and faults his handling of tragedy as "unsubstantial."[6]

What emerges most clearly from the various critical analyses of Lorca's mature plays is that the term *tragedy* does not accurately define these ambiguous and unsettling dramas. While they are not tragedies in the classical sense, they are too unique and powerful to be understood as tragedies that have failed. Lorca's folk dramas are, like Lope's *comedias*, a mixed genre in which comedy and tragedy are freely interwoven. Unlike Lope's comic scenes, however, the humorous moments in Lorca's plays are not included solely for comic relief, nor are his comic characters merely reflections of the graciosos, or comic foils, of traditional Spanish theater. Comic and grotesque humor in Lorca's serious dramas is not primarily amusing but rather reveals the dramatist's pessimistic view of reality. Lorca's mature plays derive from his experience with tragicomedy and farce, and the aggressive, often macabre humor of these early pieces remains prominent in the later dramas. In these plays humorous lines and scenes form a kind of comic counterpoint that both emphasizes and undermines the tragic agony portrayed in them.

Bodas de sangre

Bodas de sangre is the first of Lorca's serious plays that, although drawn along the lines of tragedy, does not correspond to the experience of traditional tragedy. Sexual passion rather than fate is the source of conflict in the play. Like her comic prototype in *Así que pasen*, the bride of *Bodas* is engaged to a rich young man who does not command her passions. She still loves her former fiancé, Leonardo Félix, but refused to marry him because he was poor. At her insistence Leonardo married another and now chides La novia for rejecting him: "¿Quién he sido yo para ti? Abre y refresca tu recuerdo. Pero dos bueyes y una mala choza son casi nada. Esa es la espina" [Who was I to you? Think back, refresh your memory. But a pair of oxen and a lousy hut are almost nothing. That's the rub] (p. 1213). On the eve of her wedding, the bride can no longer resist her passions. Like the petulant girl in *Así que pasen* who refuses to don her finery for her fiancé and instructs her maid to toss the flowers he brings over the balcony, the bride of *Bodas* flings away her bridal wreath in anger. Shortly after repeating her wedding vows, she escapes with Leonardo.

Personal indecision as to choice of mate is not in itself a tragic circumstance. The aura of doom is created by the ominous theme of a vicious feud between the families of the bridegroom and Leonardo Félix. The feud is prominent in the presentation of the drama, which begins and ends with lamentations by the bridegroom's mother. Her husband and older son were killed in the feud, and she voices her fears, which are later justified, that her remaining son will also be killed. But these lamentations and their accompanying symbols of foreboding and death only provide the form and not the substance of tragedy. The talk of the "mal aire" [bad blood] (p. 1227) of the Félix family is not central to the bride's dilemma of whether to marry a rich young man who bores her. There is nothing inherently tragic in the bride's conflict nor in her decision, made in full awareness of its immorality, to abandon her bridegroom and flee with Leonardo. The bride knowingly brings her dismal fate upon herself, yet disaster also befalls the innocent characters of the drama. It is the suffering of the others that gives rise to an important question: who is the central character of the play?

In considering the characters of *Bodas*, it is difficult to decide who is the protagonist. Even the leading actresses were unsure: when the play opened in Madrid, Josefina Díaz chose the part of the bride; a year later, in Buenos Aires, Lola Membrives preferred the role of La madre.[7] The older woman is not one of those most directly involved in the action; hers is the passive, consenting role. Though she tries to conquer her fears for the sake of her son's happiness, she never entirely loses her suspicions and thus does not undergo any change of character. It is she, however, who most nearly emerges as a heroic figure, for she accepts her loss, crying, "Benditos sean los trigos, porque mis hijos están debajo de ellos. . . . Bendito sea Dios, que nos tiende juntos para descansar" [Blessed are the shafts of wheat, for my sons lie beneath them, . . . Blessed is God, who lays us down to rest] (p. 1270). But the play does not end on this note of reconciliation. The dreaded symbols of death reappear in the final scene as the Madre sings of "cuchillo... un cuchillito / que apenas cabe en la mano" [a knife, a little knife / that barely fits in the hand] with which her men were slain. Perhaps because of this final scene, in which the motif of death is repeated, Roberto G. Sánchez has concluded, I think correctly, that Death is the principal character of the play.[8]

The portrayal of Death as a protagonist is neither unusual nor new. Death was the undisputed master in the medieval Spanish *Danza de la muerte*. In modern plays, such as Alejandro Casona's *La dama del alba*, the personification of death also dominates the play. The presence of

death is felt consistently throughout *Bodas*. In the opening scene of the
play La madre curses all symbols of death, such as knives and other instru-
ments that can be used as dangerous weapons. Later in Act I, Leonardo's
wife and mother-in-law sing an infant to sleep with a morbid cradle song.

> *Suegra*: Duérmete, rosal,
> que el caballo se pone a llorar.
> Las patas heridas,
> las crines heladas,
> dentro de los ojos
> un puñal de plata.
>
> .   .   .   .
>
> La sangre corría
> más fuerte que el agua.
> *Mujer*: Duérmete, clavel,
> que el caballo no quiere beber.

> [*Mother-in-law*: Sleep, my dear,
> the horse is starting to cry.
> His wounded hooves,
> his icy mane,
> in his eyes shines
> a silver knife.
>
> .   .   .   .
>
> Blood ran
> stronger than water.
> *Wife*: Sleep, my dear,
> the horse doesn't want to drink.] (Pp. 1184–1185)

This foreboding lullaby is an adaptation of one of the *nanas infantiles*
that Lorca included in his essay on cradle songs. They are discomforting,
ambiguous verses intended to lull the child to sleep with a vocabulary
of disaster and doom.

The ambiguity with which death is presented persists throughout *Bodas*.
The images used to symbolize death are ambivalent. Death is equated
with love by the symbol of the knife, which represents both virility and
destruction. Like the knife, blood is also an ambivalent symbol: when

spilled, it signifies fatality, but it is also associated with sexual passion. The horse, a source of strength, carries Leonardo to his lover, as well as to his death:

Las patas heridas	[Wounded hooves
las crines heladas	icy manes
dentro de los ojos	reflected in its eyes
un puñal de plata.	a silver knife.] (P. 1193)

Love and death are thus part of a life-death process in which opposite extremes merge in a single experience.[9]

The contradictory presentation of death, perhaps the most chilling motif of *Bodas*, culminates in Act III when death is personified as an old beggar woman. Mendiga's presence onstage is somewhat surprising since the playwright notes that "este personaje no figura en el reparto" [this character isn't listed in the cast] (p. 1250). She appears in human form, yet her human shape is totally concealed in dark green rags. The very feature that would reveal her humanity, her face, is also hidden: "Apenas si se le verá el rostro entre los pliegues" [Her face can barely be seen hidden in the folds of her rags]. Mendiga has a distinctly nonhuman look about her and calls forth the feeling of surprise, horror, and fear that Wolfgang Kayser designates as characteristic of the grotesque.[10] Alfredo de la Guardia attempts to idealize Mendiga when, recognizing her as a "bruja" [witch], he adds, "No habla como una vieja repulsiva" [She doesn't speak as a repulsive old woman].[11] Yet there is no doubt that Lorca's Mendiga is malevolent and reflects the poet's well-known horror of death. The dramatist describes her voice as a beggar's whine, a sound neither soothing nor attractive. Death in *Bodas* strongly resembles Doña Muerte of Lorca's early *Libro de poemas*:

Doña Muerte, arrugada,	[Lady Death, wrinkled,
pasea por sauzales	wanders through the willow grove
. . . .	. . . .
como un hada de cuento	like the witch of fairy tales
mala y enredadora	evil and meddling.] (P. 265)

Unlike Casona's gentle, somewhat alluring wanderer who, as the personification of death, tries to give solace in *La dama del alba*, Lorca's vision of death is, according to Jean-Louis Schonberg, a witch,[12] a cunning old hag who tricks her victims.

Mendiga is accompanied by another allegorical character, Moon, who is personified as a young woodsman. Like Moonshine in Shakespeare's *A Midsummer Night's Dream*, who stands on an improvised stage holding a lantern in Bottom's lamentable comedy, Lorca's moon-man also serves to light a darkened stage. The moon-man of *Bodas*, however, is a ghoulish creature singing verses expressing bloodthirsty anticipation of death: "Pues esta noche tendrán / mis mejillas roja sangre" [Tonight my cheeks will taste red blood]. Clearly Moon is enraptured by the vision of his victim's warm body:

¡Que quiero entrar en un pecho	[I want to cuddle close
para poder calentarme!	to warm myself!
¡Un corazón para mí!	A heart for my own!
¡Caliente!	Warm!] (P. 1250)

The prospect of death apparently delights the young moon-figure. He is eager to provide light for the grisly deed so that he can reap his grim reward:

No quiero sombras. Mis rayos	[I don't want shadows. My beams
han de entrar en todas partes,	must shine in everywhere,
. . . .	. . . .
para que esta noche tengan	so that tonight
mis mejillas dulce sangre.	my cheeks may taste sweet blood.]

The dramatist does not indicate the tone of Moon's voice, but one who lusts for the blood of another is usually considered monstrous, and his anticipation of "dulce sangre" would fittingly be sung with the ghoulish glee of a monster savoring thoughts of his victim. Marcelle Auclair characterizes this figure most accurately when she refers to him as a "lune-vampire" [moon-vampire].[13]

The enthusiastic young woodsman, singing his paean to death, and the faceless Mendiga in green rags are a ghoulish pair making preparations for the kill. In contrast to her eager accomplice, the old Mendiga seems somewhat weary and is impatient with her zealous cohort: "¡Esa luna, esa luna!" [That moon, that moon!] (p. 1251), she sighs. She instructs him

with the matter-of-fact skill of a seasoned performer who has played the
same scene innumerable times before: "Aquí ha de ser, y pronto. Estoy
cansada" [It must be here and soon. I'm tired]. When Moon asks her if
she needs anything, she replies dryly, "Nada." Beginning to sing again
of his "ansia de esta fuente de chorro estremecido" [anxiety of this shivering spurting fountain], Moon is given final orders by Mendiga, who tells
him to keep quiet. As the victim approaches, Mendiga hurriedly assumes
her pose.

Whining like a beggar, the old hag appears before the bridegroom
complaining, "Tengo frío" [I'm cold]. When he begins to question her as
to the whereabouts of his rival, she ignores him, staring absent-mindedly
at his handsome figure. "Hermoso galán" [Beautiful young man], she says.
Her appreciation of the young groom's beauty is, of course, facetious, for
she would prefer to see him dead: "Pero mucho más hermoso si estuviera
dormido" [But much more beautiful if he were asleep] (p. 1254). The
bridegroom repeats his question and is again put off by Mendiga. "Espera"
[Wait], she replies, and continues, "Qué espaldas más anchas. ¿Cómo no
te gusta estar tendido sobre ellas y no andar sobre las plantas de los pies
que son tan chicas?" [What wide shoulders. Wouldn't you like to be
stretched out on them rather than walking on your feet which are so
small?]. Mendiga's solicitude is so exaggerated that it cannot conceal her
evil purpose. Like Alacranito, who, in El maleficio, relishes the insects as
tasty morsels, Death in Bodas pauses a moment to drool admiringly over
her prey. When the bridegroom shakes her, Mendiga wakes from her
daydream and offers him assistance. Recalling Harlequin in Así que
pasen, who directs El joven to his doom with patronizing irony, saying,
"Por allí" [This way] (p. 1130), the old crone repeats the same "Por allí"
(p. 1225) as she accompanies the bridegroom on his last journey. Thus,
as the bridegroom tracks down his rival, he himself falls prey to Mendiga,
who whines and flatters her victim.

The figure of death and her sidekick Moon are grotesques whose fiend-
ish machinations and zest for blood momentarily interrupt the tragedy
with a ghastly, diabolical scene. They do not arouse laughter; yet, as
Kayser notes, the "grotesque is a play with the absurd" and is accompanied by "a faint smile [that] seems to pass rapidly across the scene."[14]
The satanic Mendiga thus borders on the comic grotesque because, by

excessively admiring the bridegroom, she appears to mock him and the gravity of his struggle. At this point, tragedy becomes indistinguishable from comic distortion, and "terror is closely joined with what is ludicrous."[15] This is the comedy of cruelty, in which man is jeered because his plight is not taken seriously by his tormentors. The tragedy begins to dissolve as human dignity is reduced to a hideous farce.

Awareness of life's absurdity seems to have overwhelmed death's remaining victim, Leonardo, who knows that he is trapped and cannot escape. Recognizing the cause of the tragedy, Leonardo blames the bride for flaunting her sexual charms:

que la culpa es de la tierra	[the fault belongs to the land
y de ese olor que te sale	and to that smell that you have
de los pechos y las trenzas.	on your breasts and hair.] (p. 1258)

The bride now begins to take stock of the debacle, knowing that she will be hated for the rest of her life. She imagines what it will be like to be jeered, as if she were a circus freak exhibiting herself in a shameful manner. With bitter sarcasm she advises Leonardo:

Llévame de feria en feria,	[Take me from fair to fair,
dolor de mujer honrada,	the pain of an honest woman,
a que las gentes me vean	so that people can stare at me
con las sábanas de boda	with my wedding sheets
al aire como banderas.	flying like flags in the air.] (p. 1259)

The scene ends as the figure of Death reappears, accompanied by Moon. She turns her back and, with a dramatic sweep, spreads her cape, looking like a great grotesque bird "de alas inmensas" [with immense wings] (p. 1261).

The death scene occupies the better part of the first scene in the final act of *Bodas*. Mendiga and Moon are on stage a comparatively short time, yet their appearance is of strategic importance. As the ultimate fate of the young men in the play, Death is central to the meaning of the work. That Death should take the form of a wheedling old beggar seems to make the struggle of the bridegroom and his rival somewhat mechanical and their destiny no more meaningful than a sick joke. The old harpy knows the fate of her victims; thus, death is as inevitable as it is in tragedy. Yet the fate of the two rivals is not noble but results from what Schonberg describes as "une grâce monstrueuse de prédestination" [the monstrous favor of predestination].[16] From the vantage point of Mendiga, and thus for the public as well, the passionate rivals in search of vengeance slay each other not as heroes but as helpless victims of some grim and fatal trick. Death leers, however, only for a moment. Having claimed her prey, Mendiga disappears, leaving the bride and the groom's mother mourning the day when "entre las dos y las tres, / se mataron dos hombres del amor" [between two and three o'clock, / two men killed each other because of a woman] (p. 1272).

However brief, the death scene of *Bodas* cannot be dismissed as incidental, for death is the ultimate ruin of the young men of the play. And their deaths leave the central characters—La novia and La madre—bereft. Generally, however, critics have either ignored Mendiga and the moon-man or have misinterpreted their significance. Guerrero Zamora, for example, views them as proof of Lorca's inability to write tragedy.[17] Yet the portrayal of death as ludicrous is merely another instance of the "ambivalence of tragic motifs"[18] in *Bodas* and is entirely in the spirit of the play. Just as the images of knives, blood, and horses are ambivalent and suggest both life and death, so death itself is presented as being both pathetic and absurd. Nor does the grotesque figure of death diminish the characters' suffering in any way. The mechanical quality of the rivals' struggle and the sardonic treatment of their doom only heighten the sense of futility of those who seek to escape despair. The juxtaposition of grotesquerie and pathos produces a disturbing moment when death appears in the closing act of *Bodas*. In his succeeding dramas, Lorca continued to exploit the unsettling effects of the unnatural and absurd.

Yerma

Of Lorca's four master plays, *Yerma* most nearly approaches the traditional classical tragedy, yet the forces that set in motion the action of this drama are the most equivocal of any in Lorca's dramaturgy. The heroine, obsessed with the desire to have children, is married to a man who does not want any. The question of who bears the guilt for this childless marriage is prominent in the play, and much of the dialogue is devoted to the discussion of it. By leaving the question unresolved, however, the playwright implies that his purpose is not to identify the guilty partner but rather to reveal Spanish attitudes toward love, sex, and marriage. The old woman who offers Yerma her own son as a mate in Act II assures the distraught heroine that "la culpa es de tu marido" [the fault is your husband's], but this is never confirmed conclusively, for Juan merely states that "sin hijos la vida es más dulce. Yo soy feliz no teniéndolos. No tenemos culpa ninguna" [without children life is sweeter. I'm happy without them. It's nobody's fault] (p. 1348). Although there are suggestions throughout that Juan is impotent, there are just as many reasons to believe that Yerma, whose name means "the barren one," is also at fault. Her character, cast in the mold of a fanatic, appears to have emerged from a petrified morality. Taunted on one hand by a distrustful husband, confronted on the other by offers to gratify her desire to have a child, and thrust at last into an atmosphere heavy with eroticism, Yerma is driven to desperation and kills her husband. Thus, in *Yerma*, as in *Don Perlimplín*, the traditional solution to the problem of dishonor is subverted. It is not the innocent wife who is murdered by her suspicious husband, but the heroine, tormented by Juan's unjustified suspicions, who is, ironically, "capaz de asesinar a su marido pero no de engañarle" [capable of killing her husband but not of deceiving him].[19]

The code of honor is the social framework for the heroine's dilemma in *Yerma*, much as in Calderón's brutal honor tragedies of the golden age. Yet, just as we are not entitled to assume that Calderón approved of the honor code he dramatized,[20] neither can we conclude that Lorca endorses the narrow and unremitting morality portrayed in *Yerma*. Calderón described an honor code so distorted that murder of an innocent victim became justified upon suspicion of infidelity. Lorca, too, presents the distortions to which a severe moral code can lead. Obsessed with the desire for children, Yerma conceives of marriage solely as a means of reproduction. That this view of marriage is determined by her conception of honor is suggested throughout the play by the juxtaposition of sensual delight, frequently associated with pagan immorality, with the austere interpretation of honor that represses human needs. Contrasting immoral and sensual behavior with Yerma's stern fidelity, Lorca emphasizes the devastating effects of his heroine's honor with comic irony.

Comic characters appear throughout the play and ridicule Yerma's attitude toward herself and toward marriage. The first of these comic figures, a young woman called "Muchacha segunda," appears in Act I and suggests that having no children to worry about should make Yerma happy. When Yerma asks the girl why she married if not to have children, the girl responds laughingly, "Porque me han casado. . . . ¿Qué necesidad tiene mi marido de ser mi marido? Porque lo mismo hacíamos de novios que ahora" [Because they married me off. . . . Why does my man need to be my husband? Because we did the same thing when we were sweethearts that we do now] (p. 1293). The girl does not feel restricted by social mores and scoffs at Yerma, who, she says, is like everyone else, "metida dentro de sus casas haciendo lo que no les gusta" [trapped in their houses, doing things they don't like] (p. 1294). Yerma thinks the girl is childish, to which she retorts, "Claro, pero no estoy loca" [Sure, but I'm not crazy].

It is this implication that repressive social conventions have helped to drive the distraught heroine to the brink of madness that brings into focus the sharp contrast between Yerma and the carefree, slightly insolent Muchacha segunda. The young girl's bemused composure accentuates Yerma's frenzy, forcing the spectator to consider Yerma's character in perspective. Yerma, while she desires children above all else, seems singularly unfit for the role of motherhood. In Act I she confesses that she derives no pleasure from intimacy with her husband and that, in fact, "me estoy llenando de odio" [I am filling up with hatred] (p. 1209). She cannot reconcile herself to life without children; yet in Act III she admits that she does not love her husband. Her lack of love or tenderness toward him appears to be a serious handicap, for she is unable to accept either Juan as he is or marriage on his terms—without children. Honorable alternatives—adoption or annulment of a childless union, long acceptable in the Catholic canon—are never considered in the play. Though Muchacha segunda is a secondary character, her positive reaction to the problem of childlessness makes Yerma's agony seem hysterical in contrast. Muchacha segunda is neither a social outcast, nor is she miserable. Ironically, she is content, and Lorca presents her pagan attitudes as being less destructive than Yerma's puritanism.

Lorca also appears to deride his heroine's religious faith. Yerma remains a good Christian until her frustration explodes into violence, but the old woman whom she consults for advice makes no pretense of religious devotion. The aged, because of their lifetime experience, are traditional sources of wisdom; Yerma, however, is shocked by the words of one of the elder women of the village. The heroine, throughout her childless marriage, has had faith that God will help her someday. But the wise old woman whom she consults advises her not to be so innocent: "Dios, no. A mí no me ha gustado nunca Dios. ¿Cuándo os vais a dar cuenta de que no existe? Son los hombres los que tienen que amparar. . . . Aunque debía haber Dios, aunque fuera pequeñito" [God, no. I've never liked God. When are you going to realize that he doesn't exist? It is men who have to help. . . . Although there ought to be God, even if he were little] (p. 1291). These mischievous remarks, echoing the poems of religious satire in *Libro de poemas*, not only ridicule Yerma's situation and thus increase her suffering, but also connote a calm wisdom markedly dissimilar to Yerma's naïveté.

The heroine's dignity is diminished further by the presence in Act II of Juan's two old-maid sisters, whom he has charged with watching Yerma to see that she does nothing dishonorable. The village washerwomen laugh at the two sisters, saying that "estaban cargadas de cuidar la iglesia y ahora cuidan de su cuñada" [they were charged with tending the church and now they tend their sister-in-law] (p. 1301). Yerma resents Juan's lack of trust in her and hates his sisters, calling them the "Figuraciones," or silent specters. She does her best to elude them, and Act II closes with her wardens searching for Yerma and calling her name.

Yerma's visit to a shrine in the second scene of Act III, the culminating scene of the play, is an occasion for satirical and Saturnalian humor. The shrine is well known as a place where "vienen las mujeres a conocer hombres nuevos. Y el santo hace el milagro" [women come to meet new men. And the saint works the miracle] (p. 1345). Beginning with a sensual song, the scene unfolds in a holiday mood, contrasting sharply with Yerma's increasing anxiety and her scrupulous fidelity. The highlight of the visit is an aphrodisian dance between two masked figures, described simply as Male and Female, who chant erotic lyrics. Since this provocative spectacle can hardly appeal to Yerma, her presence at it is somewhat inexplicable. When an old woman asks her why she came, Yerma confesses sadly that she does not know. Thus, Lorca places his heroine in circumstances that make her appear absurd, for he has already made clear that erotic pleasure is impossible for her.

Clearly, the theme of sensual delight developed throughout the play and culminating in the fertility dance is ironic and dramatizes the struggle between the two opposing moral attitudes, Christian and pagan, puritanical and carnal. Yerma, who thinks of sexual relations purely as a means of reproduction, and Juan, interested only in his good name and in making money, represent the unremitting honor-bound Christian morality. They are opposed by the carefree Muchacha segunda, who has enjoyed her husband since long before marriage, and the wise old women of the village who counsel Yerma to love her husband and accept her childless marriage, or to find another man. These women represent not only moral lenience but also the emotional fulfillment that Yerma lacks. The irony of the virtuous Yerma's viewing a sybaritic display that she must condemn is cruel indeed, but it is irony composed of comic as well as tragic elements.

Comedy originated with the festal processions and erotic songs that accompanied fertility rites,[21] and *Yerma* retains some of the bawdy comic spirit of these ancient rituals. The scene at the shrine is introduced by old crones laughing at suggestive jokes: "Venís a pedir hijos al santo y resulta que cada año vienen más hombres solos a esta romería. ¿Qué es lo que pasa? (*Rie*)" [You come to ask the saint to give you children and the result is that every year more men come alone to this shrine. What's happening? (*She laughs*)] (p. 1336). A young girl recalls the lewd revelry of a previous year when some young men pinched her sister. The fertility dance takes place amid a carnival atmosphere in which smiling onlookers clap their hands to the sensuous rhythms of the music.

Following the ritual, one of the old women assumes the role of a *celestina*, or matchmaker, and offers Yerma her own son, who waits behind the chapel. When Yerma refuses, the old woman retorts with sarcasm, "Cuando se tiene sed, se agradece el agua" [When you're thirsty, you welcome water] (p. 1345). She has ceased to take Yerma's problem seriously. Informing Yerma that she will take her offer elsewhere, she concludes, "No me das ninguna lástima, ninguna" [I don't pity you, not at all] (p. 1346). The wise old crone has rejected the so-called respectability of an artificial and life-consuming code of honor. Her sarcastic humor makes Yerma's agony more excruciating, not only by providing comic relief but also by suggesting that the idea of honor that she holds is absurd and meaningless.

By ridiculing Yerma's notion of honor, Lorca in no way suggests that the heroine debase herself, but that her austere view of fidelity has become distorted to the degree that love and marriage have lost their meaning. The puritanical belief that sexual pleasure is inappropriate, which accounts for Yerma's inability to enjoy her husband, together with her refusal to accept life without offspring, leaves her unable to resolve her dilemma. While Lorca's compassion for his heroine is unmistakable, her unbending code of honor is treated as a joke by the village women. Their satirical comments serve not only to torment the heroine and thus to increase her suffering; they also provide a comic counterpoint by which a pagan view of life directly challenges the fierce honor code to which Yerma adheres. Thus, in *Yerma*, Lorca's portrayal of an oppressive code of behavior is both satirical and tragic, an "ultimate criticism of Spanish stoical morality."[22]

Doña Rosita la soltera

If *Yerma* is a tragedy that depends upon comic irony and bawdy satire for its full effect, Lorca's next play, *Doña Rosita la soltera*, is a comedy that becomes bitter through unrelenting strokes of pathos. Focusing increasingly on the social milieu, Lorca conceived of the heroine of *Doña Rosita* as little more than a symbol, a reflection in which he felt Spanish women would recognize themselves "como en un espejo" [as in a mirror] (p. 1800). Although the play has been called a "burla cordial,"[23] a kind of fond but discreet burlesque,[24] the acid satire of the piece is unmistakable. With its gallery of caricatures, its passive rag-doll heroine, and its "atmosphere of botanical death"[25] where absolutely nothing happens, *Doña*

Rosita is an indictment of an era in which unmarried women of the middle class were trapped alive in a prison of bourgeois respectability.

In Lorca's portrait of "la cursilería española" [Spanish bad taste] (p. 1800), almost every important character in the play—with the exception of the heroine and her aunt—is a comic type. Most of these caricatures are presented in Act II as a series of visitors to Rosita's household. The first is the pedantic Señor X, who believes that the "earth is a mediocre planet" waiting to be delivered from its natural state by man's sublime scientific technology. In holy tones he invokes the names of motor cars and the dirigible and pronounces two men killed in a car race as martyrs of science who will be enshrined the day a "religion of the positive" arrives. The natural world seems hardly tolerable to Señor X, who feels himself to be "in the living Polis." He condescends to converse with Rosita's uncle but has actually come to see Rosita on her saint's day. He has brought her a gift that, as gifts often do, expresses the personality of the giver: a mother-of-pearl pendant of the Eiffel Tower that sits upon doves carrying in their beaks the wheels of industry. This gift was chosen from among others because it was in better taste, Señor X informs his host. The gift is reminiscent of the mother-of-pearl fan decorated with a picture of Pedro Romero opening his bullfight cape that Cocoliche brings to his Rosita, the puppet sweetheart in *El retablillo*; or the souvenir described in scene iv, the "barquitos de nácar . . . de Valencia, que llevan unas tijerillas y un dedal" [little mother-of-pearl boats . . . from Valencia, in which fit some little scissors and a thimble] (p. 751), which reminds Mosquito of the puppet Rosita. These florid little trinkets, used for comic effect in the puppet farce, symbolize in the mature play a Victorian society weighed down with moral as well as material trivia.

Señor X's departure is followed by the arrival of the three *solteronas*, or spinster sisters, and their mother. With fans, plumes, and dangling ribbons they are overdressed, even by the excessively ornamental standards of the early 1900's. Their gift for Rosita's saint's day is a barometer on which is mounted the figure of a girl in a rose-colored dress; the figure indicates humidity by lifting or lowering her skirts. Rosita's aunt comments with subtle sarcasm, "Es de mucho gusto" [It's very tasteful], to which the outspoken matron replies, "¡Gusto no me falta, lo que me falta es dinero!" [I don't need taste, what I need is money!] (p. 1393).

The *solteronas* are soon joined by another set of visitors, the Ayola girls, also decked out in "la moda exageradísima de la época" [the exaggerated style of the day] (p. 1396). The Ayolas, considering themselves somewhat superior, giggle uncontrollably at the garish spinsters. It is the Ayolas themselves, however, who voice the prevailing social attitude that women have only one alternative in life—marriage. When the conversation turns to the subject of Rosita's sweetheart, one of the Ayola girls urges Rosita to marry soon because "¡si soy amiga de Rosita es porque sé que tiene novio! ¡Las mujeres sin novio están pochas, recocidas y todas . . . están rabiadas!" [if I'm Rosita's friend it's because I know she has a boyfriend. Women without boyfriends are washed out, warmed over and all of them . . . frustrated!] (p. 1401).

The last of the comic types to visit Rosita's household is the forlorn don Martín, a lame and aging schoolmaster. Don Martín is designated in the stage directions as a "tipo noble, de gran dignidad" [noble sort, of great dignity], but his dignity is considerably diminished when he begins to recite from a play he has written entitled *La hija del Jefté*. From the tumid opening lines of the drama, "¡Oh Madre excelsa!" it is clear that don Martín teaches because he lacks poetic talent. When he recalls the pranks played by his mischievous pupils—such as one played on another teacher, who "había encontrado un excremento de gato sobre su lista de clase" [found cat excrement on his class roster] (p. 1419)—don Martín's own dignity reaches a new low. His visit is cut short by a request that he return to school because the pupils have punctured the water pipe and the school is being flooded. He gets up to leave, reflecting sadly that "soñé con el Parnaso y tengo que hacer de albañil y fontanero. Con tal que no me empujen o resbale" [I dreamed of Parnassus and I have to be a bricklayer and a plumber. Provided they don't push me or I fall] (p. 1424).

The Granadine society at the turn of the century, symbolized by the series of ridiculous visitors who come to call on Rosita, is portrayed by Lorca as empty, self-seeking, and ludicrous. Nor is Lorca's satirical panorama confined to outsiders—it extends into Rosita's own household. Rosita's uncle and El Ama, the housekeeper, are also comic types, though they are more sympathetic characters than the visitors. The humor that they provide serves to accentuate Rosita's misery.

The uncle is a doddering old man, an amateur botanist, who is portrayed in the opening scene, perhaps with double meaning, as having lost his seeds. He also complains that his dahlia tubers have been trampled and a flowerpot has been overturned. He is a timid sort who accepts Señor X's silly gift with effusive gratitude: "mil gracias... un millón de gracias... gracias, gracias, gracias" (p. 1378). In the final act Rosita's uncle has been dead six years; yet the aunt still complains of his excessive generosity and his inability to refuse when asked for money—traits that have left the household bankrupt. At the end of Act II Rosita's fiancé writes proposing that they be married by proxy. The bumbling uncle, overhearing Rosita speak of her marriage, cuts the fragile *rosa-mutabile* [mutable rose] growing in his greenhouse and presents it to her joyfully, a gesture that heightens the pathos of the proposed marriage by proxy.

The faithful maid, adapted from the traditionally comic graciosos of golden age drama, is also comic; yet she is portrayed as the only character who remains undaunted by the passage of time. Although she has a strong talent for seeing through the gloss of snobbery and affectation, the maid is not entirely immune to the exaggerated sentiment of the day. Her gift for Rosita's saint's day is the most preposterous of all: it is a thermometer,

> estilo Luis Quince. . . . En medio del terciopelo hay una fuente hecha
> con caracoles de verdad; sobre la fuente, una glorieta de alambre con
> rosas verdes; el agua de la taza es un grupo de lentejuelas azules, y
> el surtidor es el propio termómetro. Los charcos que hay alrededor
> están pintados al aceite y encima de ellos bebe un ruiseñor todo
> bordado con hilo de oro. Yo quise que tuviera cuerda y cantara,
> pero no pudo ser.

> [of Louis XV style. . . . In the middle of the velvet is a fountain,
> made with real shells; over the fountain is a wire arbor with green
> roses; the water is a layer of blue sequins and the waterspout is the
> thermometer. The pools that surround it are painted in oils and
> above them is a nightingale, embroidered with gold thread, drinking.
> I wanted to be able to pull a string and have it sing, but they couldn't
> make it do that.] (Pp. 1382–1383)

Ironically, the maid achieves this act of ultimate garishness only when she tries to imitate the sort of refinement cherished by her superiors. For the most part, she recognizes their pretentious mannerisms and mocks them. She announces the arrival of the Ayola girls by saying, "Ahí están las de Ayola, el fotógrafo" [Here are the Ayolas, the photographer's daughters] (p. 1395). Rosita's aunt haughtily corrects this plain-spoken presentation of the visitors: "Las señoritas de Ayola, querrás decir" [The Misses Ayola, you mean]. The maid is not fooled by this display of verbal ornamentation and makes fun of it by improvising an even more elaborate introduction: "Ahí están las señoronas por todo lo alto de Ayola, fotógrafo de Su Majestad y medalla de oro en la exposición de Madrid" [Here are the lordly ladies of Ayola, daughters of the man who is photographer to the King and the gold medal winner in the Madrid exposition]. "Hay que aguantarla" [You have to put up with her], sighs the aunt, knowing she has been upstaged by her inferior.

The servant is comic, not only because she deflates the vanity of others but also because she, too, respects the florid conventions of the day. Her gift for Rosita is more ostentatious than the rest, and she admires the inflated rhetoric of the disappointed poet don Martín. Her good-natured parody of his lectures mocks his turgid oratory. She confesses that she has eavesdropped on his classes and has heard him proclaim, " '¿Qué es idea? La representación intelectual de una cosa o un objeto.' . . . Ayer decía a voces: 'No; ahí hay hipérbaton,' y luego... 'el epinicio'... como no entiendo me dan ganas de reír. . . . Pero aunque me ría, como ignorante, comprendo que don Martín tiene mucho mérito" ["What are ideas? The intellectual representation of a thing or object." . . . Yesterday he was shouting: "No. Here is hyperbaton," and then, "the epinicion"—since I don't understand it made me laugh. . . . But even though I was laughing like a fool, I understand that don Martín is a very worthy man] (p. 1423). Through the maid's respectful admiration of the learned vocabulary glimmers Lorca's implication that the overdressed styles and effusive manners of the day had their intellectual equivalent in the bombastic and declamatory statements of academics.

As a sensible character capable of looking society in the face without the aid of its vapid rituals of politeness, the comic maid furnishes most of the amusement in *Doña Rosita*. Her primary function is the realistic one of commenting with candor upon events as she sees them, which she does with comic frankness. Her love for Rosita justifies her honesty, which is at times brutal, such as her warning that if Rosita does not marry "tendrá el pelo de plata y todavía estará cosiendo cintas de raso liberti en los volantes de su camisa de novia" [she will have silver hair and she'll still be sewing silk ribbons on her wedding skirt] (p. 1380). The maid's harsh, ironic wit creates one of the most poignant moments in the play. When she learns of the proposed marriage by proxy, she protests vigorously to Rosita's aunt: "¡Que venga en persona y se case! '¡Poderes!' . . . La cama y sus pinturas temblando de frío, y la camisa de novia en lo más oscuro del baúl. Señora, no deje usted que los 'poderes' entren en esta casa. . . . ¡Señora, que yo no quiero 'poderes!' " [Let him come in person and marry. "Powers!" . . . The bed and its pictures are shivering with cold, her wedding gown in the deepest corner of the trunk. Señora, don't you let the "powers" enter this house! . . . Señora, I don't want any "powers"!] (p. 1410). The allusion to the physical closeness of marriage, which the lonely Rosita will be denied in a marriage by proxy, intensifies the emotional disaster of such a proposal. The pathos of Rosita's enthusiasm is underlined by the maid's crude irony as she inquires pointedly, "Y por la noche, ¿qué?" [And at night, what?] (p. 1410).

In the third act, when it is clear that Rosita has been abandoned, the zealous maid expresses her anger at Rosita's fiancé by means of violent humor that resembles the comic threats of vengeance of the puppet farces. When she thinks of him she vows she would like to "coger una espada y cortarle la cabeza y machacársela con dos piedras y cortarle la mano del falso juramento" [pick up a sword and chop his head off and pound it with two stones and cut off the phony's hand] (p. 1414). Pondering ways to avenge the family's honor, the maid suggests to her mistress, "Señora, ¿y no le podríamos mandar una carta envenenada, que se muriera de repente al recibirla?" [Ma'am, couldn't we send him a poisoned letter so that he'd die the moment he received it?] (p. 1415).

There are scenes of comic relief in *Doña Rosita* that momentarily distract the spectators from the deepening pathos. Such a scene takes place in Act II between the maid and Rosita's aunt. Each professing to love Rosita more than the other, the two women begin to quarrel and quickly become angry. The aunt, feeling insulted by her maid, dismisses her, and the servant marches out triumphantly. But on her way out she drops the gift she had bought Rosita. When the aunt discovers and inspects the gift, she is ashamed to have discharged the loyal and affectionate house-keeper and admits that the maid's love for Rosita exceeds even her own. The quarrel then begins again, this time with the antagonists arguing the reverse of what they had just insisted upon. They soon tire of this mock combat, however, and leave the room, each by a different door but with their loyalty and affection for each other still intact.

Though the members of the household are more sympathetic figures than those from the world outside, they, too, with the exception of the aunt, form a comical ménage. The heroine herself is indirectly portrayed from a comic perspective, for, although seen by the spectator as pathetic, she is laughed at by others. When her aunt begs Rosita to emerge from her lonely life and search for someone who will make her happy, Rosita declares in a long monologue that she has not left her home all these years for fear of being ridiculed. Just as the spinsters are laughed at in Act II by the Ayola girls, Rosita is now mocked by others. Everyone knew that her fiancé had abandoned her, she explains: "Lo sabían todos y yo me encontraba señalada por un dedo que hacía ridícula mi modestia de pro-metida y daba un aire grotesco a mi abanico de soltera" [Everyone knew it and I found myself pointed at by people who mocked my shyness and made my spinster's fan seem grotesque] (p. 1428). That Rosita has be-come an object of derision not only accentuates her misery; it also stresses the darkly comic irony of a society—itself ludicrous in its material ostenta-tion and false gentility—declaring the timid Rosita grotesque because she is not married.

Yet Rosita is the product as well as the victim of the fatuous manners of her era. In Act III the son of one of Rosita's friends comes to bid Rosita farewell. He remembers donning one of his mother's dresses for carnival. It was an outlandish frock, a conglomeration of black laces and Nile-green flounces, at the waist a great velvet bow with streamers cascading down either side of a bustle. Costumes in *Doña Rosita* change in each act to those of a later period. Thus, costume not only measures the passage of time but also symbolizes the character of society, so that when the lad comments, "¡Qué disparate de moda!" [What a ridiculous style!], he is ridiculing the grotesque sensibility represented by the profusion of ornamentation on the dress. But this style was part of Rosita's own past, and she defends it, insisting somewhat sadly that "era una moda bonita" [it was a pretty style] (p. 1433). Rosita remembers her past with nostalgia; at the same time she is unable to avoid painful memories of unkept promises.

The heroine's life is now intolerable; if her past was melancholy, her future is equally bleak. Like the dress that is so ornate it is now used only as a fantastic carnival garb, Rosita is looked upon as an old maid, a term that generally evokes a somewhat daft, laughable creature. Rosita sympathizes with that group of women with whom she is associated in the minds of others: "Comprendo muy bien a esas viejecillas borrachas que van por las calles queriendo borrar el mundo, y se sientan a cantar en los bancos del paseo" [I understand very well those drunken little old ladies who wander the streets wanting to erase the world, and who sit down to sing on street benches] (p. 1433). Thus, Rosita's despair is total: considered unavailable while engaged, she becomes a castoff once the engagement is broken. Any indications from her that she would like to marry would now be considered indecent.[26] No longer attractive, she is treated by society like the fantastic frock in the attic—a sadly comic phantom from the past.

Doña Rosita is generally considered to be a gentle portrait of decadence. This opinion, accepted by most critics, was probably established when Angel del Río compared Lorca's play with Chekov's *The Cherry Orchard*.[27] Interesting and significant parallels exist between the Spanish and the Russian plays. Both are dramatizations of a family slowly declining into emotional and material bankruptcy because of a fundamental lack of energy and practicality. The romantic attachment to a refined but empty way of life is symbolized by both dramatists in the love for fragile botanical beauty—the uncle's hothouse and the cherry orchard both symbolize a genteel escape from reality. Both Lorca and Chekov present a society comprised of ridiculous figures: the merchant Lopakhin, who buys the cherry orchard, is as vulgar as the ostentatious Señor X; Trofimov, marked by his elegant speech as an intellectual, is as ineffectual as the hapless don Martín. Gaev, the foolish uncle, like Rosita's uncle, lacks business talent and has allowed his financial resources to slip away. As Rosita's aunt was forced to do, Mme. Ranevsky, owner of the cherry orchard, must sell her home. Both plays end with a painful scene of departure from the family residence.

Like Chekov, Lorca has created a series of caricatures representing society; but the Spanish playwright goes further in his indictment of the absurd social attitudes responsible for immobilizing women. While *The Cherry Orchard* ends, like an elegiac poem,[28] with an affectionate homage to an obsolete life style, there is no such tenderness for the past in *Doña Rosita*. Lorca's condemnation of society is far more direct and complete than Chekov's bittersweet portrayal. If Mme. Ranevsky's family goes off to face an uncertain life in Paris, there is no doubt whatever that Rosita's future is to be a kind of living death. A comparison of the final scenes of the two plays reveals Lorca's more desperate conclusion. Mme. Ranevsky leaves her family home for the last time with nostalgia and a deep sense of loss: "Oh, my orchard, my sweet, beautiful orchard! My life, my youth, my happiness, good-bye, good-bye." In contrast to this fond farewell, Rosita's aunt finds that the plants in her garden have become overgrown and misshapen. "Los cipreses . . . casi tocan las paredes de mi cuarto. Parece como si alguien quisiera poner el jardín feo para que no tuviésemos pena en dejarlo" [The cypresses . . . almost touch the walls of my room. It seems as if someone wanted to make the garden ugly, so we could leave it without regret] (pp. 1436–1437). The aunt's sadness is not so much nostalgia as it is the bitter knowledge that Rosita has been forgotten. The garden, in which Rosita was the most fragile flower, was the aunt's life. That her beloved garden is now grown ugly and deformed emphasizes the similar state of the delicate Rosita, who has become grotesque in the eyes of society. The precise emotional balance between comedy and pathos sustained in the last scene of *The Cherry Orchard* becomes in *Doña Rosita* a dissonant play between comic distortion and tragedy. While Chekov evokes the memory of a cherished past and concludes with a vague hope for the future, Lorca only remembers the cruelty of his heroine's past and the mute horror of her descent into oblivion.

Lorca's dramatization of the inhumanity of social attitudes is made particularly grim by being extended beyond the small-scale private tragedy to encompass a panoramic view of Spanish womanhood. Rosita's personal plight takes on a much larger dimension because it is not unique, but common. "Después de todo," declares Rosita, "lo que me ha pasado le ha pasado a mil mujeres" [After all, what's happened to me has happened to a thousand women] (p. 1430). Discussing the play in an interview, Lorca referred to the collective significance of his heroine's fate and implored, "¿Hasta cuándo seguirán así todas las doñas Rositas de España?" [How long will all the doñas Rositas of Spain go on this way?] (p. 1801).

La casa de Bernarda Alba

The conflict between personal aspiration and petrified social morality dramatized in *Yerma* and in *Doña Rosita* culminates in Lorca's last and greatest dramatic work, *La casa de Bernarda Alba*. As a symbol of authority grown corrupt and venomous, Bernarda Alba is probably the most memorable dramatic character in modern Spanish theater. Comparable only to Galdós's unforgettable despot, doña Perfecta, Bernarda Alba is the overwhelming personification of a social code that has become so fraudulent it is farcical. Bernarda so successfully overshadows the other characters of the play that upon her depends our understanding of the drama as a whole.

Even though critics refer automatically to *Bernarda Alba* as a tragedy, few have analyzed the protagonist of this play as a tragic figure. Díaz-Plaja is impressed by her "gigantesca lucha" [enormous struggle] and insists that "ridículo . . . es tomar partido en pro o en contra de la actitud de Bernarda" [it is ridiculous . . . to take sides for or against Bernarda's attitude],[29] yet Bernarda is not a godlike, tragic figure. Instead, she is portrayed as a hypocritical and malicious personality who has twisted the morality she represents into an instrument of repression. Her tyranny is imposed with the crude gestures of a bully and her authority is finally revealed to be hollow and cruel.

Bernarda is drawn as a symbol rather than as an individual. Her character is one-dimensional and her personal history scant. We know only that she has been married twice and that her second husband has just died. She is not involved in the family feuds that, in traditional tragedy and in *Bodas de sangre*, provide motivation for revenge. Thus, Bernarda, unlike heroically evil characters, such as Medea or Clytemnestra, cannot be considered an example of "greatness gone wrong," for she has not suffered unjustly and has nothing to avenge. She is motivated by her obsession with "lo que dirán," or "what people will say." Recalling no particular insult or injury, she justifies her behavior merely by repeating, "Así pasó en casa de mi padre" [Thus it was in my father's house]. Torrente Ballester is correct when he suggests that the reason for Bernarda's ignorance of life is unimportant;[30] the end result—tyranny—is the same. Yet, without a past, Bernarda remains depersonalized, the caricature of a social morality revealed by Lorca to be a grotesque distortion of Christian values.

Bernarda's tragic flaws—her obsessive pride and desire for respect—are not merely flaws in an otherwise balanced character; they constitute her entire personality. She acknowledges no higher law than her own, so that her desire for respect is soon recognized simply as a will to dominate others. Bernarda abuses Poncia, her maid of longstanding and her most trusted ally, calling her an "old sow." To her, the poor "son como los animales; parecen como estuvieran hechos de otras sustancias" [are like animals; they seem to be made of other stuff] (p. 1445). She accuses the neighbors of coming to her house, not from respect for her dead husband, but "para llenar mi casa con el sudor de sus refajos y el veneno de sus lenguas" [to fill my house with the sweat of their clothes and the poison of their tongues] (p. 1450). To Poncia's suggestion that they give away some of her dead husband's clothes, Bernarda responds with a miser's gusto, "Nada, ¡ni un botón! Ni el pañuelo con que le hemos tapado la cara" [Nothing, not even a button! Not even the cloth we covered his face with] (p. 1458). Bernarda's disregard for others reaches monstrous proportions in her treatment of her daughters. After the incident of the hidden photograph in Act II, she threatens them with almost medieval isolation. Clearly, Bernarda is in flagrant violation of the Christian values of charity and good will.

In her fanatical fear of gossip, Bernarda can be compared to Calderón's ghastly heroes, whose warped conception of honor is a travesty of Christian morality. Like Calderón, Lorca dramatizes a sick society, implicating figures of authority as the perpetrators of injustice and brutality.[31] Yet Lorca goes further than Calderón in condemning a decadent morality, for he ridicules tyrant and victim alike. By drawing attention to the physical repugnance of his characters, the playwright suggests that their bodies, like

their minds, have become deformed. Poncia thinks of Bernarda as "un lagarto machacado . . . que es lo es ella" [a smashed lizard . . . which is
what she is]; one of Bernarda's neighbors refers to her as a "vieja lagarta
recocida" [dried-up old lizard]; the oldest daughter, Angustias, is described as "un palo vestido" [a dressed-up stick]. María Josefa alludes to
her granddaughter and to Bernarda in "defamatory verses"[32] that she improvises in the style of children's rhymes: "Bernarda, cara de leoparda;
. . . Magdalena, cara de hiena" [Bernarda, leopard-face; . . . Magdalena,
hyena-face] (p. 1523). Physical distortion and the comparison of these
characters with animals makes them appear both pitiful and grotesque.
Perhaps, as Manuel Durán suggests, "After living in the U.S. the position
of the Spanish woman as the core of the traditional family must have
seemed somewhat absurd to [Lorca]."[33] That these distorted characters
were based on real-life models only makes the play more chilling.[34]

Bernarda is recognized by the members of her household as an arche-
type of brutality. Poncia compares her own behavior in a moment of
wrath to that of Bernarda. Explaining that her husband raised birds, Poncia entertains the daughters with a tale of exaggerated cruelty, telling
them how she handled her spouse: "Yo tengo la escuela de tu madre. Un
día me dijo no sé qué cosa y le maté todos los colorines con la mano del
almirez" [I'm of your mother's school. One day he said I don't know what
to me and I killed all his linnets with the pestle] (p. 1477). The daughters
laugh gaily at Poncia's story and at her analogy with Bernarda, whose
manner is comic as well as terrifying.

Because her behavior is so predictable, Bernarda resembles the villain
of a puppet farce, whose body jerks into stiff but automatic poses. Like a
marionette whose wooden face is carved into a grimace, she insults the
villagers, threatens her daughters with petty violence, and keeps her aged,
demented mother under lock and key. Bernarda conveys her anger with
gestures much like those of the mock-ferocious puppet Cristóbal, mentioned in the preceding chapter in the discussion of comic violence. Re-
sorting to physical blows, Bernarda assumes the gestures of a bully. In the
first act she slaps Angustias and calls her abusive names for looking out the
window in hopes of seeing Pepe, her fiancé. Later in the act, when Angustias powders her face in anticipation of seeing Pepe, Bernarda again hu-
miliates the girl by brutally scraping the powder from her face.

These harsh scenes are not humorous, yet the gestures accompanying them resemble the antics of a comic villain. However fearsome, Bernarda is also ludicrous as she knocks people about; for, as Henri Bergson points out, "Dès que notre attention se portera sur le geste et non sur l'acte, nous serons dans la comédie" [When our attention is focused on gesture and not on action, we are in the realm of comedy].[35] Always looking for trouble, Bernarda carries a cane, a counterpart of the slapstick used in farces, which serves to emphasize her commands. She pounds the floor with it and brandishes it angrily before her daughters' faces. In the last act Adela breaks the cane in two, symbolizing her defiance of the bully.

A thoroughly unsympathetic character, Bernarda is hated by the village women and by Poncia, who knows her best. Poncia's knowledge of Bernarda has been gained from many years in her service: "Treinta años lavando sus sábanas; treinta años comiendo sus sobras; noches en vela cuando tose; días enteros mirando por la rendija para espiar a los vecinos y llevarle el cuento; vida sin secretos una con otra, y, sin embargo, ¡maldita sea!" [Thirty years washing her sheets; thirty years eating her leftovers; sitting up nights when she had a cough; whole days looking through the grate to spy on the neighbors for her; a life without secrets from each other and, in spite of it, damn her!] (p. 1442). Throughout the play Poncia is an ironic contrast to the character of Bernarda. Though as a servant she cannot compete with Bernarda, her greater generosity and wisdom underscore Bernarda's lack of humanity. In spite of Bernarda's supposed independence from and superiority to Poncia, it is she on whom Bernarda must rely to keep informed of what is happening in the town. It is not Bernarda but Poncia who tries to reason with Adela, Bernarda's own daughter, when the girl insists on marrying Pepe even though she knows he is engaged to her older sister. Poncia's positive character consistently opposes Bernarda's negative one, so that her vision of violent recrimination against Bernarda is comic. Imagining the day she will get even with her mistress, Poncia vows, "Ese día me encerraré con ella en un cuarto y le estará escupiendo un año entero" [That day I'll lock myself in a room with her and I'll spit on her a whole year] (p. 1442).

Another character who defies and ridicules Bernarda is María Josefa, who is, almost literally, the skeleton in the family closet. Like Pepe el Romano, she is seldom seen (she is only onstage twice) but is a disturbing influence on the household. Her voice is heard offstage in the opening scene of the play, thus making the deep trouble in the household evident immediately. The demented old woman represents the result of generations of oppression and disregard of human needs.

María Josefa haunts Bernarda at crucial moments in the play. At the end of Act I, Angustias sees Pepe passing down the street and asks permission to go out and greet him. Bernarda refuses, proclaiming furiously, "Aunque mi madre esté loca, yo estoy en mis cinco sentidos y sé perfectamente lo que hago" [My mother may be mad, but I have my five senses and I know perfectly well what I'm doing] (p. 1469). At this point María Josefa wanders in, a living testament of Bernarda's failure. In contrast to Bernarda's cruel mistreatment of her daughters, María Josefa protests, "No quiero ver a estas mujeres solteras rabiando por la boda, haciéndose polvo el corazón" [I don't want to see these single women chafing to get married, their hearts turning to dust] (p. 1470). The timing of the old woman's appearance dramatizes Bernarda's cruelty, for the madwoman's natural sympathy makes her seem much saner than her daughter.

In Act III María Josefa pretends that a lamb she carries in her arms is her child, but in her delusion she is also aware of the truth and intimidates Martirio, one of the daughters, by telling her, "Mejor es tener una oveja que no tener nada" [It's better to have a lamb than not to have anything] (p. 1524). María Josefa's dementia is surpassed by the violence and ugliness of Bernarda and her daughters, whom the demented grandmother describes as "ranas sin lengua" [frogs without tongues]—an apt description since frogs and toads have traditionally symbolized that which is physically grotesque and repulsive.

One of the most important ironies of the play is that María Josefa is not an aunt or a distant cousin but Bernarda's own mother. Bernarda has justified her tyranny by repeating, "Así pasó en casa de mi padre," implying that she bears no personal blame for customs imposed upon her by tradition. But she is not at all like her own mother, whose madness "revela otra clase de persona" [reveals another kind of person].[36] María Josefa's gentle derangement suggests that Bernarda's cruel tactics were not learned from her mother. Poncia implies that Bernarda's father was no tyrant either; she explains in Act I that "desde que murió el padre de Bernarda no han vuelto a entrar las gentes bajo estos techos. Ella no quiere que la vean en su dominio" [since Bernarda's father died, people have not returned to this house. She doesn't want them to see her in her domain] (p. 1442). Thus, Bernarda's ferocity, excessive for simply maintaining order, was not learned in her father's house, as she claims. It can be explained only by noting that Bernarda's primary purpose is to dominate. She desires submission and uses traditional social mores to impose her will. Her devotion to morality is hypocritical, for, in her effort to prevail, she finally violates those mores by lying to society about her daughter's death. Manipulating public opinion by corrupt means has thus become a part of Bernarda's personality, and she is the willing instrument of an authoritarian society.

There are moments in the play during which Bernarda's rage subsides, and she is portrayed at ease. These scenes occur in the last act, after her tyrannical personality is indelibly impressed upon the mind of the spectator. She is seen chatting amicably with her friend Prudencia; she advises Angustias, who is soon to be married, never to question her husband; and, finally, she tells her daughters not to wonder about things of which they have no knowledge. These lines, though they do not alter the conception of Bernarda's character, indicate that she is neither insane nor irresponsible. She is quite lucid and aware of her actions, if not of their deeper significance.

There is also comic relief in the play, as in Act I when Adela models her green dress for the chickens. Permitted to wear only mourning clothes, Adela wishes to show off her new, colorful dress, so she puts it on and goes out to the chicken house. Her sisters tease her, asking how the chickens liked her frock. Adela merrily goes along with the joke, advising them that all she received from the chickens were a few fleas. This lighthearted gaiety, however, is merely incidental, while the ridicule evoked by Bernarda is central to Lorca's conception of her character.

The grim comic effect of Bernarda coincides with chilling horror in the final scene of the play. Having shot at Adela's fleeing lover, Bernarda gives the impression that she has killed him and announces to Adela, "Atrévete a buscarlo ahora" [Dare to go look for him now]. Thinking her lover is dead, the girl commits suicide. Bernarda never tells Adela the truth—that she did not hit Pepe and that he is safe—and is thus directly responsible for her daughter's death. Nor does Bernarda grieve for Adela.

Staring at her daughter's body hanging from the rafters, Bernarda can only think of her own reputation: "Mi hija murió virgen. . . . ¡Nadie diga nada! Ella ha muerto virgen" [My daughter died a virgin. . . . No one say anything! She has died a virgin] (p. 1532). There is a kind of horrible absurdity in these lines, not only because they are false, but also because they are preposterous. Bernarda might be expected to defend her daughter's reputation, but that her concern for respectability totally supplants any expression of grief is not only monstrous but grotesquely comic.

Interpreted as a tragedy, *Bernarda Alba* is indeed a degeneration of the tragic experience in which neither tragic enlightenment nor acceptance of tragic destiny is achieved. Commenting that "la falsedad se cierne la obra, pero aun así la tenebrosa tragedia subsiste" [The play ends on a false note, but even so, the tenuous tragedy is sustained],[37] Valbuena Prat, who treats the play as a tragedy, is rightly disturbed that tragedy should end with the reinforcement of a gigantic lie. If, however, we understand *Bernarda Alba* not as a traditional tragedy but as a new kind of farcical or "slapstick" tragedy, the last scene becomes a powerful revelation: Bernarda's subordination of compassion to concern for respectability remains unjustified, as it has been throughout the play, and she is finally revealed to be an automaton who continues churning out false signals even after the truth has been told ("Nadie diga nada" [No one is to say anything], she interjects, realizing that her statement is false and that her command will not be obeyed). To see this final scene as farcical does not require that we laugh at it, although some audiences in Madrid responded with laughter at the final line, but only that Bernarda be recognized for what she has been throughout the play—the searing caricature of a repressive morality.

Like a doddering old general who keeps giving orders after the battle is lost, Bernarda is ludicrous in her defeat. Her failure stems not so much from Adela's immorality as from her own lack of power to prevent it. Her words evoke neither pity nor fear, but only amused horror at her hypocrisy and insensibility. Bernarda's hope that the townspeople will believe what she tells them is slim indeed, for the outside world is represented in this scene by Poncia, who knows the truth and who hates Bernarda. In the town where Adela's lover still lives, Bernarda's words will sound as fraudulent and foolish as they do to the spectators of the play.

Bernarda is easily ridiculed because she is, like Molière's misanthrope, self-centered and devoid of a sense of humor. Unlike Alceste, however, Bernarda is not to be pitied; she bears direct guilt for Adela's death. Comparing her to another Molière character, Roy Campbell describes Bernarda as "a cross between a tiger and Molière's Tartuffe."[38] Bernarda resembles Molière's ambiguous characters who, in spite of their cruelty, inspire laughter because they are psychologically deformed and grotesque.

Laughter at Bernarda's ludicrous behavior, however, rings hollow, expressing only anguish and defeat, because there is no final victory over her. She is a preposterous figure in the final scene, shrieking out her orders while Adela's corpse hangs before her eyes. The spectator, though shocked at the rebellious girl's demise, is struck not so much with her death but with Bernarda's grotesqueness. The remaining daughters have gained nothing from their sister's rebellion and suicide: oppressed and embittered, their lives are hopeless, and they are ruined along with Bernarda.

In this terrifying figure Lorca has not projected a balanced, indifferent characterization. He has, on the contrary, created an extraordinary caricature of oppression. If Bernarda were, like Calderón's villains, merely evil, it would be easy to agree that Lorca "no toma partido; presenta" [doesn't take sides; he merely presents them].[39] But Lorca reveals his villain to be absurd as well as evil. Bernarda's exaggerated behavior produces a grim comic effect, which, according to Bergson, indicates critical intent, since laughter serves as a "geste social. Par la crainte qu'il inspire il réprime les excentricités. . . . Cette raideur est le comique et le rire en est la châtiment" [social gesture. Through the fear it inspires it represses eccentricities. . . . This stiffness is the comic act and laughter is its punishment].[40] Bergson's description of the comic character as rigid, unsociable, and automatic defines the character of Bernarda Alba more adequately than do the criteria of the tragic heroine.

Because of its distorted protagonist and its static characters, *La casa de Bernarda Alba* not only reflects the honor tragedies of Calderón but also foreshadows the Theater of the Absurd. Like the dramatists of the Absurd, Lorca suggests that there is no such thing as human dignity in a depraved society. As in some Absurdist farces, Lorca's symbol of authority is perverse and repulsive; her final command "es sólo una impotente y patética continuación de la farsa fracasada" [is only a weak and pathetic continuation of a farce which has failed].[41] *Bernarda Alba* is a drama of revolt whose chilling *humour noir* lends the play its thoroughly modern spirit. Yet comic distortion has been historically characteristic of the Spanish mind. In his last play Lorca joins Quevedo, Goya, Valle-Inclán, and Camilo José Cela in hopeless laughter at the absurdity and misery of mankind.

CONCLUSION

Lorca's mature dramas reveal a new conception of the tragic experience in which humor is used to reveal despair. In addition to the Aristotelian prerequisites of pity and fear, Lorca's dramas also provoke derisive laughter and a comic awareness of man's frailty. The response to these plays is, therefore, not the purgative experience traditionally ascribed to tragic drama but the unsettling sense of conflict still unresolved.

Even though Lorca's heroines are pitiable creatures, they fall short of tragic dimension. If they are indecisive (La novia), hysterical (Yerma), and intimidated (Rosita), their struggles are not conflicts whose tragic inevitability we can accept without question. The compassion with which these trapped heroines are drawn is unmistakable, yet our sense of loss at their demise is ambivalent, for their struggles inspire not only pity but also grim laughter. This is not the curative laughter of comic relief; it derives from the heart of Lorca's tragic sense of life.

The traditional purpose of comic relief has been twofold: to give the spectator brief but necessary respite from action that cannot be sustained at the peak of emotional intensity, and to underline or intensify the tragic action. Lorca's comic scenes serve both these purposes. The maid's insinuating remarks to the bridegroom in *Bodas de sangre* and Adela's modeling of her new frock for the chickens in *Bernarda Alba* are moments in which dramatic tension is relaxed and the spectator is briefly invited to enjoy himself. Lorca also intensifies tragic action by use of comic irony in his characterization of María Josefa in *Bernarda Alba*. In *Doña Rosita* the heroine's suffering is more poignant because it is made to appear comic, as when the maid asks Rosita what happens at night in a marriage by proxy.

There is, however, another more complex use of the comic that alone seems to account for the disturbing impact of Lorca's master plays. These comic moments, as J. L. Styan remarks, are not happy afterthoughts but reveal an essential ambivalence in the dramatist's conception of tragic action.[42] That the figure of Death, which hovers over the characters of *Bodas de sangre*, should leer at their downfall at once reduces them to the dimension of puppets and makes their struggles seem absurd. Just as we are compelled by Shakespeare to give equal weight both to King Lear's madness and to his saner mind, we are asked by Lorca to give equal importance both to Yerma's severe Christian principles and to the paganism which she rejects.

While Lorca's comic spirit is present in *Bodas de sangre* and *Yerma*, his grim humor becomes increasingly critical in his last two more socially oriented plays. No longer engaged in purely personal conflict, the heroines of *Doña Rosita* and *Bernarda Alba* now struggle against a decadent morality that imprisons them in a tight cocoon. Doña Rosita becomes a passive member of a society of fools, while Adela and her sisters lose an emotional and psychological combat with the ferocious bully who is their mother. The highly wrought tension between humor and anguish in these two plays is too incongruous to be described by the rather nondescript term "tragicomedy." At the same time amusing and terrifying, *Doña Rosita* and *Bernarda Alba* recall Lorca's puppet plays and the tragic farce *Don Perlimplín*. Like *Don Perlimplín*, these last two plays seem best described as, to borrow a phrase from Tennessee Williams, "slapstick tragedy."[43]

Lorca is horrified by the hypocrisy and cruelty of established morality and expresses his dismay not only by creating rigid, one-dimensional characters, but also by adapting scenes and gestures from ancient farce for the purpose of serious criticism. Although not a polemical dramatist, Lorca never ceases to rebel against the web of social injustice, hurling satirical barbs at what he considers outmoded social attitudes that might be changed. His outlook on life, however, is darkly pessimistic. Using grim humor to depict social paralysis and decay, he joins other modern playwrights in suggesting that anguish in a morally bankrupt culture is absurd and meaningless.

6. Historical Perspective:
Lorca and Twentieth-Century Spanish Theater

Not often is it necessary to stress the modernity of a modern author. Such, however, is the case with Lorca; his plays have won critical acclaim not for their expression of modern life but for their affinity with the theater of the golden age. Perhaps because Lorca portrays characters in rural scenes, critics have assumed that he is more concerned with the revival of traditional dramatic forms than with dramatizing social problems of the present day. Alfredo de la Guardia concludes that Lorca's dramatic art is entirely unrelated to twentieth-century theater: "Es indudable que, apartando la mirada de todo el teatro moderno de su país, buscó en aquellas comedias y tragedias [del siglo de oro] y también en pasos y entremeses, las pautas que le sirvieran para componer sus producciones dramáticas" [Without doubt, (Lorca), turning away from his country's modern theater, sought in those comedies and tragedies (of the golden age) and also in the *pasos* and *entremeses*, the models for his own dramatic works].[1] Yet, as we have seen, Lorca's theater is modern in spirit and reflects contemporary social and artistic preoccupations. Among those who, like Lorca, dramatized a serious view of life by means of comic techniques are at least three of Spain's best playwrights, who can be considered his precursors. Carlos Arniches, the writer of critical burlesques; Jacinto Benavente, who satirized the upper classes; and Valle-Inclán, whose bitter *esperpentos* parody Spanish political and social customs—all helped to modernize the twentieth-century Spanish stage. Without their contributions, the theater of García Lorca would have been impossible.

Modern theater begins in Spain with Jacinto Benavente, often considered Spain's equivalent to George Bernard Shaw. An extraordinarily versatile dramatist who wrote everything from children's theater to rural tragedies similar to Lorca's folk plays, Benavente is best known for his realistic bourgeois comedies satirizing aristocratic boredom and middleclass snobbery. Benavente was a widely read, thoroughly cultivated dramatist who was inspired not so much by the Spanish theater of the golden age as by the drama of Shakespeare and of modern European playwrights, such as Shaw, Ibsen, and Maeterlinck. His conception of theater was in the intellectual manner of his predecessors in France, such as Henri Lavedan, François de Curel, and Henri Becque. Action in Benavente's plays is conveyed primarily by dialogue rather than by the more emotional and theatrical techniques used by Lope, who relied heavily upon the use of spectacle to communicate the meaning of his works. Benavente's plays are full of brilliant repartee and witticisms. Even his peasant characters are loquacious and articulate. Their speech, full of proverbs, reflects the ellipsis of rural pronunciation.

Though no one questions the fact that Benavente is the father of modern Spanish theater, his plays have faded quickly. Berated by critics of his own day for writing dramas alien to traditional Spanish theater and to the national ethos, he is today accused of creating facile portrayals of aristocratic and bourgeois life. Yet Benavente, like Lorca, was essentially an artist. Although his plays focused upon a decadent morality, his primary concern was not with philosophy or ideology but with maintaining his position as the most successful dramatist of the day. Luring audiences to the theater to see plays that disparaged their morality and customs demanded the restrained, genteel satire at which Benavente excelled. With an outlook best described as "entre desprecio y piedad" [between scorn and pity],[2] Benavente became a master of irony who presented the follies of both sides of a situation.

Lorca began his career as a dramatist in revolt against the tired, realistic comedies that Benavente had made popular. By turning to the golden age dramatists and to the popular tradition of puppetry, Lorca was seeking a more spontaneous and lively theater that would appeal to rural audiences as well as to the urbane spectators of Madrid: "Sé muy bien cómo se hace al teatro semi-intelectual, pero eso no tiene importancia," he declared.

"Por eso yo . . . me he entregado a lo dramático que nos permite un contacto más directo con las masas" [I know very well how semi-intellectual theater is made, but that is not important. That's why . . . I've devoted myself to the kind of drama that allows us more direct contact with the masses] (p. 1771). Despite his aversion to bourgeois theater, Lorca's plays reveal the careful balance of sympathy and satire achieved by Benavente. Behind the traditional atmosphere that Lorca created with folksongs and dances is an often critical view of society and an unmistakably sympathetic portrayal of the problems of women.

For both Lorca and Benavente, the struggle between the individual and society seemed most intense in the lives of women. Both dramatists also challenged conventional conceptions of morality. Although their heroines seek orthodox lives of marriage and motherhood, the institution of marriage is at times portrayed as a farce that oppresses and isolates the lives of women. In *La escuela de princesas* (1909), Máximo gently ridicules the young Costanza's protests against an arranged marriage: "Después de algunos años de matrimonio, todos los maridos son lo mismo. . . . El matrimonio es una especie de danza de los siete velos; antes de terminar la luna de miel, que es la danza, no queda un velo" [After a few years of marriage, all husbands are the same. . . . Marriage is a kind of dance of seven veils; before the honeymoon, which is the dance, is over, the veil is gone].[3] These words of advice recall Poncia's skeptical warning to Bernarda's daughters that in only two weeks after the wedding a man "deja la cama por la mesa y la mesa por la taberna, y la que no se conforma se pudre llorando en un rincón" [leaves the bed for the table and the table for the tavern, and whoever doesn't like it can rot, crying in a corner] (p. 1476).

Both Benavente and Lorca portray heroines who refuse to conform to the behavior expected of women. Pepa Doncel does not apologize for her shady past but gains respectability by marrying a rich bourgeois; though Nené of *El hombrecito* (1903) is unable to marry Enrique, she continues to meet him secretly. Most of Lorca's rebellious characters, unlike those of Benavente, are unable to compromise. Some—Muchacha segunda in *Yerma* and the undaunted *zapatera*—survive unharmed; more often, however, their confrontation with conventional moral standards leads to disaster. But if Mariana Pineda, the bride of *Bodas*, and Bernarda's daughter

Adela refuse to submit to the dictates of respectable morality, their rebellion is nevertheless portrayed sympathetically.

Dramatization of rebellious females was prominent in the theater of the golden age. Heroines asserted their equality with men, as in Calderón's *Afectos de odio y amor*; they prided themselves on their immunity to love, as Tisbea does in Tirso's *El burlador de Sevilla*. Bellicose and determined types such as doña Juana in *Los milagros del desprecio* and Laura of *La vengadora de las mujeres* gave particular force to Lope's portrayal of the war between the sexes. But in golden age theater, antagonism between men and women was always resolved by love, the universal master.[4] Those heroines of the golden age who rejected love or social convention finally submitted willingly to persistent suitors or lost their lovers to more receptive rivals, as in Lope's *La dama boba*. In Lorca's plays, however, women's attempts to control their lives is not a convention used solely for the development of intrigue and coquetry. It is rather the central dramatic conflict in which final harmony is, with the exception of *La zapatera*, never achieved.

Lorca's strident and forceful females are thus more akin to Benavente's protagonists than to the heroines of the golden age. His attitudes toward women are inherited not from Lope, but from Ibsen and Chekov by way of the theater of Benavente. Neither Benavente nor Lorca portrayed female characters with a specific social purpose in mind; nor did they have any interest in the furthering of women's rights. Lorca's sympathy for women, like that of Benavente, is part of a more general critical attitude. Their dramatization of human conflict transcends the personal struggle of the individual heroine and implicates society at large.

Benavente criticized all segments of society, especially the upper classes, of which he was a member. He invented an imaginary kingdom called Suavia, a name that alludes to the life of comfort enjoyed by bored aristocrats in *La noche del sábado*. The fictitious town of Moraleda was the scene of middle class hypocrisy in *La gobernadora* and *Pepa Doncel*. In *La escuela de princesas*, class consciousness and snobbery are characteristic of the nobility. Scandalized at the prospect of Costanza's marriage to Alejandro, a duchess exclaims: "Es un súbdito, y si los súbditos por nobles que sean, hallan la posibilidad de elevarse por el amor de princesas,

¿dónde iríamos a parar?" [He's a subject, and if subjects, however noble they may be, find it possible to further their careers with the love of princesses, where will it all end?] (Benavente, III, 513).

Like Benavente, Lorca satirized the class to which he himself belonged —the upper class. Social hierarchy is particularly rigid in the mind of Bernarda Alba, the rich provincial who considers the poor to be "como los animales" (p. 1445). Bernarda disdains suitors who cannot match her daughters' wealth or status and discourages all the available men of the town. Poncia taunts her by suggesting sarcastically that Bernarda might move to another town in search of eligible husbands, except for the risk that "claro que en otros sitios ellas resultan las pobres" [of course, in other places, they'll be the poor ones] (p. 1457). Bernarda recognizes that Poncia's suggestion is insolent; although she resents her maid, she must continue to rely on her to keep informed of what is happening in the town.

Lorca's portrayal of social decadence echoes Benavente's deep skepticism. *Doña Rosita* parallels *La gobernadora* as a play in which nearly every character is satirized. Just as Benavente ridicules both liberals and conservatives in Moraleda, Lorca presents both the bumbling old aesthete, Rosita's uncle, and Señor X, who is obsessively on the side of progress, as comic types. While Benavente's social commentary is expressed by witty and ironic dialogue, Lorca goes beyond the use of satiric dialogue to create preposterous caricatures. Benavente's frivolous socialites in *La gata de angora* (1900), who explain that a friend's engagement was broken because "a última hora se averiguó que Aguado no tiene una peseta" [at the last minute it was discovered that Aguado hadn't a cent] (Benavente, I, 471), are prototypes of the three overdressed *solteronas* who, according to their mother, prefer to spend their money on reserving chairs in the park than on food. While Benavente presents both sides of Moraleda's petty politics as corrupt and self-seeking, Lorca ridicules the exaggerated manners and the oppressive morality of an entire society in *Doña Rosita*.

Though most of Benavente's plays are in the tradition of nineteenth-century realism, he saw the innovative possibilities in ancient farce and, as Lorca was later to do, experimented with the characters from the Italian *commedia dell'arte*. In *Los intereses creados* (1907), considered his best play, Benavente attempted to escape the confines of realism in order to give fresh dramatic expression to his view of life. He did not entirely succeed. Just as the country dialect of the peasants in *Señora Ama* and *La malquerida* cannot conceal their urban middle-class morality, the names of sixteenth-century comic types from the commedia do not alter the characters of *Los intereses creados*. Like most of Benavente's dramatis personae, the Italianate figures are members of the upper class. As in his other works, they indulge in much witty, satirical dialogue. The most exaggerated character is the stingy villain, Polichinela, who resembles Lorca's ferocious puppet, don Cristóbal, and who is derived from the same Italian mask. Crispín, the hero, is a clever opportunist who, like Manolo in *La gobernadora*, plays one interest against the other. Characteristically, Benavente satirizes not only the miser but also the penniless poet, Leandro, who loves Silvia, Polichinela's daughter. As in most of his plays, Benavente achieves a delicate balance in *Los intereses*. The practical Crispín manages to bring his master Leandro and Silvia together, thus satisfying both their own idealistic love and the cynical materialism of himself and Polichinela. Far from the obscene, slapstick humor of the commedia, *Los intereses* is a play of intrigue and intellectual badinage. In it, however, Benavente proved that simple comic types could be used to dramatize a serious, even subtle commentary on life. It was this revaluation of the ancient farce as a serious dramatic form that Lorca continued in his own effort to revitalize Spanish theater.

Farce began to reappear on the twentieth-century Spanish stage in Benavente's subtle and rhetorically elegant rendering of the Italian commedia. But *Los intereses creados*, like the works of dramatists who continued the style of Benavente—Martínez Sierra, Alejandro Casona, and Jacinto Grau—was a highly sophisticated play intended for cultivated audiences. There was, in contrast, another sort of farce that drew a different public and existed solely for the sake of entertainment. This was the *género chico*, the short satirical one-act play, often accompanied by music, which dealt not with the upper class but with the low life of Madrid. Its characters were *majas* and *chulos*—young men and women of the street— the frequently unemployed *cesante*, and the impudent *fresco* who often worked at avoiding employment. Directly descended from the traditional Spanish *entremeses*, the *sainete*, or short musical satire, relied on the stock jokes that were old when Cervantes tried his hand at them: comic use and abuse of language, foreign words, jargon, and parody of social customs and petty officialdom. Endless repetition and unimaginative handling of stale plots had brought the *entremés* to the brink of oblivion in the eighteenth century, but in the last two decades of the nineteenth century the short farce revived and became so popular that twenty theaters sprang up in Madrid to meet the demand. After 1910 the *sainete* began to decline again; soon vaudeville and operetta had superseded it as the most popular forms of stage entertainment.

Many playwrights of Benavente's generation began as *saineteros*, churning out the frivolous farces for a voracious public that demanded only laughs. Benavente himself wrote several, including one entitled *Todos somos unos*. With its touch of melancholy in the midst of merriment, this *sainete* is similar to Lorca's *La zapatera*, in which the heroine becomes reflective and expresses her sadness and fears. Like the *zapatera*, Benavente's heroine tries to be brave: "Yo soy, me basto / y todo el mundo me sobra" [I am, I'm enough / and I can do without the whole world]. Her friends recognize that her bravado is a mask, telling her, "Por no llorar lo cantas" [You sing so you won't cry]. But Benavente's subtle wit generally was too refined for the crude, often obscene jokes of the *género chico*. The undisputed master of this genre was Carlos Arniches.

Unlike Benavente, Arniches was not an intellectual and had no artistic pretensions. He was, however, a keen observer of social customs and was particularly adept at satire, so that in his hands the *género chico* gained artistic stature and psychological depth. Arniches devised plays he called *tragedias grotescas*. These were actually farces lengthened into full three-act plays in which the old comic tricks were retained but put to unexpectedly serious use. Ridicule, caricature, puns, and distorted language were no longer merely empty amusements but revealed the genuine suffering of characters who were not only hilarious but who also evoked sympathy and compassion. The nonsense and frivolity of traditional farce assumed a new and complex dimension in Arniches's masterpiece, *La señorita de Trevélez* (1916). The creation of Flora Trevélez is a consummate portrayal of the virtuous but awkward spinster, still unloved yet capable of exaggerated passion. A group of malicious young men send her a fake love letter supposedly signed by Galán, who is their rival for the attention of another girl. Though Galán is the butt of the joke, it is Flora who suffers from it. Having received the letter, Flora, blushing and smiling modestly, sallies forth to find Galán. In the course of their courtship she sings "Torna a Sorrento" to him and reminds him bashfully of a movie called *Fighting in the Darkness* in which the lovers exchange "uno de esos besos del 'cine' durante los cuales todo se atenúa, se desvanece, se esfuma, se borra y . . . aparece un letrero que dice Milano Films" [one of those movie kisses during which everything slows down, fades, goes up in smoke, disappears and . . . letters saying Milano Films appear].[5]

Flora's ludicrous sentimentality is surpassed only by the crudity of her brother don Gonzálo, who is ecstatic when he thinks his sister has at last attracted a suitor. He bestows upon Galán a copy he has painted of the famous *Rendición de Breda* by Velásquez, which he has enlarged to include eight extra meters of lances (Act I). As in *Doña Rosita*, the absurdity of the gift is a clue to the personality of the giver. Gonzálo also considers giving Galán a statue of Saturn consuming his offspring, the grotesque theme of one of Goya's most horrifying canvases. Don Gonzálo is somewhat disconsolate because the statue "está algo deteriorada porque al hijo que Saturno está comiendo le falta una pierna; . . . pero, en fin, así está más en carácter" [is somewhat worn because the son whom Saturn is eating is lacking a leg; . . . but, anyhow, that way he's more in character] (Arniches, p. 139). This amusing but grotesque statue is significant, for its excessive gesture of devouring suggests not only the overanxiousness of the giver, don Gonzálo, but also that of his sister. Like the statue, Flora is both amusing and repulsive, inspiring one of the characters in the play to comment "¡Qué esperpento!" [What a fright!] (Arniches, p. 103).

The cruel joke is finally admitted, and Flora is once again left hopelessly alone. Similar to Lorca's Rosita, Flora is only a type; for it is the treatment this pathetic creature receives that interests the dramatist rather than her inner thoughts, which can be easily imagined. Arniches's portrayal of the spinster in society is more excruciating than is Lorca's; Rosita is not such an exaggerated caricature as Flora, and the ridicule she suffers is not enacted upon the stage but is merely narrated by her. Both Rosita and Flora, however, suffer undeserved disaster, and both dramatists make their attitude toward the spinster's fate incontrovertibly clear: Arniches dilutes his disgust for the pranksters with Christian hope and charity, declaring that "la manera de acabar con este tipo nacional de guasón es difundiendo la cultura" [the way to stop this typically Spanish kind of joker is to educate people] (Arniches, p. 154). Flora's brother realizes the futility of avenging his honor in the traditional manner, that is, by killing the pranksters. He resolves his anger by wishing only "que Dios, como castigo llene de este dolor mío el alma de todos los burladores" [that God, as punishment, fill all pranksters' hearts with the sadness that I feel] (Arniches, p. 154). Rosita also copes with her own desolation by resigning herself to her fate.

Although Lorca admired Arniches, whom he considered "más poeta que casi todos los que escriben teatro en verso" [more of a poet than almost any who write verse plays], and respected his inventiveness—"fantasía hay en el sainete más pequeño de don Carlos Arniches" [there is fantasy in the shortest farce by don Carlos Arniches] (p. 1775)—I do not suggest that he was directly influenced by the *género chico*, which was hardly more than light entertainment. Arniches's accomplishment, however, bears directly upon the kind of theater Lorca tried to create. It was Arniches who restored the *género chico* to its traditional stature as a comic view of man's inhumanity and stupidity. In the eighteenth century the *género chico* had been more than light entertainment; Ramón de la Cruz, for example, described one of his *sainetes* as "una tragedia para reír o un sainete para llorar" [a funny tragedy or a sad farce].[6] By returning to this complex comic spirit, Arniches derived what he called the "tragedia grotesca," which both amused and criticized. Arniches not only laughed at typical speech and customs but also, through laughter, expressed horror and disgust at more serious traits, such as typical prejudices and social attitudes. Like the Italian *teatro del grottesco*, Arniches's *tragedia grotesca* is a farcical portrayal of man's depravity and corruption. Arniches, together with Benavente, thus preceded Lorca in making the farce a complex dramatic genre, accessible to a wide audience yet capable of expressing suffering as well as delight.

If the *tragedias grotescas* are amusing farces with tragic implications, the *esperpentos* of Valle-Inclán are farces in which amusement is hollow and detachment from the characters is complete. For Valle-Inclán, who admitted that "mi teatro es el género chico multiplicado por cuatro" [my theater is the *género chico* multiplied by four],[7] Arniches's *tragedia grotesca* was a point of departure from which farce became increasingly grave. Arniches laughed at ordinary, unloved, and uninspiring human creatures yet dignified them by implying that they suffered unjustly; Valle-Inclán laughed at traditionally respected figures—poets, kings, and state officials—implying that suffering could not bring them dignity but only absurdity and defeat. In the *esperpento* traditionally heroic characters are transformed as if by a concave mirror into distorted images and pitiful freaks. Valle-Inclán presented his theory of *esperpentismo* in 1920 in the twelfth scene of *Luces de bohemia*: "El esperpentismo lo ha inventado Goya. . . . mi estética actual es transformar con matemática de espejo cóncavo las normas clásicas. . . . deformemos la expresión en el mismo espejo que nos deforma las caras y toda la vida miserable de España" [Goya invented *esperpentismo*. . . . my present aesthetic is to transform with the mathematics of a concave mirror the classical norms. . . . let's deform expression in the same mirror that deforms our faces and the whole miserable life of Spain]. Like the *género chico*, then, the *esperpento* is historical and circumstantial, a burlesque of events in the literary, political, and social life of the day. But Valle-Inclán eliminated much explanatory dialogue and character delineation from his farces so that they appear, in contrast to Arniches's plays, stark, corrosive caricatures of entirely negative intent.

La reina castiza (1920), although written before Valle had defined the aesthetics of *esperpentismo*, is a typical *esperpento*. A parody of the nineteenth-century court of Isabel II, *La reina castiza* presents a gallery of caricatures. The young student Sopón, who seeks to blackmail the queen; the equine and effeminate consort; the flatulent general don Tragamundos; the queen's lover don Gargalito; and the queen herself are the ludicrous inhabitants of a "Realm of Fools" in *La reina castiza*. This bitter panorama parallels the series of ridiculous creatures in *Doña Rosita*. Lorca wrote that in this play Spanish women could see themselves reflected "como en un espejo" [as in a mirror] (p. 1800). But Rosita's friends and, in the eyes of others, the heroine herself, are ridiculous figures. Thus, Lorca's mirror can be compared to the concave mirror used by Valle-Inclán to distort his heroes. If Lorca's characters are not as grotesque as Valle's, they nevertheless are distorted figures who make up a society that has itself become cruel and indifferent to the suffering of others.

Valle-Inclán caricatured not only political, social, and literary personages of his day but also literary themes and ideas. *Las galas del difunto* is a burlesque of the traditional don Juan; *Los cuernos de don Friolera* parodies the theme of honor as it was portrayed in golden age theater. By presenting the traditional honor theme, not in the tragic mode as Calderón had done, but in the insolent manner of farce, Valle-Inclán degraded the traditional conception of honor and renewed the importance of farce as a keen instrument of satire and ridicule.

Lorca's criticism is never as topical or direct as Valle's, yet he, too, found that the traditional theme of honor lent itself naturally to comic treatment. Both Valle's don Friolera and Lorca's don Perlimplín represent the typical aging husband deceived by his wife. Both characters are puppetlike, easily manipulated by others: Perlimplín's maid persuades him to marry Belisa; Friolera, described as a puppet by the author, dutifully follows his superiors' orders and attempts to shoot his unfaithful wife. Both Lorca and Valle-Inclán undermine the Calderónian solution to the dilemma of dishonor: the victim is not the wife but the husband, who has become, in the modern honor farce, a ridiculous puppet.

Yet neither Perlimplín nor Friolera is merely a buffoon. As Ricardo Gullón explains, "The concept of character as a multiple being is basic to the creation of the *esperpento*";[8] and the puppet heroes of Valle and Lorca assume dimensions not ordinarily contained within the ancient comic types. The mind of Perlimplín becomes unexpectedly complex; he invents the elaborate scheme in which he disguises himself as a dashing youth. Winning a moment of Belisa's love, Perlimplín kills himself, knowing she cannot be faithful to an old man. Valle presents three versions of his hero's fate; in the most important one, Friolera, full of anger and remorse when he realizes he has missed his target and killed his daughter instead of his wife, asks to be sent away to a hospital. Thus, both Lorca and Valle-Inclán convert the traditional defender of honor into a pathetic clown in order to reveal that honor based on vengeance is both horrible and absurd.

Both Lorca and Valle-Inclán used the farce as a vehicle for serious social commentary. Implying that traditional interpretations of honor were ruthless and cruel, they created puppetlike characters to suggest that human life, like that of a one-dimensional type, is not free but is manipulated so that men become dehumanized and powerless to control their own actions. Roberto Sánchez comments that the characters in Lorca's plays who most resemble the mechanical figures of the *esperpento* are the puppet-bully don Cristóbal and the grotesque don Mirlo of *La zapatera*.[9] But Lorca's play that most nearly coincides with Valle's formula of deformation of heroic figures is *La casa de Bernarda Alba*. Its protagonist, Bernarda, is Lorca's most "esperpentic" as well as his most effective dramatic personage.

Like most of the characters of the *esperpentos*, Bernarda Alba is drawn from life. Yet Lorca, like Valle-Inclán, eliminated from his dramatic portrait any features that might have lent perspective to the characterization, so that Bernarda can be described as a caricature, an "exaggeration of actually existing disproportions."[10] Bernarda is entirely ferocious; she abuses the maids and the neighbors as well as her own mother and daughters. There are traces of farce in her thoroughly noxious personality, which suggest that Bernarda derives not only from Lorca's earlier puppet figures but also from the caricatures of the *esperpentos*. Bernarda represents and upholds the strict moral code of Spanish rural society; yet she has become a distorted reflection of that society, thereby corresponding to Valle's definition of an "esperpentic" character. Her appearance on stage could be announced by merely changing to the feminine form the last two words of Valle's description of the absurd prime minister in *La reina castiza*:

¡Vuelta de fantoche	[The puppet turns
golpe de bastón,	pounds his cane,
mirada de feroche	and casts around
del viejo mandón!	his tyrant's frown!]

Bernarda, like Valle's prime minister, shouts or speaks loudly more often than she participates in normal conversation. She appears onstage for the first time and also ends the play shouting, "Silence!" This command is the key to her personality, indicating her desire for total submission from others. Like some of Valle's caricatures who are described as having the physical traits of animals, Bernarda is compared to a lizard and a snake. But she resembles an "esperpentic" character primarily because her personality does not alter. She complains, but her suffering is not so profound that it brings her tragic recognition of her mistakes. Her bellicose defense of a primitive and bloodthirsty morality is fearful yet mechanical. The only clue as to how she became a tyrant, a hypocrite, and a snob is her own explanation of the eight-year period of mourning that her daughters must observe: "Así pasó en casa de mi padre." Because she remains a bully, her defeat arouses no pity. Like the characters of the *esperpento*, Bernarda is a caricature whose fearful shadow looms large against the whitewashed walls that surround her.

With the exception of Poncia, who tries to reason with both Bernarda and the rebellious Adela, the secondary characters in the play are as one-dimensional as Bernarda and serve primarily to reflect some important ironies: the moral distortions of a decadent tradition assume a physical reality in the humpbacked Martirio; the dementia of the grandmother does not produce brutality or violence, such as Bernarda indulges in, but only causes her to express in an extravagant and somewhat clownish manner her desire for freedom and her wish to satisfy normal human needs. It is not María Josefa who threatens the daughters, for "if the mind of the *abuela* is at times intellectually unsound, her utterances often have the truth of a higher reality."[11]

In his final play, then, Lorca's reaction to the traditionally distorted conception of honor imposed by vengeance is similar to that of Valle-Inclán. Like the characters of the *esperpento*, Bernarda is an automaton who continues to do what she has always been told. Both Friolera and Bernarda bear guilt for the deaths of their daughters, and the traditional honor code is again found to be not only deformative, but murderous as well.

Perhaps because Lorca's plays have been studied almost exclusively in terms of their similarity to the theater of Lope, their satirical and critical moments have been overlooked; for there is little social criticism in Lope's drama. The devices Lorca borrowed from Lope's works were those that increased the sensual appeal of theater: lyrical moments in dramatic dialogue, folkloric settings, and the use of music and dances—all of which aided in the creation of spectacle and thus encouraged greater audience participation in the theater. Yet entirely apart from these acquired theatrical techniques is a satirical undertone in Lorca's plays that grows more pronounced as he matures as a dramatist. In *Mariana Pineda* the nuns who give the heroine refuge believe she is being sought by the police because she is a Mason, and Masons were considered subversive "free thinkers" in nineteenth-century Spain. In his puppet plays as well as in *La zapatera*, Lorca's humor, confined within the limits of harmless caricature, is directed against figures of authority who abuse others. But in *Yerma* the heroine herself is ridiculed, her dilemma made to seem absurd not only to the carefree young girl whose views of marriage conflict with Yerma's, but also to the wise old women of the village. In Lorca's last two plays, music and spectacle are entirely subordinate to the bitter presentation of social decay.

Just as Lorca's lyric poetry cannot be understood apart from the poetic developments of the avant-garde, his dramatic art cannot be fully appreciated outside the context of the theater of his day. Lorca, who dramatized his critical view of life by use of comedy and farce, was not the only twentieth-century playwright to attempt to renovate traditional comic techniques. His theater did not appear "de la casi nada" [from almost nowhere][12] but emerged from the interpretations of farce developed by the modern dramatists who preceded him. Benavente's carefully balanced but sharp satires of middle-class boors and snobs and Arniches's serious use of crude jokes and traditional comic types were important precedents for Lorca, who attempted not only to amuse but also to awaken his audience to the cruelty of certain social attitudes. Valle-Inclán's conception of farce as a genre capable of dramatizing misery and despair seems to have influenced Lorca directly. The parodies of the *esperpentos* are prototypes of the complex comic figure of Perlimplín and the psychologically grotesque Bernarda Alba. In these two plays, as well as in *Doña Rosita*, Lorca, like Valle-Inclán, presents a desperate view of life by means of caricature and bitter *humour noir*.

Lorca succeeded more than any other Spanish dramatist in synthesizing the divergent directions of modern theater in Spain and in breathing fresh life into traditional dramatic forms. Through his comic spirit, a mixture of gaiety and despair, Lorca not only expressed the anxieties of his day but also announced the anguish and disillusionment of the Theater of the Absurd.

Lorca and the Theater of the Absurd

Nearly forty years after his death, Lorca seems to represent a dead end rather than a new trend in Spanish drama. Ricardo Doménech finds that Lorca's theater occupies a kind of historical limbo representing "una difícil frontera entre 'los clásicos' y 'los contemporáneos' " [a difficult borderline between "the classics" and "the contemporaries"].[13] It is true that Lorca's highly theatrical mixture of tragedy and farce is not being continued by the best contemporary dramatists in Spain—Buero Vallejo and Alfonso Sastre, whose plays began to appear after the Civil War. Perhaps only tragedy, unmitigated even by the grim humor of despair, could follow holocaust. On the other hand, comic dramatists, such as Jardiel Poncela, Miguel Mihura, and Alfonso Paso, have produced amusing and inventive comedies generally lacking the tragic outlook that characterizes Lorca's art.[14] Even though Lorca's theater is related to the oldest Spanish and Italian farce and to the theater of the golden age, it also announces the newest innovations in European drama. The comic violence and puppet-like characters that Lorca borrowed from ancient farce to dramatize his dark view of life have been similarly adopted, not in Spain, but in France, by dramatists of the Absurd, such as Eugène Ionesco, Jean Genet, and Fernando Arrabal.

Lorca's conventional plays are so distinct from Ionesco's extravagant, nonsensical farces that to compare the works of these two dramatists would seem impossible. Lorca's full-blown lyrical and visual scenes, through which move characters speaking rational, often poetic lines, appear to have sprung from an ancient and orderly universe quite remote from Ionesco's disoriented, unreal chaos tottering on the brink of insanity and populated by characters who mutter a kind of gibberish. Despite these obvious differences, Lorca's drama anticipates that of Ionesco in several respects. Although Lorca's world appears antique and stable, he reveals that it nevertheless has begun to putrefy. As Ionesco was to do two decades later, Lorca revived techniques of farce to dramatize the modern experience of isolation, helplessness, and solitude. Though strongly critical of the society of his day, Lorca's theater, like that of Ionesco and Genet, remains essentially poetic. While ridiculing social conventions, Lorca eschews a specifically political orientation, refusing to allow his art to serve what Ionesco calls "ce féroce engagement" [this ferocious commitment].[15] Lorca's protagonists are, like those of Ionesco, victims; their own weaknesses and illusions, together with stale and senseless social mores, predictably bring about their downfall. Most importantly, however, Lorca announces the theater of Ionesco by observing the lack of distinction between comedy and tragedy. Lorca's assertion that "if in certain scenes the audience doesn't know what to do, whether to laugh or to cry, that will be a success for me"[16] represents the same dramatic sensibility expressed by Ionesco when he admits that "Je n'ai compris . . . la différence que l'on fait entre comique et tragique" [I've never understood . . . the difference that is made between the comic and the tragic].[17] The dislocation of traditional dramatic modes that lies beneath the conventional appearance of Lorca's plays becomes one of the predominant characteristics of the theater of Ionesco.

Ionesco's characters derive, as do many of Lorca's, from puppet theater. In an early farce, *Le Tableau* [The painting], which Ionesco calls a "guignolade," the protagonist is a buffoon identified only as "The Stout Man." When the play begins, the Stout Man is a rich bully, descended from the same puppet tradition as don Cristóbal. As in the Marx brothers' comedies and in Lorca's puppet farces, violence is freewheeling but harmless. Shooting a gun results not in killing but in instant transformation of character. Ionesco uses farcical devices for serious purposes as well. Suddenly ennobled by love, the Stout Man, like Perlimplín, unexpectedly becomes aware of his ugliness. *Le Tableau* ends with the Stout Man imploring someone in the audience to shoot him so that he may transcend his boorish nature. Inspired by the beautiful painting, the Stout Man wishes, like don Perlimplín, that his own likeness could be transformed into a beautiful one.

While *Le Tableau* is more violent than Lorca's somewhat nostalgic period piece, *Don Perlimplín*, these two farces represent experiments with the same dramatic effect: the sudden revelation of sympathetic human traits in a clown. Yet, if clowns can become human, the process can also be reversed: humans can be reduced to laughingstocks or automatons by the terrible power of conformity, as Lorca and Ionesco suggest in two other plays. In *Doña Rosita*, Lorca portrays the triviality and neglect of human needs by burlesque of middle-class concern for outward appearances. Ionesco's Old Man and Old Woman enact a similar burlesque in *Les Chaises* [The chairs], subtitled a "farce tragique". As Lorca does in *Doña Rosita*, Ionesco employs the device of the arrival of a series of eccentric guests for satiric purposes. The guests in Doña Rosita's household—Señor X and the old school teacher, don Martín—are visible representatives of the smug and pedantic bourgeois at the turn of the century. That Ionesco's guests are invisible does not alter the possibilities for revealing the absurdities of both the guests and their hosts as well. Ionesco's old couple receive an imaginary stage-full of guests—Belle, an aging beauty whose hair is now white ("mais sous les blancs il y a les bruns, les blues, j'en suis certain" [but beneath the white hairs are brown and blue ones, I'm sure];[18] a general in bemedalled uniform, who enters to the sound of martial fanfare, and His Majesty the Emperor. This assemblage is to be addressed by the only visible guest, the Orator, who is a deaf mute.

The guests in *Doña Rosita* and *Les Chaises* are only slightly more ridiculous than the hosts themselves. Just as Lorca satirizes not only those who visit Rosita's household but also its inhabitants, Ionesco directs laughter at the aged couple, who live empty, isolated lives. Rosita's aunt mocks her husband's lack of business sense in much the same way the Old Woman of *Les Chaises* decries her husband's lack of ambition. With cruel, comic irony, both Ionesco and Lorca remind the spectator of their characters' dignity after they have ridiculed them in the eyes of others. The spectator is thus disturbed and confused by characters with whom he can neither fully sympathize nor whom he can entirely dismiss. Like Rosita, who proclaims pathetically in Act III that "lo único que me queda es mi dignidad" [the only thing I have left is my dignity], the Old Woman of *Les Chaises* insists to her guests that "Nous avons notre dignité, un amour-propre personnel" [We have our dignity, our self-esteem] (Ionesco, *Théâtre*, I, 177).

The aggressive, grotesque humor of Lorca's prose tales, the kind of humor that André Breton and the surrealists valued as a means of conquering adversity (see chapter four), becomes Ionesco's most characteristic dramatic mode. The French playwright acknowledges the positive effect of *humour noir* when he observes that "prendre conscience de ce qui est atroce et en rire, c'est devenir maître de ce qui est atroce" [to become aware of what is atrocious and laugh at it is to have power over the atrocious].[19] It is with this laughter at distortion and deformity that Lorca and Ionesco shock their public into awareness of the emptiness of conventional morality.

Lorca dramatizes the emotional starvation in Bernarda's household by laughing at psychological deformation through the comic remarks of María Josefa. In *Amédée, ou comment s'en débarrasser* [Amédée, or how to get rid of it], Ionesco points to the atrophied love between Amédée and Madeleine by means of the comic grotesque—the corpse that grows to enormous proportions in the couple's apartment.

Lorca treats María Josefa in the same way that Ionesco treats the corpse: both are symbols of something gone wrong and are highly embarrassing to the households they occupy. Like Bernarda, who insists that her mother not be allowed to wander where the neighbors can see her, Amédée and Madeleine take elaborate precautions to insure that no one discovers the corpse in their flat. But the two skeletons in the closet are not easily contained. María Josefa escapes at inopportune moments and, decked out in flowers and earrings, sings of her plans to be married. The corpse, though inert, imposes itself upon the couple by assuming immense size and by causing mushrooms to grow throughout the flat. As David I. Grossvogel explains, the "monster implicit in the bourgeois interiors" of Ionesco's play finally becomes explicit and takes over the entire room.[20] The fact that no affection exists between Amédée and Madeleine is manifest when the corpse can no longer be hidden; it soon becomes the central fact of their lives. As the same sort of comic presence, María Josefa, singing of her repressed need for human warmth, escapes her cell and confronts Bernarda and her daughters with insults and accusations of oppression.

The emergence of a skeleton in the closet creates both surprise and amusement. We smile at the daft grandmother as she shows off a lamb she carries in her arms, saying it is the child she just had. Similarly, the growing corpse is ludicrous as it gradually consumes the lives of Amédée and Madeleine. Yet our laughter becomes more hollow as the tragic meaning of these two shocking figures becomes apparent. María Josefa's amusing attempts at glamour and husband hunting also emphasize the repression and hypocrisy that threaten to engulf the household. Ionesco, too, focuses first upon the comic effect of the corpse. But, as it floats off into the sky with Amédée, it is Madeleine who finally receives the dramatist's full attention. Like Bernarda, Madeleine is incapable of realizing her error. In the second of the two possible endings of the play, she repeats, "Non, non, je n'ai pas soif, je n'ai pas soif!" [No, no, I'm not thirsty, I'm not thirsty!] (Ionesco, *Théâtre*, I, 333), thus symbolically refusing to recognize the elementary human desires for sympathy and companionship. Bernarda, too, misses the point of her daughter's death. She refuses to admit her own complicity in it and, seeing Adela's body, automatically shifts the blame, insisting "No. ¡Yo, no! Pepe . . ." [No, not I, Pepe . . .].

In most formal respects, of course, *Bernarda Alba* and *Amédée* are entirely dissimilar works. The Spanish play is traditional realistic theater; the later French farce, sheer fantasy. Both playwrights, however, are portraying a society coming apart. Lorca reveals only glimpses of the lunatic world that looms behind a tightly controlled façade. Ionesco penetrates the façade, treating directly the lunatic realm beyond. Yet these two playwrights, focusing with different styles upon opposite views of a sinking civilization, share a similar comic vision. Both not only use the skeleton-in-the-closet motif to symbolize the dementia lurking behind empty respectability, but they also exploit the comic resources of this motif. For Lorca, as for Ionesco, humor becomes a means by which a public may be forced to recognize the bankruptcy of its social and moral attitudes.

Lorca's adaption of the techniques of farce to present a tragic view of life has been advanced considerably by Ionesco. The French playwright has reduced language to meaningless cliché and converted dramatic characters into robots. While Lorca's heroines are uncomplicated, puppetlike creatures dominated by their passions, Ionesco's creatures switch from one mood to the next abruptly and without explanation. The professor of *La Leçon* changes from docility to criminality with the easily discernible movements of a marionette whose strings are plainly visible to the public. Lorca leads us to suspect, but only confirms in the final scene, that Bernarda is puppetlike in her ferocity; Ionesco's professor is, from the beginning, an automaton who shifts from servility to ferocity with jerky but irreversible movements. Thus, while Lorca reveals by subtle analogies that humans are wooden creatures with little control over their passions, the futility of modern life is, for Ionesco, a point of departure from which all human action appears blatantly absurd.

The unconventional subtitles Lorca gave to his plays—"aleluya erótico" [lace-paper valentine], "farsa violenta" [violent farce], and "leyenda del tiempo" [legend of time]—result from his effort to classify the hybrid mood of his plays in which characters are wooden, yet still human; comic, and at the same time, pitiable. Ionesco reflects a similar attitude in his equally hybrid definitions of his works, such as "anti-pièce" and "pseudo-drame." Thus, the resemblance that Lorca tried to suggest in the 1930's between tragedy and farce develops two decades later into what Martin Esslin has termed Ionesco's "favorite theme of the identity of comedy and tragedy."[21]

By reducing dialogue to nonsense and non sequitur and by portraying characters as one-dimensional puppets, Ionesco has created amusing but stark dramatic images of the monotony and isolation of middle-class life. Jean Genet also presents a negative view, not of the life of the bourgeois, but of the social reject. Genet has given dramatic form to a demimonde ordinarily noticed only by sociologists. Yet Genet's portrayals of servants, sexual deviants, and criminals resemble Lorca's violent dramas in many ways. Genet's characters, like those of Lorca, suffer in double measure, losing their struggle for existence as well as their social respectability. Genet's attention to costume and spectacle is extravagant, and his plays, like those of Lorca, are not reduced to dialogue but are highly theatrical experiences. Besides their choice of outcast characters and their talent for histrionics, Lorca and Genet share the violent, macabre humor with which they hope to jolt their audience. Lorca's use of comic violence to shock conventional sensibility and morality is a step toward Genet's conception of the theater as being "not a mirror, nor entertainment, but an act of aggression . . . performed . . . against society."[22]

Neither Lorca nor Genet is interested in analyzing the psychological make-up of dramatic characters; they seek instead to portray human relationships and the passions they generate. Their protagonists are outcasts, not because outcasts are more interesting, but because they elicit from society a more virulent and brutal reaction than respectable bourgeois; it is cruelty, hatred, and persecution that spark the imaginations of these two playwrights. The relationships between maid and mistress in *Les Bonnes* [The maids] and in *Bernarda Alba* provide them numerous opportunities to dramatize the suffering of the underdog by means of comic violence and parody.

For Poncia, as for Claire and Solange of *Les Bonnes*, mockery of her mistress is a necessary means of venting hostility and vindictiveness. Poncia entertains the daughters in Act II by telling them of the day she became angry at her husband. Comparing her own gruesome vengeance with that of Bernarda, she laughingly declares, "Yo tengo la escuela de tu madre. Un día me dijo no sé qué cosa y le maté todos los colorines con la mano del almirez." [I'm of your mother's school. One day he said I don't know what to me and I killed all his linnets with the pestle] (p. 1477). With unmistakable gusto, Poncia imagines herself punishing Bernarda, using the same ferocity Bernarda has shown toward her for thirty years. In *Les Bonnes* this comic yet violent mockery becomes the predominant motif of the play, in which the two servant girls dress in their mistress's clothing and ape her condescending manners. Poncia imagines Bernarda "squashed like a lizard"; Claire and Solange actually attempt to poison their despised "Madame." Like Poncia, they dream of retribution and take sadistic delight in their gory plan: "Nous l'enterrerons sous les fleurs dans nos *parterres* que nous arroserons le soir avec un petit *arrosoir!*" [We'll bury her beneath the flowers, in the flower beds, that we'll water at night, with a little watering can].[23]

The savage parodies in *Bernarda Alba* and *Les Bonnes* reveal the hatred inspired by the mutual dependence of underlings and their superiors. Lorca and Genet also explore the attitudes of inferiors toward each other. Bernarda's daughters are her inferiors no less than Poncia, and their hostility toward each other is as vicious as that between Claire and Solange, who are sisters as well as maids. Jealousy between Bernarda's daughters is expressed through insults and tricks, such as the hiding of Pepe's photograph. Claire and Solange conspire to deceive Madame, but at the same time express their hatred of each other. Like the bitter Magdalena who describes her older sister Angustias as "un palo viejo" [an old stick], Claire tells Solange, "Tu es ma mauvaise odeur!" [You're my bad smell!].[24] Solange, in turn, seeks her own identity apart from that of her sister. Bernarda's daughters and Claire and Solange are all suffocated by relationships that trap them into isolation and offer them no possibilities to pursue lives of their own.

Like Lorca, Genet seems fascinated by the inability to live life fully. Not only maids and adolescents, but also the passive young man of *Así que pasen* and the blacks of *Les Nègres* are consumed by frustration. The psychological paralysis from which they suffer is symbolized by a kind of danse macabre. El Joven of *Así que pasen* hopes to marry but falls victim to two leering clowns who perform a sinister dance and lead him to his demise. A similar grim humor is displayed in Genet's farce by blacks who have assumed the identity manufactured for them by white society. Expressing their bitter frustration, they cavort around a coffin and gleefully condemn five white victims to death in a mock trial.

Lorca's theater, like that of Genet, is intended not so much to amuse as to agitate the emotions and sensibilities of the audience. Lorca's incendiary treatment of inverted love in *El público* has been discussed in chapter four. The extent to which this play anticipates the disturbing humor of the Theater of the Absurd can best be understood by comparing it to the theater of Genet. Martínez Nadal has remarked that much of the dramatic symbolism of *El público* parallels that of *Le Balcon*;[25] yet the theme, the obscene humor, and the sinister but farcical tone of *El público* are also echoed with striking similarity in *Les Nègres*.

Les Nègres and *El público* are dramatizations of the themes of hatred and persecution—in Genet's farce, between blacks and whites; in *El público*, between society and sexual deviants. Both playwrights present their themes by means of the ancient device of a play within a play. While this technique creates aesthetic distance by presenting scandalous action as only make-believe, both Lorca and Genet deliberately assault the notions of conventional morality. The actor who plays Juliet is not a girl but a young boy (Genet instructed that the two servant girls in *Les Bonnes* be played by boys); and the dialogue between the Figura de Pámpano and the Figura de Cascabeles is at times scatological and sadistic. In the scene satirizing the Christian faith, Christ appears as a nude. Referred to as the "Desnudo rojo," he is propped up in a perpendicular bed. Surrounded by the three thieves and a nurse, the nude figure repeats the famous words of the Passion, now absurdly out of place:

Desnudo: Padre mío, perdónalos, que no saben lo que se hacen.
Enfermo (a los ladrones): Porqué llegáis a esta hora?
Ladrones: Se ha equivocado el traspunte.

[*The Nude*: Father forgive them for they know not what they do.
Nurse (*to the thieves*): Why are you coming in now?
Thieves: The prompter goofed.]

Both playwrights ridicule accepted, so-called respectable behavior by creating a make-believe audience that is a caricature of middle-class society. In *El público* the audience is presented first as a group of four horses;[26] later it becomes a bloodthirsty mob that mounts a revolution and demands the death of the director and actors responsible for the inverted love scene.

The make-believe audience in *Les Nègres* is a caricature of white figures of authority. It is composed of six blacks who wear white masks representing roles of white imperialists—a queen, her valet, a missionary, a judge, a general, and a governor. Mocking white values and culture, the black actors hold a phony funeral. As they gather round the coffin of a white woman, they sing verses from a nursery rhyme and improvise a "Litanie des Blêmes" [Litany of the livid]. The make-believe whites repeat lines that parody the sentiments of white racists. The judge and the governor plan to punish the rebellious blacks with a violence both grandiose and absurd. The governor asserts, "Je l'exécute: une balle dans la tête et dans les jarrets, jets de salive, couteaux andalous, baïonnettes, revolver à bouchon, poisons de nos Médicis" [I'll execute him: a bullet in his head and in his calves, streams of saliva, knives, bayonets, popguns, poisons of our Médicis], while the judge mumbles, "Articles 280–8, 927–17–18–16–4–3–2–1–0." Finally the Queen, characteristically pronouncing the blacks guilty, commands, "Qu'on les passe au fil de l'épée!" [Put them to the sword!].[27] These visions of revenge, like the vengeance of the mob in *El público*, are justified, ironically, in a society "defending its decency."

The differences between *Les Nègres* and *El público* are too varied to enumerate, yet the intention of both playwrights is identical: an exaggerated, farcical portrayal of the violence and savagery that erupts when an established morality is threatened. When the director of *Romeo and Juliet* hopes to show the public that love can be authentic and intense in relationships not traditionally sanctioned by society, he is set upon by a mob in the name of decency. Genet reveals the violence lurking behind longstanding racial views.

Both *El público* and *Les Nègres* are radical denunciations of the social order. Just as Genet slanders religious and racial attitudes, Lorca challenges attitudes that prevail throughout Western society toward sex.

Such extreme attacks on established morality are perhaps permissible only when presented in the artificial atmosphere of farce, and both Lorca and Genet have gone to considerable lengths to insist upon the artificiality of their theater. Not only the device of the play within the play but also the exaggerated farcical gestures are used to dazzle the audience into remaining to view a spectacle intended to torment them. All the ancient rules of farce are scrupulously observed by both Lorca and Genet. Characters are not sympathetic studies but are types dressed in bizarre costumes. Dramatic action is rapid and proceeds, not logically and coherently, but in a series of quick tableaux. Music, mime, mask, and dance are all combined to produce a visual sleight of hand in which heroes are outcasts, dialogue is verbal joust, and the audience is the villain of the play. Lorca's experiments in puppet farce and surrealism equipped him with the technical means to create *El público*; this audacious satire in the guise of farce is almost uncanny in its resemblance to Genet's *Les Nègres*, *clownerie*, written twenty-eight years later.

The most direct Spanish counterpart to the French dramatists of the absurd is Fernando Arrabal. Although he writes in French because his works cannot be published uncensored in Spain, Arrabal insists that he is a Spanish writer and is annoyed by those of his countrymen who treat his works as foreign literature.[28] It is not surprising that Arrabal's vicious satires mocking the religious and cultural values of Western civilization would not be tolerated by a touchy officialdom. Like Lorca's plays, those of Arrabal are not doctrinaire in their criticism, yet they deride the most sacred images of Spanish culture—motherhood, the Church, and almost any figure of authority.

Perhaps it was inevitable that such a writer as Arrabal—whose works are full of the most uninhibited sadism, masochism, and moral confusion —should emerge from the Spanish Civil War. Lorca's plays dramatizing the suffering that a decayed morality can produce are in a sense forerunners of Arrabal's farces—Kafka-like pieces portraying a world cluttered with the meaningless cultural and moral detritus of the past. Writing before society disintegrated into the total chaos that was the Spanish Civil

War, Lorca was able to reflect poetry and beauty in a way no longer possible to postwar dramatists like Arrabal. Lorca's characters, although puppetlike, inhabit a landscape still intact. Arrabal's dramatis personae are like cartoons of homeless creatures who move about in wasteland scenes, such as the rubble of war (*Pique-nique en campagne* and *Guernica*), a maze of hanging blankets (*Le Labyrinthe*), or a vast junk heap of rusting car bodies (*Le cimetière des voitures*). The mischievous satire, searing caricatures, and *humour noir* with which Arrabal confronts his derelict world are themselves a measure of hope, and serve, as they do in Lorca's plays, as a refuge from cruelty, injustice, and futility. Arrabal has followed the example of modern playwrights, including Lorca, who employ techniques of farce to dramatize man's inhumanity.[29] Francisca, the vicious mother in *Les deux bourreaux* [*The Two Executioners*], who masquerades as a martyr to her family, is a preposterous caricature and, as such, is a direct descendant of Bernarda Alba. Bernarda, who collaborates with Martirio to give Adela the false information that leads the girl to kill herself, proclaims with studied disregard, "Es mejor así" [It's better this way]. Such extreme complacency seems comic, yet its consequences are fatal. Arrabal's Francisca exhibits the same farcical but tragic disregard for her husband, explaining to her husband that she delivered him to his torturers because, "Tu est coupable. . . . Tu dois remercier même les bourreaux qui te traitent avec tant d'égards" [You're guilty . . . You should appreciate the executioners who treat you with such consideration].[30] When Bernarda learns that a woman has given birth to and then killed her illegitimate child, her brutal thirst for vengeance masquerades as moral outrage. Shrieking, "Sí, que vengan con varas de olivo y mangos de azadones, que vengan todos para matarla" [Let them come with olive switches and hoe handles, let everyone come and kill her] (p. 1505) as the woman is dragged through the streets by the townspeople, Bernarda becomes a kind of comic demon. Her delight at physical torture is again evident when, like a frenzied Roman spectator calling for the blood of a gladiator, she incites the villagers by shouting "¡Acabad con ella antes que lleguen los guardias! ¡Carbón ardiendo en el sitio de su pecado!" [Finish her before the guards come! Burning coals in the place where she sinned!] (p. 1506). Arrabal, too, dramatizes the sadism that appears in the guise of righteous indignation. Francisca advises her moaning husband to accept torture as punishment for being a rebel: "C'est ta purification. Repens-toi de tes fauts et promets que tu ne retomberas pas dans l'erreur" [It is your purification. Repent your sins and promise you won't fall into error again] (Arrabal, I, 41). She is the same kind of comic monster as Bernarda when, with "enthusiasme hystérique," she pours salt and vinegar on Juan's wounds "pour les désinfecter" (Arrabal, I, 42). The contrast between Francisca's sadistic treatment of Juan and her motherly rhetoric becomes hilarious when she coos piously, "La famille est une chose sacrée" [The family is a sacred thing] (Arrabal, I, 44).

Bernarda Alba is only one of the figures of authority whom Lorca frequently ridicules. In Arrabal's plays, authority in any form is "synonymous with gratuitous persecution."[31] Not only the mother, but also the father in *Labyrinthe*, as well as officials of any sort, are portrayed as outrageous or villainous caricatures. But Arrabal's favorite target seems to be the Church and the symbols of Christianity, which he mocks with a wide variety of farcical devices. Recalling the upright bed in Lorca's parody of the Passion in *El público*, the emperor in *L'Architecte et L'Empereur* mimes the crucifixion during a fantastic charade with the architect. Echoing the pagan woman who tells Yerma that she does not like God, the emperor signs a series of blasphemous verses and declares that he hates God and all his miracles. This kind of humor—mockery of parental and religious authority, scatological jokes, and blasphemy—which amuses Lorca and obsesses Arrabal, is, of course, childish, expressing fear and horror of institutions and persons that threaten the existence of one who is dependent upon them. The laughter of horror and desperation is particularly important in the plays of Lorca and Arrabal because it serves as the futile yet comic protest of those who refuse to submit without a struggle to what has been forced upon them.

Comic protest in Lorca's plays is most often expressed by subservient characters—maids, wives, and daughters, who have no choice but to accept what is meted out to them. The demented but harmless María Josefa frequently escapes from her prison room and sings of freedom and marriage; El ama protests in behalf of Rosita, whom she loves, against a marriage she knows will never be fulfilled; Poncia warns Bernarda's daughters of the mechanical relationship that develops in marriage and tries to deflate Bernarda's overpowering air of superiority. In *Bodas* it is the bride who responds with sardonic humor to her fate. Protest, however, has no effect on the relentless tide of events that engulfs Lorca's dramatic characters.

Similarly, Arrabal's creatures are puny dolls who shake their fists in defiance at the wave of disaster rising about them. Zapo, the unwilling soldier in *Pique-nique en campagne*, is so bored with the war that he knits during lulls in the fighting. When his parents come to visit him, they take their picnic lunch to the battlefield and decide to stop the fighting simply by telling all the soldiers to go home. They put a record on the Gramophone and begin to dance, but then are mowed down by machine-gun fire. With bitter sarcasm Arrabal makes clear the futility of their lives as two stretcher bearers, eager to increase their daily body-count record, approach with an empty stretcher. Comic futility is also of central importance in *Guernica*, in which the elderly couple, Fanchou and Lira, amuse themselves during an air raid by playing with a blue balloon. When the balloon is punctured by a bullet, Lira shouts, "Quelles brutes! D'abord, ils nous démolissent la maison et maintenant, pour comble de bonheur, ils nous crèvent le ballon" [What brutes! First they demolish our house and now, to crown their kindness, they pop our balloon] (Arrabal, II, 31). In the final scene the old couple disappears, but two balloons rise from the spot where they were last seen. This comic treatment of death parallels that in *Así que pasen* where death is announced by the flashing image of an ace of hearts. Arrabal's heroes, like those of Lorca, are losers whose only triumph is persistent rebellion in the face of total defeat.

CONCLUSION

A comparison of Lorca's plays to the Theater of the Absurd is useful in several respects. Such a perspective leads to an understanding of Lorca's art in relationship to trends in contemporary theater. It also illustrates the fundamentally modern outlook of this dramatist, renowned for his renovation of the dramatic traditions of the golden age. In adapting age-old comic techniques for the modern stage, Lorca presents an attitude toward life that is neither that of Spanish stoic resignation nor the more hopeful acceptance and forgiveness of Christianity. Through humor, Lorca conveys a deeply pessimistic world view. This hopelessness, essentially non-Christian, is characteristic of the twentieth century and was inherited by Lorca from the Generation of '98. Yet Lorca's pessimism is more desolate than that of his immediate predecessors. The undercurrent of humor that runs throughout *Yerma, Bernarda Alba,* and *Doña Rosita* challenges and ridicules conventional figures of authority and traditional social values. Like the old woman in *Yerma* who claims she does not like God, Lorca laughs at sacred religious symbols beginning with his earliest verses in *Libro de poemas.*

In spite of his skepticism, Lorca was capable of artistic merriment and produced works intended solely for the entertainment of himself and his public. He wrote amusing farces, such as *La zapatera prodigiosa,* and delighted in nonsense verses and children's rhymes in *Canciones.* Although his surrealist prose tales, in *Narraciones,* at times hint at more serious purposes, Lorca composed them, as he did his puppet plays, with great exuberance. Frivolity and mischief dominate these works, in which the poet is at play with his craft. The nonsense lyrics and the prose tales are pieces of apprenticeship; *La zapatera* and the puppet plays are works of a virtuoso taking pleasure in casting his spell upon an audience.

As he matured, however, Lorca increasingly put the techniques of comedy and farce to more serious use. Problems of honor and personal anguish are introduced by means of laughter and bawdy farce in *Don Perlimplín.* The tragic consequences of social injustice are worked into the drawing-room comedy, *Doña Rosita.* While he dramatized grave situations in his comedies, Lorca added a new dimension to his serious plays with comic sequences. Within the stark, primitive context of folk drama, anguish is mixed with amusement and horror is expressed with a strange sort of gaiety. The specter of death in *Bodas de sangre,* accompanied by her exultant accomplice, leers at her victims. The brutal Bernarda Alba seems at times to be a grotesque bully, while old crones crack obscene jokes at the desperate Yerma. The effect produced by this incongruous mixture of tragedy and farce is a kind of hysteria at the helplessness of human beings to control their destiny.

Because of the mingling of tragedy with farce, it is an oversimplification to view Lorca's mature dramas as tragedies. Their disturbing complexity requires another perspective, for the criteria of tragedy do not explain their underlying critical and satirical moods. It was probably Martin Esslin, in the original (1961) edition of his definitive study, who first included Lorca among the forerunners of the Theater of the Absurd.[32] Esslin presumably recognizes Lorca on the basis of the dramatist's experimental plays, for he only mentions these works in his text. The unconventional dialogue and characterization of *Así que pasen*, *El público*, and the skits of *Teatro breve* undoubtedly anticipate the form of Absurdist farce. Yet the dislocation of traditional comic and tragic modes beneath the conventional façade of Lorca's mature dramas also foreshadows the Absurdist view of the human condition as both pathetic and ludicrous. Like the plays of Ionesco, Genet, and Arrabal, Lorca's folk dramas are negative in their revolt against established values. Lorca's heroines are not heroic, and their sacrifice is in no way glorified. The social order is not affirmed but is found to be corrupt and oppressive. Yet it is not Lorca's dark philosophical view, held by countless twentieth-century writers, nor his highly theatrical conception of dramatic arts, shared by many contemporary playwrights, that link him to Absurdist drama. It is rather his habit of dramatizing his pessimistic outlook with elements of farce that marks Lorca as an important forerunner of the Theater of the Absurd.

Writing at a moment in which Spain neared the brink of violent dissolution, Lorca understood what later dramatists who emerged from catastrophe have made palpably clear: that traditional distinctions between laughter and despair, good and evil, tragedy and farce, are no longer valid. By mocking such pathetic figures as Yerma and don Perlimplín, Lorca reveals tragic sacrifice to be futile. When such preposterous and sadistic figures as Bernarda Alba and Arrabal's Francisca represent motherhood, infinite maternal goodness has become hopelessly contorted into evil. When society has become as insensitive and cruel as that in *Doña Rosita*, in Arrabal's war farces, and in Genet's *Les Nègres*, tragic suffering is indistinguishable from farce, and the only reaction possible is the laughter of despair. Such was Lorca's laughter—as Gabriel Celaya recalls, "Un rire peut-être plus terrible que la tragédie" [A laugh perhaps more terrible than tragedy].[33]

Finally, comparison of Lorca's works with the Theater of the Absurd may also help clarify reasons why Lorca's dramatic art has not been continued in Spain. Beneath their conventional exterior, Lorca's mature dramas are disturbing, often suggesting a satirical view of Spanish social morality and institutions. If such a view were still tolerated in Spain, Fernando Arrabal would be writing today in his native tongue rather than in French.

Perhaps the unique quality of Lorca's mature plays is that they are never consoling. For Aristotle, tragedy was a purgative experience from which the spectator could derive strength from suffering. Lorca adds a new dimension to the tragic experience. For him, as for the dramatists of the Absurd, the theater is a volatile synthesis of disparate moods calculated not to purge the spectator of his fears but to aggravate them.

A Lorca Chronology

1898   Born in Fuentevaqueros, near Granada.

1918   *Impresiones y paisajes* is published.

1919   Begins studies at the Residencia de Estudiantes in Madrid.

1920   *Maleficio de la mariposa* is produced at the Teatro Eslava in Madrid.

1921   *Libro de poemas* is published. Begins writing *Canciones*.

1922   Completes a version of *Los títeres de Cachiporra*.

1925   Writes *El paseo de Buster Keaton*; *Mariana Pineda* in preparation.

1927   *Canciones* is published. Premier of *Mariana Pineda*. Exposition of drawings at Dalmau Gallery in Barcelona. Publishes "Santa Lucía y San Lázaro."

1928   Publishes *Romancero gitano*, "Historia de este gallo," "Suicidio en Alejandría," and "Nadadora sumergida." Begins writing "Las tres degollaciones." *El amor de Don Perlimplín* in preparation.

1929   Publishes "Degollación de los inocentes"; *Don Perlimplín* is censored. Departs in June for New York.

1930   *Así que pasen cinco años* and *El público* in preparation. Arrives back in Spain in June. Premier of *La zapatera prodigiosa* in December.

1931   Publishes *Poema del cante jondo. El retablillo de don Cristóbal* in preparation.

1932   Begins work with *La Barraca. Bodas de sangre* in preparation.

1933   Premier of *Bodas de sangre* at Teatro Beatriz in Madrid. Departs in October for Buenos Aires to direct performances of his plays there. Premier of *El retablillo de don Cristóbal*.

1934   Returns in March from Buenos Aires. Publishes two scenes from *El público*. Premier in December of *Yerma* at Teatro Español in Madrid.

1935   Premier of *Doña Rosita la soltera* in Barcelona. *La casa de Bernarda Alba* is completed. *Los títeres de cachiporra* is performed.

1936   Presentation of *Así que pasen cinco años* is planned by Club Anfistora in Madrid. On August 19 Lorca is executed near Granada by Falangists.

Note: Based, to a large extent, on Marie Laffranque, "Pour l'étude de Federico García Lorca: Bases Chronologiques," *Bulletin Hispanique* 65 (July–December): 333–377.

Notes

PREFACE

1. Luigi Pirandello, *L'Umorismo*, pp. 50–51.

2. Vivian Mercier, *The Irish Comic Tradition*, p. 5.

INTRODUCTION

1. Full documentation given in Bibliography.

2. Jean-Louis Schonberg, *Federico García Lorca*.

3. Susan Smith Blackburn, "Humor in the Plays of Federico García Lorca," in *Lorca*, ed. Manuel Durán, pp. 155–166. Also, David Bary, "Preciosa and the English," *Hispanic Review* 37 (October 1969): 510–517.

4. Guillermo de Torre, "Federico García Lorca y sus orígenes dramáticos," *Clavileño* 5 (March–April 1954): 14–18. Also, see François Nourissier, *Federico García Lorca*.

5. William I. Oliver, review of *Lorca: A Collection of Critical Essays*, *Modern Drama* 8 (September 1965): 234.

6. Eugène Ionesco, *Notes et contre-notes*, p. 99.

7. Plato, *Symposium*, p. 64.

8. Robert W. Corrigan, "Comedy and the Comic Spirit," in *Comedy*, ed. Robert W. Corrigan, p. 3.

9. Charles Baudelaire, "Some Foreign Caricaturists," in *The Mirror of Art*, trans. and ed. Jonathan Mayne, p. 182.

10. Francisco Goya, *Los desastres de la guerra*, plate 61.

11. Benito Pérez Galdós, *Obras completas*, V, 1002.

12. Miguel de Unamuno, "Malhumorismo," in *Ensayos*, II, 603–610.

13. Pío Baroja, *Obras completas*, II, 527.

14. Ibid., II, 226.

15. Baroja, "La caverna del humorismo," in ibid., V, 393–487.

16. Ramón Gómez de la Serna, *Antología*, p. 136.

17. Rodolfo Cardona, *Ramón*, p. 66.

18. Ramón Gómez de la Serna, "Humorismo," in *Ismos*, p. 163.

19. Santiago Vilas, *El humor y la novela española contemporánea*, p. 182.

20. Camilo José Cela, *La obra completa*, II, 87.

1. LYRIC POETRY

1. Federico García Lorca, *Obras completas*, p. 184. All references to Lorca's works, as well as to remarks by other authors included in this edition, are followed in the text by page numbers.

2. Henri Louis Bergson, *Le rire*, p. 3.

3. Roy Campbell, *Lorca*, p. 34.

4. Carlos Morla Lynch, *En España con Federico García Lorca*, p. 429.

5. Ibid.

6. Ramón Gómez de la Serna, *Greguerías*, p. 141.

7. Ibid., p. 60.

8. Arturo Berenguer Carisomo, *Las máscaras de Federico García Lorca*, p. 37.

9. Jean-Louis Schonberg, *Federico García Lorca*, p. 194.

10. Arturo Barea, *Lorca*, p. 75.

11. Schonberg, *Federico García Lorca*, p. 202.

12. David Bary, "Preciosa and the English," *Hispanic Review* 37 (October 1969): 510–517.

13. Doris Margaret Glasser, "Lorca's 'Burla de don Pedro a caballo,'" *Hispania* 47 (May 1964): 297.

14. Schonberg, *Federico García Lorca*, p. 194.

15. Wylie Sypher, "Our New Sense of the Comic," in *Comedy*, ed. Wylie Sypher, p. 195.

16. Jean-Louis Flecniakoska, *L'Universe poétique de Federico García Lorca*, p. 103.

17. Octavio Ramírez, "El poeta en tres tiempos," Literary Supplement to *La Nación* (Buenos Aires), November 19, 1933.

18. Berenguer Carisomo, *Las máscaras*, p. 48.

2. TRAGICOMEDIES AND FARCES

1. See José Mora Guarnido, *Federico García Lorca y su mundo*, pp. 123–131, for a full account of the staging of *El maleficio*.

2. Ibid., p. 125. Mora Guarnido recalls that Lorca and his fellow poets were "allergic" to the word *maleficio* and other terms relating to spells and magic.

3. Sumner M. Greenfield, "The Problem of Mariana Pineda," *Massachusetts Review* 1 (August 1960): 753.

4. Wm. Shaffer Jack, *The Early Entremés in Spain*, p. 51.

5. Ibid., pp. 51–71, *passim*.

6. Aubrey F. G. Bell, *Cervantes*, p. 48.

7. Francisco García Lorca, Intro-

duction to *Five Plays*, trans. J. Graham-Luján and Richard O'Connell, p. 6.

8. Alfredo de la Guardia, *García Lorca*, p. 307.

9. Kathleen M. Lea, *Italian Popular Comedy*, I, 17.

10. García Lorca, Introduction to *Five Plays*, p. 6.

11. Gustave Lanson, "Molière and Farce," trans. Ruby Cohn, *Tulane Drama Review* 2 (Winter 1963): 153.

12. Luigi Pirandello, *L'Umorismo*, p. 195.

13. Ibid.

14. Rafael Martínez Nadal, *El público*, p. 271.

15. Luigi Pirandello, *Così è (se vi pare)*, p. 159.

16. Pirandello, *L'Umorismo*, p. 195.

17. Ricardo Gullón, "Reality of the Esperpento," in *Valle-Inclán Centennial Studies*, ed. Ricardo Gullón, p. 131.

18. Marie Laffranque, *Federico García Lorca*, p. 43.

3. AVANT-GARDE PROSE AND PLAYS

1. Jorge Guillén, "Federico en persona," in *Obras completas*, by Federico García Lorca, p. lvii.

2. To Arturo Berenguer Carisomo, Lorca was indulging in a "pecado ultraísta" [an *ultraísta* sin] when he wrote the poems of New York (Arturo Berenguer Carisomo, *Las máscaras de Federico García Lorca*, p. 160). Other writers, including Guillermo de Torre and Ricardo Gullón, have generally dismissed surrealism as an important influence upon Lorca.

3. Jean-Louis Schonberg, *Federico García Lorca*, p. 125.

4. Isidore Ducasse, *Oeuvres complètes*, p. 199.

5. According to J. Francisco Aranda, *Luis Buñuel*, fn. p. 53, this now famous title originated as a derogatory epithet applied by Dalí and Buñuel to works of poets they thought too traditional.

6. Yves Duplessis, *Le Surréalisme*, p. 22.

7. Pierre Renaud, "Symbolisme au second degré: *Un Chien andalou*," *Etudes cinématographiques* 22–23 (1963): 154.

8. André Breton, *Anthologie de l'humour noir*, p. 14.

9. Fernando Vásquez Ocaña, *García Lorca*, p. 235.

10. Eric Bentley, "On Farce and Satire," in *Comedy*, ed. Robert W. Corrigan, p. 292.

11. Georges de Coulteray, *Sadism in the Movies*, p. 166.

12. Marianne Alexandre, trans., *"L'age d'or" and "Un Chien andalou,"* p. 65.

13. Gino Nenzioni, "Il 'Teatro breve' di Federico Lorca," *Letterature Moderne* 10 (March–April 1960): 192.

14. J.-P. Lebel, *Buster Keaton*, trans. P. D. Stovin, p. 122.

15. Federico García Lorca, "A Trip to the Moon," trans. Bernice G. Duncan, in *New Directions 18*, pp. 35–41. Also see my article, "El viaje de García Lorca a la luna," *Insula* 23 (January 1968): 1, 10. The original Spanish version of this scenario still remains unpublished.

16. Berenguer Carisomo, *Las máscaras de Federico García Lorca*, p. 96.

17. Marie Laffranque, *Federico García Lorca*, p. 60.

18. R. G. Knight, "Federico García Lorca's *Así que pasen cinco años*," *Bulletin of Hispanic Studies* 43 (January 1966): 32–46.

19. Rafael Martínez Nadal, *El público*, pp. 121–122.

20. Raymond Durgnat, *Luis Buñuel*, pp. 24–25.

21. Roberto G. Sánchez, *García Lorca*, p. 47.

22. Durgnat, *Luis Buñuel*, pp. 22–35.

23. Carl G. Jung, *Symbols of Transformation*, p. 185.

24. García Lorca, *Obras completas*, pp. 1755–1756.

25. The similarity between the two aged characters is also noted by Martínez Nadal in *El público*, p. 128.

26. Allardyce Nicoll, *The World of the Harlequin*, p. 69.

27. *Holbein's Dance of Death*, introduction by Francis Douce.

28. Thanks to Martínez Nadal's recently published synopsis of the piece in *El público*.

29. Martínez Nadal, *El público*, p. 75.

30. Wilma Newberry, "Aesthetic Distance in García Lorca's *El público*: Pirandello and Ortega," *Hispanic Review* 37 (April 1969): 276–296. Newberry maintains that aesthetic autonomy is the central theme of *El público*.

31. Martínez Nadal, *El público*, p. 41.

32. Ibid., p. 19.

33. F. Lázaro Carreter, "Apuntes sobre el teatro de García Lorca," *Papeles de Son Armadans* 18 (July 1960): 16.

34. John Brande Trend, "Lorca," in *Lorca*, ed. Manuel Durán, p. 43.

35. Anna Balakian, *Surrealism*, p. 143.

4. PUPPET FARCES

1. Michael Benedikt and George E. Wellwarth, eds., introduction to *Modern French Plays*, pp. ix–xv.

2. Wallace Fowlie, *Climate of Violence*, p. 224.

3. Luigi Pirandello, *Il beretto a sonagli*, p. 160.

4. Joseph Spencer Kennard, *Masks and Marionettes*, p. 110.

5. Jean-Louis Schonberg, *Federico García Lorca*, p. 286.

6. William I. Oliver, "Lorca: The Puppets and the Artist," *Tulane Drama Review* 7 (Winter 1962): 95.

7. Guillermo de Torre, "Federico García Lorca y sus orígenes dramáticos," *Clavileño* 5 (March–April 1954): 14–18.

8. François Nourissier, *Federico García Lorca*, p. 59.

9. Oliver, "Lorca: The Puppets and the Artist," p. 90.

10. Ibid., p. 95.

11. Alfredo de la Guardia, *García Lorca*, p. 261.

12. Oliver, "Lorca: The Puppets and the Artist," p. 82.

13. Francisco García Lorca, introduction to *Three Tragedies*, trans. J. Graham-Luján and Richard O'Connell, p. 21.

14. A. A. Parker, *The Approach to the Spanish Drama of the Golden Age*.

15. Oliver, "Lorca: The Puppets and the Artist," p. 78.

5. MASTER PLAYS

1. Arturo Berenguer Carisomo, *Las máscaras de Federico García Lorca*, pp. 87, 99.

2. Pedro Laín Entralgo, *Teatro y vida*, I, 114.

3. Alfredo de la Guardia, *García Lorca*, p. 279.

4. Monalisa Lina Pérez Marchand, "Apuntes sobre el concepto de la tragedia en la obra dramática de García Lorca," *Asomante* 4 (1948): 86–96.

5. William I. Oliver, "The Trouble with Lorca," *Modern Drama* 7 (May 1964): 12.

6. Juan Guerrero Zamora, *Historia del teatro contemporáneo*, III, 91.

7. Guardia, *García Lorca*, p. 349. See also Jean-Louis Schonberg, *Federico García Lorca*, p. 314.

8. Roberto G. Sánchez, *García Lorca*, p. 107.

9. Eva K. Touster, "Thematic Patterns in Lorca's *Blood Wedding*," *Modern Drama* 7 (May 1964): 20.

10. Wolfgang Kayser, *The Grotesque in Art and Literature*, trans. Ulrich Weisstein, p. 31.

11. Guardia, *García Lorca*, p. 182.

12. Schonberg, *Federico García Lorca*, p. 305.

13. Marcelle Auclair, *Enfances et mort de García Lorca*, p. 312.

14. Kayser, *Grotesque in Art and Literature*, p. 188.

15. Wylie Sypher, "Our New Sense of the Comic," in *Comedy*, ed. Wylie Sypher, p. 208.

16. Schonberg, *Federico García Lorca*, p. 305.

17. Guerrero Zamora, *Historia del teatro contemporáneo*, III, 91, 92.

18. Touster, "Thematic Patterns," p. 19.

19. Angel Valbuena Prat, *Historia del teatro español*, p. 643.

20. A. A. Parker, *The Approach to the Spanish Drama of the Golden Age*, p. 5.

21. James K. Feibleman, *In Praise of Comedy*, pp. 25–26.

22. Edwin Honig, *García Lorca*, p. 178.

23. Rafael Martínez Nadal, *El público*, p. 154.

24. Marie Laffranque, *Federico García Lorca*, p. 80.

25. Honig, *García Lorca*, p. 193.

26. See Gonzalo Torrente Ballester, *Teatro español contemporáneo*, pp. 261–263, for an interesting discussion of the range of behavior allowed women in provincial Spanish society.

27. Angel del Río, *Vida y obras de Federico García Lorca*, p. 127.

28. George Rapall Noyes, introduction to *Masterpieces of the Russian Drama*, I, 16.

29. Guillermo Díaz-Plaja, *Federico García Lorca*, p. 223.

30. Torrente Ballester, *Teatro español*, p. 248.

31. Calderón's critical view of the code of honor has been discussed by A. A. Parker in the work listed in the Bibliography.

32. Honig, *García Lorca*, p. 224.

33. Manuel Durán, introduction to *Lorca*, ed. Manuel Durán, p. 10.

34. Lorca's account of how he came to write *Bernarda Alba* is recounted by Carlos Morla Lynch in *En España con Federico García Lorca*, pp. 488–489.

35. Henri Louis Bergson, *Le rire*, p. 147.

36. Torrente Ballester, *Teatro espa-*

ñol, p. 248.

37. Valbuena Prat, *Historia del teatro*, pp. 646–647.

38. Roy Campbell, *Lorca*, p. 88.

39. Díaz-Plaja, *Federico García Lorca*, p. 224.

40. Bergson, *Le rire*, pp. 20–21.

41. Emma Susana Speratti Piñero, "Paralelos entre *Doña Perfecta* y *La casa de Bernarda Alba*," *Revista de la Universidad de Buenos Aires* 4 (July–

September 1959): 371.

42. J. L. Styan, *The Dark Comedy*, p. 268. My presentation of comic relief is based on Styan's illuminating discussion on pp. 266–268.

43. See Tennessee Williams's two one-act farces included under the title *Slapstick Tragedy* as referred to in *A Look at Tennessee Williams* by Mike Steen, p. 15.

6. HISTORICAL PERSPECTIVE

1. Alfredo de la Guardia, *García Lorca*, p. 253.

2. Alfredo de la Guardia, *El teatro contemporáneo*, p. 349.

3. Jacinto Benavente, *Obras completas*, III, 521–522. Subsequent references to Benavente's plays are followed by page numbers in the text.

4. Barbara Matulka, "The Feminist Theme in the Drama of the *Siglo de Oro*," *Romanic Review* 26 (1935): 231.

5. Carlos Arniches, *Teatro completo*, II, 84. Subsequent references to this edition are followed by page numbers in the text.

6. *Manolo* in *Teatro selecto de don Ramón de la Cruz*, p. 91.

7. Antonio Otero Seco, "Sobre Valle-Inclán y el esperpento," *Asomante* 20 (April–June 1964): 16.

8. Ricardo Gullón, "Reality of the Esperpento," in *Valle-Inclán Centennial Studies*, ed. Ricardo Gullón, p. 151.

9. Roberto G. Sánchez, *García Lorca*, p. 144.

10. Wolfgang Kayser, *The Grotesque in Art and Literature*, p. 30.

11. Sumner M. Greenfield, "Poetry

and Stagecraft in *La casa de Bernarda Alba*," *Hispania* 38 (December 1955): 458.

12. Domingo Pérez Minik, *Debates sobre el teatro español contemporáneo*, p. 268.

13. Ricardo Doménech, "A propósito de *Mariana Pineda*," *Cuadernos Hispanoamericanos* 70 (June 1967): 608.

14. Phyllis Z. Boring, "Incongruous Humor in the Contemporary Spanish Theater," *Modern Drama* 11 (May 1968): 86.

15. Eugène Ionesco, "La démystification par l'humour noir," *L'Avant Scène*, February 15, 1959, p. 5.

16. Francisco García Lorca, introduction to *Three Tragedies*, trans. J. Graham-Luján and Richard O'Connell, p. 13.

17. Eugène Ionesco, *Notes et contre-notes*, p. 13.

18. Eugène Ionesco, *Théâtre*, I, 149. Further references to Ionesco's works are by page numbers in the text. All translations my own.

19. Ionesco, "La démystification par l'humour noir," p. 6.

20. David I. Grossvogel, *The Blas-*

phemers, p. 79.

21. Martin Esslin, *The Theatre of the Absurd*, p. 142.

22. Grossvogel, *The Blasphemers*, p. 138.

23. Jean Genet, *Les Bonnes*, p. 51.

24. Ibid., p. 48.

25. Rafael Martínez Nadal, *El público*, p. 260 n. 24.

26. Here the horse is a symbol of negation and death, according to Martínez Nadal, *El público*, p. 230.

27. Jean Genet, *Les Nègres, clownerie*, pp. 144–152.

28. José Monleón, "Correspondencia con Fernando Arrabal," in *El cementerio de automóviles, Ciugrena, Los dos verdugos*, by Fernando Arrabal, p. 41.

29. No direct influence upon Arrabal can be attributed to Lorca. It is interesting to note, however, that the "poete assasiné" in *Et ils passerent des minottes aux fleurs* is identified as Federico García Lorca. Thus Arrabal, imprisoned for a time by the Spanish Government, appears to acknowledge Lorca at least as a kind of spiritual predecessor.

30. Fernando Arrabal, *Théâtre*, I, 41. Subsequent references to this edition are followed by page numbers in the text.

31. Allen Thiher, "F. Arrabal and the New Theatre of Obsession," *Modern Drama* 13 (September 1970): 182.

32. Esslin, *Theatre of the Absurd*, p. 287.

33. Marie Laffranque, *Federico García Lorca*, p. 114.

Bibliography

Acerete, Julio C. "Homenaje a García Lorca." *Primer Acto* 55 (August 1964): 57–59.

Aguado, Emiliano. "Catarsis y humor." *Revista de Ideas Estéticas* 12 (October–December 1954): 301–317.

Aguirre, J. M. "El sonambulismo de Federico García Lorca." *Bulletin of Hispanic Studies* 44 (October 1967): 267–285.

Alberich, J. "El erotismo femenino en el teatro de García Lorca." *Papeles de Son Armadans* 39 (October 1965): 9–36.

Alberti, Rafael. "Federico García Lorca, poeta en Nueva York." *Sur* 9 (December 1940): 247–251.

Alfaro, María. "Tres heroinas nefastas de la literatura española." *Cuadernos Americanos* 140 (May–June 1965): 246–254.

Allen, Rupert. "An Analysis of Narrative and Symbol in Lorca's 'Romance sonámbulo.'" *Hispanic Review* 36 (October 1968): 338–352.

———. "A Commentary on Lorca's *El paseo de Buster Keaton.*" *Hispanófila* 48 (May 1973): 23–25.

———. "Una explicación simbológica de 'Iglesia abandonada' de Lorca." *Hispanófila* 27 (January 1966): 33–44.

———. *Psyche and Symbol in the Theater of Federico García Lorca.* Austin: University of Texas Press, 1974.

———. *The Symbolic World of Federico García Lorca.* Albuquerque: University of New Mexico Press, 1972.

Allison, Alexander W. Introduction to *The House of Bernarda Alba.* In *Masterpieces of the Drama*, edited by Alexander W. Allison. New York: Macmillan Co., 1957.

Alonso, Dámaso. *Poetas españoles contemporáneos.* Madrid: Gredos, 1958.

Aranda, J. Francisco. *Luis Buñuel: Biografía crítica.* Barcelona: Ed. Lumen, 1969.

Arce, Margot. "Palabras de introducción." *La Torre* 3 (1955): 175–178.

Arniches, Carlos. *Teatro completo.* 4 vols. Madrid: Aguilar, 1948.

Arrabal, Fernando. *El cementerio de automóviles, Ciugrena, Los dos verdugos.* Madrid: Taurus, 1965.

————. *Théâtre*. 7 vols. Paris: Julliard, 1958.

Ashmore, Jerome. "Interdisciplinary Roots of the Theater of the Absurd." *Modern Drama* 14 (May 1971): 72–83.

Auclair, Marcelle. *Enfances et mort de García Lorca*. Paris: Editions du Seuil, 1968.

Babín, María Teresa. "García Lorca, poeta del teatro." *Asomante* 4 (1948): 48–57.

————. "La prosa mágica de García Lorca." *Asomante* 18 (1962): 49–69.

Balakian, Anna. *Surrealism: Road to the Absolute*. New York: Noonday Press, 1959.

Barea, Arturo. "El lenguaje poético de Federico García Lorca." *Bulletin of Hispanic Studies* 31 (October 1944): 3–15.

————. *Lorca: The Poet and His People*. New York: Grove Press, 1949.

Barnes, Robert: "The Fusion of Poetry and Drama in *Blood Wedding*." *Modern Drama* 2 (February 1960): 395–402.

Baroja, Pío. *Obras completas*. 8 vols. Madrid: Biblioteca Nueva, 1946.

Bartra, Agustín. "Los temas de la vida y de la muerte en la poesía de Antonio Machado, García Lorca y Miguel Hernández." *Cuadernos Americanos* 21 (September–October 1962): 191–212.

Bary, David. "Preciosa and the English." *Hispanic Review* 37 (October 1969): 510–517.

Baudelaire, Charles. *The Mirror of Art: Critical Studies*. Translated and edited by Jonathan Mayne. New York: Doubleday, 1956.

Beaumont, Cyril W. *Puppets and the Puppet Stage*. London: Studio Publications, 1958.

Bell, Aubrey F. G. *Cervantes*. New York: Collier Books, 1961.

Benavente, Jacinto. *Obras completas*. 10 vols. Madrid: Aguilar, 1950.

Benedikt, Michael, and Wellwarth, George E., eds. *Modern French Plays: An Anthology from Jarry to Ionesco*. London: Faber and Faber, 1965.

Bentley, Eric. *The Playwright as Thinker: A Study of Modern Theatre*. New York: Noonday Press, 1955.

————. "The Poet in Dublin." In *In Search of Theater*, pp. 215–232. New York: Knopf, 1953.

————. "The Psychology of Farce." In *The Genius of the French Theatre*, edited by Albert Bermel. New York: Mentor Books, 1961.

Berenguer Carisomo, Arturo. *Las máscaras de Federico García Lorca*. Buenos Aires: Ed. Universitaria de Buenos Aires, 1969.

Bergamín, José. Introduction to *Poet in New York*. Translated by Rolph Humphries. New York: W. W. Norton, 1940.

Bergson, Henri Louis. *Le rire: Essai sur la signification du comique*. Paris: F. Alcan, 1924.

Bishop, Thomas. *Pirandello and the French Theater*. New York: New York University Press, 1960.

Blackburn, Susan Smith. "Humor in the Plays of Federico García Lorca." In *Lorca: A Collection of Critical Essays*, edited by Manuel Durán. Englewood Cliffs, N.J.: Prentice-Hall, 1962.

Blanco-González, Manuel. "Lorca: The Tragic Trilogy." *Drama Critique* 60 (Spring 1966): 91–97.

Bodini, Vittorio. *I poeti surrealisti spagnoli*. Turin: Giulio Einaudi, 1963.

Borel, Jean-Paul. *Théâtre de l'impossible: Essai sur une des dimensions fonda-*

mentales du théâtre espagnol au XXe siècle. Neuchatel, Switzerland: Ed. A la Baconnière, 1963.

Boring, Phyllis Z. "Incongruous Humor in the Contemporary Spanish Theater." *Modern Drama* 11 (May 1968): 82–86.

Bosch, Rafael. "El choque de imágenes como principio creador de García Lorca." *Revista Hispánica Moderna* 30 (January 1964): 35–44.

Bowra, C. M. *The Creative Experiment*. New York: Grove Press, 1948.

Breton, André. *Anthologie de l'humour noir*. Paris: Editions du Sagittaire, 1950.

Brustein, Robert. *The Theatre of Revolt*. Boston: Little, Brown, 1964.

———. "Tragedy on a Trampoline." *New Republic*, May 12, 1973, pp. 25–26.

Büdel, Oscar. *Pirandello: Studies in Modern European Thought and Literature*. New York: Hillary House, 1966.

Buero Vallejo, Antonio. "García Lorca ante el esperpento." In *Tres maestros ante el público*. Madrid: Alianza, 1973.

Bull, Judith M. "Santa Bárbara and *La Casa de Bernarda Alba*." *Bulletin of Hispanic Studies* 47 (April 1970): 117–123.

Burton, Julianne. "Society and the Tragic Vision in Federico García Lorca." *Dissertation Abstracts International* 33 (1972): 2362 A.

Busette, Cedric. *Obra dramática de García Lorca: Estudio de su configuración*. New York: Las Américas Publishing Co., 1971.

Campbell, Roy. *Lorca: An Appreciation of His Poetry*. New Haven: Yale University Press, 1952.

Cangiotti, Gualtiero. "Federico García Lorca, poeta del 'desengaño.'" *Litteratura Moderni* 2 (1961): 34–55.

Cannan, Gilbert. *Satire*. London: Martin Secker, 1914.

Cannon, Calvin. "The Imagery of Lorca's *Yerma*." *Modern Language Quarterly* 21 (June 1960): 122–130.

———. "*Yerma* as Tragedy." *Symposium* 16 (1962): 82–93.

Cano, José Luis. "De *El Maleficio* a *Mariana Pineda*." *Cuadernos Americanos* 23 (July–August 1962): 201–213.

———. *García Lorca: Biografía ilustrada*. Barcelona: Ediciones Destino, 1962.

Cano Ballesta, Juan. "García Lorca y su compromiso social: el drama." *Insula* 290 (January 1971): 3, 5.

Carbonell Bassett, Delfín. "Tres dramas existenciales de Federico García Lorca." *Cuadernos Hispanoamericanos* 64 (October 1965): 118–130.

Cardona, Rodolfo. *Ramón: A Study of Gómez de la Serna and His Works*. New York: Eliseo Torres, 1957.

Carrier, Warren. "Poetry in the Drama of Lorca." *Drama Survey* 2 (Winter 1963): 297–304.

Cavalheiro, Edgard. *García Lorca*. São Paulo: Martins, 1946.

Cela, Camilo José. *Obra completa*. Vol. 2. Barcelona: Ediciones Destino, 1964.

Cernuda, Luis. *Estudios sobre poesía española contemporánea*. Madrid: Guadarrama, 1957.

Chica-Salas, Susan. "Synge y García Lorca: Aproximación de dos mundos poéticos." *Revista Hispánica Moderna* 27 (1961): 128–137.

Cirre, José Francisco. "Algunos aspectos del 'Jardín cerrado' en las *Canciones* de Federico García Lorca." *Cuadernos Americanos* 132 (January–February 1964): 207–217.

Cohn, Ruby. "Terms of the Tragicomic Mixture." *Drama Survey* 5 (Summer 1966): 191.

Colecchia, Frances. "Doña Rosita—una heroina aparte." *Duquesne Hispanic Review* 2 (Autumn 1967): 37–43.

Correa, Gustavo. "Honor, Blood and Poetry in *Yerma.*" *Tulane Drama Review* 7 (Winter 1962): 96–110.

———. *La poesía mítica de Lorca.* Eugene, Oreg.: University of Oregon Press, 1957.

———. "Significado de *Poeta en Nueva York* de Federico García Lorca." *Cuadernos Americanos* 18 (January–February 1959): 224–233.

———. "El simbolismo del sol en la poesía de Federico García Lorca." *Nueva Revista de Filología Hispánica* 14 (1960): 110–119.

Corrigan, Robert W., ed. *Comedy: Meaning and Form.* San Francisco: Chandler Publishing Co., 1965.

———. *Theatre in the 20th Century.* New York: Grove Press, 1963.

Cotarelo y Mori, E. *Colección de entremeses, loas, bailes: Nueva biblioteca de autores españoles.* Vol. 17. Madrid: Bailly-Bailliére, 1911.

Coulteray, Georges de. *Sadism in the Movies.* New York: Medical Press, 1965.

Croce, Benedetto. "L'Umorismo." *The Journal of Comparative Literature* 1 (1903): 220–228.

Crow, John A. *Federico García Lorca.* Los Angeles: University of California Press, 1945.

Cuadra Pinto, Fernando. "Para un análisis de *Bodas de sangre.*" *Revista Signos de Valparaiso* 3 (January–February 1969): 97–115.

Davis, Barbara Sheklin. "El teatro surrealista español." *Revista Hispánica Moderna* 33 (January–April 1967): 309–329.

Devoto, Daniel. "*Doña Rosita la soltera*: estructura y fuentes." *Bulletin Hispanique* 69 (1967): 407–440.

———. "García Lorca y Darío." *Asomante* 2 (April–June 1967): 22–31.

———. "Lecturas de García Lorca." *Revue de Littérature Comparée* 33 (1959): 518–528.

———. "Notas sobre el elemento tradicional en la obra de García Lorca." *Filología* 2 (1950): 292–341.

Díaz-Plaja, Guillermo. *Federico García Lorca.* Buenos Aires: Espasa-Calpe, 1954.

Diers, Richard. Introduction to "A Trip to the Moon." In *New Directions 18.* New York: New Directions Press, 1964.

Díez-Canedo, Enrique. *Artículos de crítica teatral: El Teatro Español de 1914 a 1936.* Mexico City: Ed. Joaquín Mortiz, 1968.

Doménech, Ricardo. "*La casa de Bernarda Alba.*" *Primer Acto* 50 (February 1963): 14–16.

———. "A propósito de *Mariana Pineda.*" *Cuadernos Hispanoamericanos* 70 (June 1967): 608–613.

Doubrovsky, J. S. "Le rire d'Eugène Ionesco." *Nouvelle Revue Francaise* (February 1960): 313–323.

Ducasse, Isidore. *Oeuvres complètes.* Paris: Au Sans Pareil, 1927.

Duplessis, Yves. *Le Surréalisme.* Paris: Presses Universitaires de France, 1967.

Durán, Manuel. *La ambiguedad en el Quijote.* México: Universidad Veracruzana, 1960.

————. "García Lorca, poeta entre dos mundos." *Asomante* 18 (January–March 1962): 70–77.

————. "El surrealismo en el teatro de Lorca y Alberti." *Hispanófila* (September 1957): 61–66.

————, ed. *Lorca: A Collection of Critical Essays.* Englewood Cliffs, N.J. Prentice-Hall, 1962.

Durgnat, Raymond. *Luis Buñuel.* Berkeley: University of California Press, 1968.

Eich, Christoph. *Federico García Lorca: Poeta de la intensidad.* Madrid: Gredos, 1958.

Enck, J.; Forter, E.; and Whitley, A., eds. *The Comic in Theory and Practice.* New York: Appleton-Century Crofts, 1960.

Espina, Antonio. *El genio cómico y otros ensayos.* Madrid: Cruz del Sur, 1965.

Esslin, Martin. *The Theatre of the Absurd.* New York: Doubleday, 1969.

Falconieri, John V. "Tragic Hero in Search of a Role: *Yerma's* Juan." *Revista de Estudios Hispánicos* 1 (1967): 17–33.

Feal-Deibe, Carlos. "Crommelynck and Lorca: Variaciones sobre el mismo tema." *Revue de Littérature Comparée* 3 (1970): 403–409.

————. *Eros y Lorca.* Barcelona: Edhasa, 1973.

Feibleman, James K. *In Praise of Comedy: A Study in its Theory and Practice.* New York: Russell and Russell, 1962.

Fergusson, Francis. *The Human Image in Dramatic Literature.* New York: Doubleday, 1957.

————. *The Idea of a Theatre.* New York: Doubleday, 1949.

Fernández Flores, Wenceslao. "El humor en la literatura española." In *Obras completas.* Vol. 5. Madrid: Aguilar, 1950.

Flecniakoska, Jean-Louis. *L'Universe poétique de Federico García Lorca.* Paris: Bière, 1952.

Florit, Eugenio. "Apostillas al Romancero gitano." *Asomante* 18 (January–March 1962): 46–48.

————. Introduction to *Lorca: Obras escogidas.* New York: Dell Publishing Co., 1965.

Flys, Jaroslaw M. *El lenguaje poético de Federico García Lorca.* Madrid: Gredos, 1955.

Fowlie, Wallace. *Climate of Violence: The French Literary Tradition from Baudelaire to the Present.* New York: Macmillan Co., 1967.

Frazier, Brenda. *La mujer en el teatro de Federico García Lorca.* Madrid: Ed. Plaza Mayor, 1973.

García Lorca, Federico. *Cartas a sus amigos.* Preface by Sebastián Gasch. Barcelona: Ed. Cobalto, 1950.

————. *Obras completas.* 6th ed. Madrid: Aguilar, 1963.

————. "A Trip to the Moon." Translated by Bernice G. Duncan. In *New Directions 18*, pp. 35–41. New York: New Directions Press, 1964.

García Lorca, Francisco. Introduction to *Five Plays.* Translated by J. Graham-Luján and Richard O'Connell. New York: New Directions Press, 1961.

————. Introduction to *Three Tragedies.* Translated by J. Graham-Luján and Richard O'Connell. New York: New Directions Press, 1955.

García-Luengo, Eusebio. "Revisión del teatro de Federico García Lorca." *Política y literatura* 3 (1951): 7–34.

Gaskell, Ronald. "Theme and Form: Lorca's *Blood Wedding.*" *Modern Drama* 5 (February 1963): 431–439.

Gassner, John. *Masters of the Drama*. 3rd ed. New York: Dover, 1954.
————. *The Theatre in our Times*. New York: Crown Publications, 1954.
Genet, Jean. *Les Bonnes*. Sceaux: Pauvert, 1954.
————. *Les Nègres, clownerie*. L'Arbalete: Décines, 1958.
Gershator, David. "Federico García Lorca's Trip to the Moon." *Romance Notes* 9 (Spring 1968): 213–220.
Gibson, Ian K. "Federico García Lorca en Burgos: Más textos olvidados." *Bulletin Hispanique* 49 (1967): 179–194.
Gicovate, Bernard. "Serenidad y conflicto en la poesía de Federico García Lorca." *Asomante* 18 (January–March 1962): 7–13.
Girard, René. "Perilous Balance: A Comic Hypothesis." *Modern Language Notes* 87 (December 1972): 811–826.
Glasser, Doris Margaret. "Lorca's 'Burla de don Pedro a caballo.'" *Hispania* 47 (May 1964): 295–301.
Glicksburg, Charles I. *The Tragic Vision in 20th Century Literature*. Carbondale: Southern Illinois University Press, 1963.
Gómez de la Serna, Ramón. *Ántología*. Buenos Aires: Losada, 1955.
————. *Greguerías: Selección, 1910–1960*. Madrid: Espasa-Calpe, 1960.
————. *Ismos*. Buenos Aires: Ed. Brújula, 1968.
Gómez Lance, Betty Rita. "Muerte y vida en el drama de Federico García Lorca." *Hispania* 43 (September 1960): 376–377.
González Guzmán, Pascual. "Los dos mundos de don Perlimplín." *Revista do livro* 4 (December 1959): 39–60.
Goya, Francisco. *The Disasters of War*. New York: Dover, 1967.
Granell, Eugene F. "Esquema interpretivo." *La Torre* 3 (1955): 178–188.
Grant, Mary A. *The Ancient Rhetorical Theories of the Laughable: The Greek Rhetoricians and Cicero*. University of Wisconsin Studies in Language and Literature. Vol. 21. Madison: University of Wisconsin Press, 1924.
Green, Otis H. "A Hispanist's Thoughts on the *Anatomy of Satire* by Gilbert Highet." *Romance Philology* 17 (1963): 123–133.
Greenfield, Sumner M. "Poetry and Stagecraft in *La casa de Bernarda Alba*." *Hispania* 38 (December 1955): 456–461.
————. "The Problem of Mariana Pineda." *Massachusetts Review* 1 (August 1960): 751–763.
Grismer, R. L. *The Influence of Plautus in Spain*. New York: Hispanic Institute of America, 1944.
Grossvogel, David I. *The Blasphemers*. Ithaca, N.Y.: Cornell University Press, 1965.
————. *The Self-Conscious Stage*. New York: Columbia University Press, 1958.
————. *20th Century French Drama*. New York: Gordian Press, 1961.
Grotjahn, Martin. *Beyond Laughter*. New York: Blakiston Division, 1957.
Guardia, Alfredo de la. *García Lorca: Persona y creación*. Buenos Aires: Editorial Schapire, 1944.
————. *El teatro contemporáneo*. Buenos Aires: Editorial Schapire, 1947.
Guerrero Zamora, Juan. *Historia del teatro contemporáneo*. 4 vols. Barcelona: J. Flors, 1961–1967.
Guillén, Jorge. *Federico en persona: Semblanza y epistolario*. Buenos Aires: Editorial Emecé, 1959.
Gullón, Ricardo. "Lorca en Nueva York." *La Torre* 18 (1957): 161–170.

———. "Reality of the Esperpento." In *Valle-Inclán Centennial Studies*, edited by Ricardo Gullón. Austin: University of Texas Press, 1968.

Guthke, Karl S. *Modern Tragicomedy: An Investigation into the Nature of the Genre*. New York: Random House, 1966.

Hadow, W. H. *The Use of Comic Episodes in Tragedy*. Oxford: Oxford University Press, 1915.

Halliburton, Charles Lloyd. "García Lorca, the Tragedian: An Aristotelian Analysis of *Bodas de sangre*." *Revista de Estudios Hispánicos* 2 (1968): 35–40.

Herrick, Marvin T. *Tragicomedy: Its Origin and Development in Italy, France and England*. Illinois Studies in Language and Literature. Vol. 39. Urbana: University of Illinois Press, 1955.

Higginbotham, Virginia. "Bernarda Alba—A Comic Character?" *Drama Survey* 6 (Summer 1968): 258–265.

———. "Lorca and Twentieth-Century Spanish Theater: Three Precursors." *Modern Drama* 15 (September 1972): 164–174.

———. "Lorca's Apprenticeship in Surrealism." *Romanic Review* 61 (1970): 109–122.

———. "Reflejos de Lautréamont en *Poeta en Nueva York*." *Hispanófila* 46 (September 1972): 59–68.

———. "El viaje de García Lorca a la luna." *Insula* 23 (January 1968): v, 1, 10.

Highet, Gilbert. *The Anatomy of Satire*. Princeton, N.J.: Princeton University Press, 1962.

Hogan, Robert, and Molin, Sven Eric. *Drama: The Major Genres. An Introductory Critical Anthology*. New York: Dodd, Mead, 1962.

Holbein's Dance of Death. Introduction by Francis Douce. London: n.p., 1858.

Honig, Edwin. *García Lorca*. New York: New Directions, 1963.

———. "Lorca to Date." *Tulane Drama Review* 7 (Winter 1962): 120–126.

Hume, Robert D. "Some Problems in the Theory of Comedy." *Journal of Aesthetics and Art Criticism* 31 (Fall 1972): 87–100.

Iglesias Ramírez, Manuel. *Federico García Lorca, el poeta universal*. Barcelona: Ed. Dux, 1955.

Ionesco, Eugène. "La démystification par l'humour noir." *L'Avant Scène*, February 15, 1959, pp. 5–6.

———. *Notes et contre-notes*. Paris: Gallimard, 1962.

———. *Théâtre*. 3 vols. Paris: Gallimard, 1954.

Jack, Wm. Shaffer. *The Early Entremés in Spain: The Rise of a Dramatic Form*. Philadelphia: University of Pennsylvania Press, 1923.

Jackson, Richard L. "La presencia de la greguería en la obra de García Lorca." *Hispanófila* 9 (September 1965): 51–55.

Jones, C. A. "Honor in Spanish Golden Age Drama: Its Relation to Real Life and to Morals." *Bulletin of Hispanic Studies* 35 (July 1958): 199–210.

Jung, Carl G. *Symbols of Transformation*. Princeton, N.J.: Princeton University Press, 1970.

Kayser, Wolfgang. *The Grotesque in Art and Literature*. Translated by Ulrich Weisstein. New York: McGraw-Hill, 1966.

Kennard, Joseph Spencer. *Masks and Marionettes*. New York: Macmillan Co., 1935.

Kierkegaard, Søren. "Repetition." In *A Kierkegaard Anthology*, edited by Robert Bretall. New York: Modern Library, 1946.

Knight, G. Wilson. *The Wheel of Fire*. London: Methuen, 1949.
Knight, R. G. "Federico García Lorca's *Así que pasen cinco años.*" *Bulletin of Hispanic Studies* 43 (January 1966): 32–46.
Kott, Jan. *Shakespeare Our Contemporary*. New York: Doubleday, 1964.
Kovacci, Ofelia, and Salvador, Nélida. "García Lorca y su leyenda del tiempo." *Filología* 7 (1961): 77–105.
Kris, Ernest. *Psychoanalytic Explorations in Art*. New York: International Universities Press, 1952.
Laffranque, Marie: *Federico García Lorca*. Paris: Seghers, 1966.
————. "Federico García Lorca: Le théâtre et la vie." In *Realisme et poésie au théâtre*, edited by Jean Jacquot. Paris: Centre National de la Recherche Scientifique, 1960.
————. *Les idées esthétiques de Federico García Lorca*. Paris: Centre de Recherches Hispaniques, 1967.
————. "Lorca: études, souvenirs et documents." *Bulletin Hispanique* 69 (January–February 1967): 195–197.
————. "Pour l'étude de Federico García Lorca. Bases chronologiques." *Bulletin Hispanique* 65 (July–December 1963): 333–377.
"L'age d'or" and "Un Chien andalou": Films by Buñuel. Translated by Marianne Alexandre. New York: Simon and Schuster, 1968.
Laín Entralgo, Pedro. "Tras el amor y la risa." In his *Teatro y vida*. Vol. 1. Barcelona: Delos-Aymá, 1967.
Lamont, Rosette C. "The Metaphysical Farce: Beckett and Ionesco." *French Review* 32 (February 1959): 319–328.
Lanson, Gustave. "Molière and Farce." Translated by Ruby Cohn. *Tulane Drama Review* 2 (Winter 1963): 133–154.
Lauter, Paul, ed. *Theories of Comedy*. New York: Doubleday Anchor, 1964.
Lázaro Carreter, F. "Apuntes sobre el teatro de García Lorca." *Papeles de Son Armadans* 18 (July 1960): 9–33.
Lea, Kathleen M. *Italian Popular Comedy: A Study in the Commedia dell'arte, 1560–1620*. 2 vols. Oxford: Clarendon Press, 1934.
Lebel, J.-P. *Buster Keaton*. Translated by P. D. Stovin. New York: Barnes and Co., 1967.
Lewis, Allan. *The Contemporary Theatre: The Significant Playwrights of Our Time*. New York: Crown Publishers, 1962.
Lima, Robert. *The Theater of García Lorca*. New York: Las Americas Publishing Co., 1963.
Lisboa, J. Carlos. *Lorca e "Bodas de sangre."* Río de Janeiro: n.p., 1961.
Lópe-Delpecho, Luis. "Perfiles y claves del humor barojiano." *Revista de Occidente* 62 (1968): 129–150.
Lott, Robert. "Tragedy of Unjust Barrenness." *Modern Drama* 8 (May 1965): 20–27.
Lumley, Frederick. *New Trends in 20th Century Drama: A Survey since Ibsen and Shaw*. London: Barrie and Jenkins, 1972.
Machado Bonet, Ofelia. *Federico García Lorca: Su producción dramática*. Montevideo: Imprenta Rosgal, 1951.
Magnin, Charles. *Histoire des marionettes en Europe*. Paris: M. Lévy, 1862.
Marcilly, C. *La "Burla de don Pedro a caballo" de Federico García Lorca*. Paris: Libraire des éditions Espagnoles, 1957.
Marinello, Juan. *García Lorca en Cuba*. La Habana: Ed. Belic, 1965.

Martínez, Miguel. "Realidad y símbolo en *La casa de Bernarda Alba.*" *Revista de Estudios Hispánicos* 4 (April 1970): 55–66.

Martínez Nadal, Rafael. *El público: Amor, teatro y caballos en la obra de Federico García Lorca.* Oxford: Dolphin Book Co., 1970.

Matulka, Barbara. "The Feminist Theme in the Drama of the *Siglo de Oro.*" *Romanic Review* 26 (1935): 191–231.

Mazzara, Richard A. "Dramatic Variations on Themes of *El sombrero de tres picos*; *La zapatera prodigiosa* and *Una vida difícil.*" *Hispania* 41 (May 1958): 186–189.

Mercier, Vivian. *The Irish Comic Tradition.* London: Oxford University Press, 1969.

Meredith, George. *An Essay on Comedy.* New York: Scribner's, 1918.

Mignon, Paul-Louis. *Le Théâtre contemporain.* Paris: Hachette, 1969.

Miralles, Enrique. "Concentración dramática en el teatro de Lorca." *Archivum* 21 (January–December 1971): 77–94.

Mirlas, Leon. *Panorama del teatro moderno.* Buenos Aires: Editorial Sudamericana, 1956.

Moncayo, Hugo. *Federico García Lorca.* Quito: La Universidad Central, 1937.

Monleón, José. "Correspondencia con Fernando Arrabal." In *El cementerio de automóviles, Ciugrena, Los dos verdugos,* by Fernando Arrabal. Madrid: Taurus, 1965.

Montaner, Carlos Alberto. *Galdós, humorista, y otros ensayos.* Madrid: Ed. Partenon, 1969.

Monte, Alberto del. "Il realismo di *La casa de Bernarda Alba.*" *Belfagor* 20 (March 1965): 130–148.

Mora Guarnido, José. *Federico García Lorca y su mundo.* Buenos Aires: Losada, 1958.

Morla Lynch, Carlos. *En España con Federico García Lorca: Páginas de un diario íntimo, 1928–36.* Madrid: Aguilar, 1958.

Morris, C. B. *A Generation of Spanish Poets: 1920–1936.* Cambridge: At the University Press, 1969.

————. "Lorca's *Yerma*: Wife without an Anchor." *Neophilologus* 56 (July 1972): 285–297.

————. *Surrealism and Spain, 1920–1936.* Cambridge: At the University Press, 1972.

Muller, Herbert J. *The Spirit of Tragedy.* New York: Washington Square Press, 1965.

Murcia, Juan Ignacio. "Les aboutissants du gran guignol dans Federico García Lorca." In *Le théâtre moderne: hommes et tendences,* edited by Jean Jacquot. Paris: Centre National de la Recherche Scientifique, 1958.

Nenzioni, Gino. "Il 'Teatro breve' di Federico García Lorca." *Letterature Moderne* 10 (March–April 1960): 189–198.

Newberry, Wilma. "Aesthetic Distance in García Lorca's *El público*: Pirandello and Ortega." *Hispanic Review* 37 (April 1969): 276–296.

Nicoll, Allardyce. *Masks, Mimes and Miracles: Studies in the Popular Theatre.* New York: Cooper Square Publications, 1963.

————. *The World of the Harlequin: A Critical Study of the Commedia dell' arte.* Cambridge: At the University Press, 1963.

Nieva, Francisco. "García Lorca: Metteur en scène: Les intermèdes de Cervantes." In *La mise en scène des oeuvres du passé*, edited by Jean Jacquot. Paris: Centre Nacional de la Recherche Scientifique, 1957.

Nimetz, Michael. *Humor in Galdós*. New Haven: Yale University Press, 1968.

Nonoyama, Minako. "Vida y muerte en *Bodas de sangre*." *Arbor* 83 (December 1972): 307–315.

Nourissier, François. *Federico García Lorca: Dramaturge*. Paris: L'Arche, 1955.

Noyes, George Rapall. Introduction to *Masterpieces of the Russian Drama*. Vol. 1. New York: Dover, 1961.

Obrdlik, Antonio J. "Gallows Humor—A Social Phenomenon." *American Journal of Sociology* 47 (1942): 709–716.

Oliver, Edith. "Yerma, the Walking Sahara." *New Yorker*, October 28, 1972, pp. 119–120.

Oliver, William I. "Lorca: The Puppets and the Artist." *Tulane Drama Review* 7 (Winter 1962): 76–96.

———. Review of *Lorca: A Collection of Essays*. *Modern Drama* 8 (September 1965): 233–234.

———. "The Trouble with Lorca." *Modern Drama* 7 (May 1964): 2–15.

Olmos, Francisco. "García Lorca, el teatro clásico, y Lope de Vega." *Primer Acto* 37 (November 1962): 15–27.

Olson, Elder. *The Theory of Comedy*. Bloomington: Indiana University Press, 1968.

Ortega, José. "Cela y tremendismo." *Hispania* 48 (March 1965): 21–27.

Otero Seco, Antonio. "Sobre Valle-Inclán y el esperpento." *Asomante* 20 (April–June 1964): 15–27.

Otis, Mary. "Lorca's Audience." *Theater Arts* 36 (May 1951): 37–39.

Palley, Julian. "Archetypal Symbols in *Bodas de sangre*." *Hispania* 50 (March 1967): 74–79.

Palmer, John. *Comedy*. London: Martin Secker, n.d.

Paolucci, Anne and Henry, eds. *Hegel on Tragedy*. New York: Anchor Books, 1962.

Parker, A. A. *The Approach to the Spanish Drama of the Golden Age*. London: Diamante, 1964.

———. "Toward a Definition of Calderonian Tragedy." *Bulletin of Hispanic Studies* 39 (October 1962): 222–237.

Pérez Galdós, Benito. *Obras completas*. 6 vols. Madrid: Aguilar, 1949–1951.

Pérez Marchand, Monalisa Lina. "Apuntes sobre el concepto de la tragedia en la obra dramática de García Lorca." *Asomante* 4 (1948): 86–96.

Pérez Minik, Domingo. *Debates sobre el teatro español contemporáneo*. The Canary Islands: Ediciones Goya, 1953.

Pirandello, Luigi. *Il beretto a sonagli*. Florence: Bemporad et Figlio, 1925.

———. *Così è (se vi pare)*. Florence: Bemporad et Figlio, 1927.

———. *L'Umorismo*. La Nuova Italia, Editrice. Venice, n.d.

Plato. *Symposium*. Translated by Benjamin Jowett. New York: Liberal Arts Press, 1950.

Pradal, Gabriel. "La paloma y el leopardo o lo humano y lo inhumano en la obra de Federico García Lorca." *Cuadernos americanos* 16 (July–August 1957): 193–207.

Prieto, Gregorio. *Dibujos*. Madrid: A. Aguado, 1950.

Pronko, Leonard Campbell. *Avant-garde: The Experimental Theatre in France*. Berkeley: University of California Press, 1962.

Radcliff-Umstead, Douglas. "Pirandello and the Puppet World." *Italica* 44 (March 1967): 13–27.

Ramírez, Octavio. "El poeta en tres tiempos." Literary Supplement to *La Nación* (Buenos Aires), November 19, 1933.

Ramos-Gil, Carlos. *Claves líricas de García Lorca.* Madrid: Aguilar, 1967.

Raphael, David D. *The Paradox of Tragedy.* Bloomington: Indiana University Press, 1960.

Renaud, Pierre. "Symbolisme au second degré: *Un Chien andalou.*" *Etudes cinématographiques* 22–23 (1963): 147–157.

Riley, Edward C. "Sobre *Bodas de sangre.*" *Clavileño* 7 (January–February 1951): 8–12.

Rincón, Carlos. "*Yerma* de Federico García Lorca: Ensayo de interpretación." *Beiträge zur Romanischen Philologie* 5 (1966): 66–99.

Río, Angel del. *Vida y obras de Federico García Lorca.* Saragossa: Heraldo de Aragón, 1952.

Roberts, Gemma. "La intuición poética del tiempo finito en *Las Canciones* de Federico García Lorca." *Revista Hispánica Moderna* 33 (1967): 250–261.

Roberts, James L. "The Role of Society in the Theatre of the Absurd." In *Literature and Society,* edited by Bernice Slote. Lincoln: University of Nebraska Press, 1964.

Rocamora, Pedro. "Imagen lírica y teatro pasional en García Lorca." *Arbor* 67 (December 1967): 5–18.

Rodríguez Chícharro. "La tragedia del amor y del tiempo." *Estudios literarios: Cuadernos de la Facultad de filosofía, letras y ciencias* 20 (1963): 153–167.

Roux, Lucette Elyane. "*Así que pasen cinco años*" de Federico García Lorca ou le désir d'éternité. Perpignan: Imprimerie Catalane, 1966.

Ruiz Ramón, Francisco. *Historia del teatro español, 2: Siglo XX.* Madrid: Alianza, 1971.

Salinas, Pedro. "Lorca and the Poetry of Death." In *Lorca: A Collection of Critical Essays,* edited by Manuel Durán. Englewood Cliffs, N.J.: Prentice-Hall, 1962.

Sánchez, Alberto. "Aspectos de los cómico en la poesía de Góngora." *Revista de Filología Española* 44 (January–June 1961): 95–138.

Sánchez, Roberto G. *García Lorca: Estudio sobre su teatro.* Madrid: Ed. Jura, 1950.

———. "García Lorca y la literatura del siglo XIX: Apuntes sobre *Doña Rosita la soltera.*" *Insula* 270 (January 1971): 1, 12, 13.

———. "Lorca, the Post War Theater and the Conflict of Generations." *Kentucky Romance Quarterly* 1 (1972): 17–29.

———. "La última manera dramática de Federico García Lorca." *Papeles de Son Armadans* 50 (January 1970): 83–102.

Sapojnikoff, Victor K. "La estructura temática de *Así que pasen cinco años.*" *Romance Notes* 12 (Autumn 1970): 11–20.

Scarpa, Roque Esteban. *El dramatismo de Federico García Lorca.* Santiago: Ed. Universitaria, 1961.

Schonberg, Jean-Louis. *Federico García Lorca: L'homme—L'oeuvre.* Paris: Librairie Plon, 1956.

Schwartz, Alfred. "Toward a Poetic of Modern Realistic Tragedy." *Modern Drama* 9 (September 1966): 136–146.

Sewall, Richard B. *The Vision of Tragedy*. New Haven: Yale University Press, 1959.

Sharp, Thomas F. "The Mechanics of Lorca's Drama in *La casa de Bernarda Alba*." *Hispania* 44 (May 1961): 230–233.

Shaw, D. L. "*Humorismo y angustia* in Modern Spanish Literature." *Bulletin of Hispanic Studies* 35 (July 1958): 165–176.

Siebenmann, Gustav. *Los estilos poéticos en España desde 1900*. Madrid: Gredos, 1973.

Silverstein, Norman. "Chekhov's Comic Spirit and *The Cherry Orchard*." *Modern Drama* 1 (September 1958): 91–100.

Skloot, Robert. "Theme and Image in Lorca's *Yerma*." *Drama Survey* 5 (Summer 1966): 151–161.

Smith, Robert Metcalf. *Types of World Tragedy*. New York: Prentice-Hall, 1928.

Speckman, William Henry. "Literature and the Grotesque." *Dissertation Abstracts International* 32 (1971): 933A.

Speratti Piñero, Emma Susana. "Paralelos entre *Doña Perfecta* y *La casa de Bernarda Alba*." *Revista de la Universidad de Buenos Aires* 4 (July–September 1959): 369–387.

Spiegel, N. "On Aristotle's Definition of Tragedy." *Revue Belge de Philologie et d'histoire* 49 (1971): 14–30.

Starkie, Walter. *Luigi Pirandello*. Berkeley: University of California Press, 1965.

Steen, Mike. *A Look at Tennessee Williams*. New York: Hawthorn Books, 1969.

Steig, Michael. "The Grotesque and the Aesthetic Response in Shakespeare, Dickens and Günter Grass." *Comparative Literature Studies* 6 (June 1969): 167–180.

Steiner, George. *The Death of Tragedy*. New York: Knopf, 1961.

Styan, J. L. *The Dark Comedy: The Development of Modern Comic Tragedy*. Cambridge: At the University Press, 1968.

Sullivan, Patricia L. "The Mythic Tragedy of *Yerma*." *Bulletin of Hispanic Studies* 69 (July 1972): 265–278.

Swabey, Marie Collins. *Comic Laughter: A Philosophical Essay*. New Haven: Yale University Press, 1961.

Sypher, Wylie. "The Meanings of Comedy." In *Comedy*, edited by Wylie Sypher. New York: Doubleday, 1956.

Teatro selecto de don Ramón de la Cruz: Colección completa de sus mejores sainetes. Madrid: Hijos de Alvarez, 1902.

Thiher, Allen. "F. Arrabal and the New Theatre of Obsession." *Modern Drama* 13 (September 1970): 174–183.

Thompson, Alan Reynolds. *The Dry Mock*. Berkeley: University of California Press, 1948.

Torre, Guillermo de. "Federico García Lorca y sus orígenes dramáticos." *Clavileño* 5 (March–April 1954): 14–18.

———. *El fiel de la balanza*. Madrid: Taurus, 1961.

———. *Tríptico del sacrificio*. Buenos Aires: Editorial Losada, 1948.

Torrente Ballester, Gonzalo. "Bernarda Alba y sus hijas, o un mundo sin perdón." In *Teatro español contemporáneo*, by Gonzalo Torrente Ballester. Madrid: Guadarrama, 1968.

Touster, Eva K. "Thematic Patterns in Lorca's *Blood Wedding*." *Modern Drama* 7 (May 1964): 16–27.

Trend, John Brande. *Lorca and the Spanish Poetic Tradition*. Oxford: Blackwell, 1956.

Umbral, Francisco. *Lorca: Poeta maldito*. Madrid: Biblioteca Nueva, 1968.

Unamuno, Miguel de. *Ensayos*. 2 vols. Madrid: Aguilar, 1951.

Valbuena Prat, Angel. *Historia del teatro español*. Barcelona: Noguer, 1956.

Valle-Inclán, Ramón del. *Opus Completas*. 2 vols. Madrid: Ed. Plenitud, 1952.

Vásquez Ocaña, Fernando. *García Lorca: Vida, cántico, y muerte*. México: Atlante, 1957.

Victoria, Marcos. *Ensayo preliminar sobre lo cómico*. Buenos Aires: Losada, 1958.

Vilas, Santiago. *El humor y la novela española contemporánea*. Madrid: Guadarrama, 1968.

Vittorini, Domenico. *The Drama of Luigi Pirandello*. New York: Russell and Russell, 1969.

Vivanco, Luis Felipe. "Federico García Lorca, poeta dramático de copla y estribillo." In *Introducción a la poesía española contemporánea*, by Luis Felipe Vivanco. Madrid: Guadarrama, 1957.

Wells, C. Michael. "The Natural Norm in the Plays of Federico García Lorca." *Hispanic Review* 38 (July 1970): 299–313.

Williams, Raymond. *Drama from Ibsen to Brecht*. New York: Oxford University Press, 1969.

Young, Raymond A. "García Lorca's *Bernarda Alba*: A Microcosm of Spanish Culture." *Modern Languages* 50 (June 1969): 66–72.

Zardoya, Concha. "La técnica metafórica de Federico García Lorca." *Revista Hispánica Moderna* 20 (October 1954): 295–326.

Zdanowicz, Casimir Douglass. "Molière, and Bergson's Theory of Laughter." *University of Wisconsin Studies in Language and Literature* 20 (1924): 99–125.

Zdenek, Joseph M. "La mujer y la frustración en las comedias de García Lorca." *Hispania* 38 (March 1955): 67–69.

Zimbardo, R. A. "The Mythic Pattern in Lorca's *Blood Wedding*." *Modern Drama* 10 (February 1968): 364–371.

Ziomeck, Henryk. "El simbolismo del blanco en *La casa de Bernarda Alba* y en *La Dama del alba*." *Symposium* 24 (1970): 81–85.

Zuleta, Emilia de. "Relación entre la poesía y el teatro de Lorca." In *Cinco poetas españoles (Salinas, Guillén, Lorca, Alberti, Cernuda)*, by Emilia de Zuleta. Madrid: Gredos, 1971.

Index